Collected Reports
1949–1965

Also Published

Collected Reports 1966–1975
Collected Reports 1976–1985

Collected Reports
of the Jane Austen Society
1949–1965

With an Introduction by
ELIZABETH JENKINS

The Jane Austen Society

First published in 1967
by Wm. Dawson & Sons Ltd, London
Reprinted in 1990
by The Jane Austen Society
c/o The Hon. Secretary
Yield House, Overton
Hampshire RG25 8HT

ISBN 0 9511035 2 0

Printed by Antony Rowe Ltd, Chippenham, Wiltshire

CONTENTS

iii

LIST OF ILLUSTRATIONS

MISCELLANEOUS

INTRODUCTION

to

The Jane Austen Society was founded by the late Dorothy Darnell in 1940. Its object was to gain posession of Chawton Cottage where Jane Austen lived from 1809 till her death in 1817, and to make it available as a showplace and museum. The house at this time was let in three tenements, the rent of each tenement being half-a-crown a week. It was the property of Major Edward Knight of Chawton House, the descendant of Jane Austen's brother Edward who had taken the name of Knight on the death of Mrs. Thomas Knight who had made over to him the properties of Godmersham in Kent and Chawton in Hampshire.

Edward Knight gave Chawton Cottage to his mother and his sisters Cassandra and Jane, after the death of his father the Rev. George Austen. The house stands at a junction of the London, Winchester and Portsmouth Roads, a short distance from the park gates of Chawton House. It is L-shaped.; the long arm, lying parallel with the garden and the Winchester road, joins the short arm to form the large room used by the Austens as a living-room; the rest of the arm runs into a series of small unidentified rooms. The short arm fronts the village street, and this is the important part of the house as it contains the rooms identified by contemporary description.

Jane Austen's nephew Edward Austen-Leigh, the son of her eldest brother James, the Rector of Steventon, published his *Memoir of Jane Austen* in 1870. This, compiled from the recollections of his sister Caroline Austen and himself, is, apart from the brief notice contributed by Jane Austen's brother Henry to the posthumous edition of *Northanger Abbey* and *Persuasion*, the only memoir written by someone who had known her. Edward Austen-Leigh describes the house as it was in his aunt's life-time. It was said once to have been an inn, its situation, the number of its small rooms and the extent of its outbuildings, on two sides of a large gravel yard, supporting this idea. He says: "A good-sized entrance and two sitting-rooms made the length of the house, all intended to look upon the road ", but he adds that Edward Knight blocked up the existing drawing room window and cut another looking into the garden. This confirms that the large room on the left as one faces the house was the Austens' living room and that on the right of the front door, the dining parlour. The degree to which the latter was overlooked explains the blocking-up of the living-room window. Mrs. Thomas Knight, writing on October 26th, 1809, says: " I heard of the Chawton party looking very comfortable at breakfast from a gentleman who was travelling by their door in a postchaise ten days ago."

The *Memoir* is the source of the famous description of Jane Austen's method of writing. " She had no separate study to retire to, and most of the work must have been done in the general sitting-room ... she was careful that her occupation should not be suspected by servants or visitors or any person beyond her own family party. She wrote upon small sheets of paper which could be easily put away or covered with a piece of blotting-paper. There was, between the front door and the offices, a swing-door which creaked when it was opened, but she objected to having this little inconvenience removed because it gave her notice when someone was coming."

Where this vanished door was sited is now difficult to decide. The front of the house shows that the position of the front door has at some time been altered. The present front door opens into the dining-parlour, or rather into a narrow passage made out of the latter by a partition. John White of Chawton who died in 1921 aged one hundred, said: "The front door of Jane Austen's house used to open into a sitting room, but cannot recollect whether it was the dining or the drawing room. The partition was put up afterwards when the house was turned into cottages for labourers." (See *My Aunt Jane Austen* by Caroline Austen, printed for the Jane Austen Society, 1952). This was done after Cassandra Austen's death in 1845. It would seem therefore as if some alteration had been made between 1817 and 1845. Before 1817, according to Edward Austen Leigh there had been " a good sized entry ", which according to John White had disappeared after 1821. There is now a small room with a sash window overlooking the street, between the living room and the dining room; this was presumably made out of the entry, and the front door moved to clear it.

The *Memoir* says and John White confirms that after 1845 the house became labourers' tenements; it continued in this occupation for over a hundred years, but it had always enjoyed some degree of celebrity as the house in which Jane Austen had re-written *Sense and Sensibility* and *Pride and Prejudice*, and composed *Mansfield Park*, *Emma* and *Persuasion*.

A wooden tablet on the front of the house bears an inscription, undated, commemorating the fact that Jane Austen lived there from 1809–1817, and saying: " Her admirers in this country and in America have united to erect this tablet."

Of the three households which occupied the premises in 1940, Mrs. Stevens, aged 80 and her daughter Miss Stevens, included in their share the dining parlour and two bedrooms, of which they knew by tradition which was Mrs. Austen's and which was the one used by Jane and Cassandra. The length of this tradition, over a hundred years of occupation, seemed to give it considerable value. The room called Jane Austen's has a neat little grate with hobs, two built in cupboards with wooden pegs and a leaded casement overlooking the yard. Edward Austen-Leigh says that the sisters " shared the same bedroom till separated by death," and this room though rather small for the purpose could reasonably accommodate two people. The master-bedroom, an excellent room with two sash-windows overlooking the street, is said by the same authority to be Mrs. Austen's. That the latter should occupy the best bedroom was of course very probable, if not an absolute certainty.

Dorothy Darnell had had the ambition of restoring the house for a long time; what gave it impetus was the sight of the cast-iron grate from the Austens' dining parlour lying on the scrap-heap by the local forge. It had been wrenched out to make way for a gas fire, and its future was uncertain. She consulted Hugh Curtis, the curator of the Curtis Museum in Alton, and he housed the grate in the Museum until the day when the Jane Austen Society were able to restore it to its original position. This piece of rescue-work, performed before she had even founded the Society, was characteristic of everything she did afterwards. In May 1940, the Jane Austen Society held its first meeting; Hugh Curtis was Chairman, Beatrix Darnell treasurer, Dorothy Darnell and I, joint secretaries.

Major Knight was on active service, but he approved of the Society's scheme, and said finally that he was prepared to sell the freehold for £3,000. This seemed at the time a formidable sum to people quite without resources, and even if it were found, as we never doubted it would be in the end, to get vacant possession of the premises appeared next door to impossible as the inmates were protected tenants. All we could acquire at first was the tenancy of the living room; this had been let to the Chawton Village Library, who kindly made way for us.

We were told on all hands that we should never accomplish anything while the war lasted, but we did not agree. We secured the interest, approval and guidance of Dr. R. W. Chapman, and this was one of the greatest benefits we could have gained, while the Reports printed here show what Dorothy Darnell was able to do during these years, in which we had been told that we could not expect to do anything. Her conviction was justified that there would be wide support for such a society once it were known to exist, and news of it spreading merely by word of mouth resulted in small but steadily increasing membership. The annual subscription was then half a crown. The second piece of work she carried on during these years was the searching out and recording of every piece of local tradition about Jane Austen and the discovery of the whereabouts of any object which had a good pedigree of association with her. Unlike the possessions of the Brontës which had been kept intact by Charlotte Brontë's husband, the entire contents of Chawton Cottage were dispersed in the sale of 1845 which was held after Cassandra Austen's death. It seemed once as if nothing would ever come to light. But Dorothy Darnell always maintained that once Chawton Cottage were established as a Museum, people who had relics in their private possession would be encouraged to give or lend them or at least to say where they were. How right she was will be seen in these Reports, which also record what she did in collecting local memories. The most prized of her discoveries was the recollection of Mrs. Luff who was over 80 in 1942 and whose grandmother as a little girl remembered to have seen Jane Austen.

The progress of the Society reached a high water mark after December 1946. In that month an appeal published in *The Times* for help in collecting the purchase money brought in £1,400; but it also attracted the attention of Mr. Thomas Edward Carpenter, J.P., who visited the house in May 1947, and agreed to buy it for £3,000, creating the Jane Austen Memorial Trust to administer it in memory of his son Lieutenant John Philip Carpenter who was killed in action in July 1944. This arrangement made it possible for the Society to spend the money subscribed by readers of *The Times* appeal, as well as some previously collected, on immediate repairs to the property, £1,000 of which were needed for the roof alone.

From this time, the development of Chawton Cottage as a showplace and museum has been continuous. Mr. Carpenter has not only spent large sums renovating and decorating the interior; he also secured vacant possession of one of the tenements by buying a house in Alton in which he offered the inmates alternative accommodation. The exhibits he has bought and placed on view as well as gifts and loans from other sources are recorded in the following pages.

With the financial and administrative burden removed from the Jane Austen Society to the Jane Austen Memorial Trust, the function of the former is now to arrange the Annual General Meeting and to produce the Annual Report. The latter has turned into something more important than was once forseen. Many of its items are of limited interest, but some are of such value that no new life of Jane Austen should be written without reference to them: such as, the transcripts from the ledgers of Hoare's Bank dealing with the accounts of the Austen family, made available to the Society by the kindness of one of the Directors, the late Ronald Griffin, and the article on Jane Austen's death by Sir Zachary Cope, F.R.C.S.

The house was formally opened to the public at a General Meeting on July 23rd, 1949, and the Society has held an Annual General Meeting ever since, addressed by a guest speaker. We much regret that we did not adopt the practice of printing the speaker's address at full length until the printing of Sir Harold Nicolson's in 1956, so we have no verbatim record of Miss Elizabeth Bowen's in 1950, Lord David Cecil's in 1951, Miss Margaret Kennedy's in 1952, the Duke of Wellington's in 1953, Lady Cynthia Asquith's in 1954, and Mr. Arthur Bryant's in 1955. The speakers' names show what a loss has been entailed on the reader.

The early transactions of the Jane Austen Society were of a very amateur kind, and never intended for anything except private circulation, but perhaps that makes them the more interesting, as showing from what simple beginnings a seemingly-impossible goal can be achieved.   ELIZABETH JENKINS.

JANE AUSTEN
AND
JANE AUSTEN'S HOUSE

Photo, Sydney Newbury

Reproduced by the kind permission of Miss Louisa Lefroy, from the coloured drawing in her possession, in the MS. notebook of family history, compiled by her grandmother Anna Lefroy, Jane Austen's niece. Identified as a portrait of the authoress, by her sister Cassandra (C.E.A. 1804). See Dr. R. W. Chapman, "Jane Austen. Facts and Problems." Oxford. 1948. Appendix : The Portraits, p. 213-114.

Issued by The Jane Austen Society, in commemoration of the formal opening of Jane Austen's House, July 23rd, 1949.

FOREWORD

by

Dr. R. W. CHAPMAN, M.A., HON. D.LITT., HON. LL.D.

" Nescio qua natale solum dulcedine cunctos
Ducit, et immemores non sinit esse sui."

BUT the Ovidian maxim is truer of Jane Austen than of most, for she had roots deep in her native soil. She was not quickly reconciled to her first transplantation to Bath, which she left " with what happy feelings of escape ! " She made the best of the years at Southampton ; it was her nature to make the best of everything. But it is easy to see that she felt an alien there. The return to her own part of Hampshire, at the end of a long exile, moved her to expression in verse :

> Cassandra's pen will paint our state,
> The many comforts that await
> Our Chawton home, how much we find
> Already in it, to our mind ;
> And how convinced, that when complete
> It will all other Houses beat
> That ever have been made or mended,
> With rooms concise, or rooms distended.

At Chawton Cottage her talent came at last to full flower. Thence she launched the three books of her early twenties ; there she wrote the second three, the fruit of her maturer genius.

In so far as the house is now made free to lovers of Jane Austen it is rather concise than distended ; but that may be thought a type of the limits within which she confined her work—" infinite riches in a narrow room."

JANE AUSTEN, ALTON AND CHAWTON

by

ELIZABETH JENKINS

────────

WHEN the visitor arrives at Alton he will see that the High Street has still so many shop fronts, façades and doorways of late eighteenth century and early nineteenth century date that it presents very much the appearance which it had in 1809. Three notable buildings familiar to Jane Austen's view are on the right hand as one goes down the High Street, the Crown Inn, Normandy Hill next door (the house of Mr. Curtis, the Austens' surgeon-apothecary), and further down still the beautiful Lansdowne House with its early Georgian front and garlanded pediment.

2

The road from Alton to Chawton is the one followed by Jane Austen on her shopping expeditions to Alton. As the village is approached a green lane on the right of the road can be seen. This is Mounter's Lane, up which Jane Austen rode on donkey back, with Cassandra walking beside her, on her last airing before she was taken to Winchester.

On the outskirts of the village, standing in a meadow to the right of the road, is the remains of the house known as " Prowtings." From a cottage on the left of the road, the family used to see Jane Austen crossing the field which adjoins the garden of the Austens' House, when she went to call on her friends, the Misses Prowting.

Jane Austen's House stands at the cross-roads of the Winchester, Portsmouth and London roads. On the facade of the house to the left of the front door there will be noticed the place of the window which Edward Knight blocked up and replaced by the one overlooking the garden, when his mother and sisters went to the house in 1809. In this space was erected the Tablet (designed by Ellen G. Hill) subscribed for by Anglo-American friends to commemorate the Jane Austen Centenary in 1917. When the drawing room was redecorated by the Society in 1949, fragments were discovered of a wall paper which had been pasted on the actual plaster filling up the window. These fragments, which visitors will see framed on the drawing room wall, must be a part of the paper hung in 1809 and intimately familiar to Jane Austen on the walls of the family living room.

The various objects of interest which the room contains at present have descriptive labels attached.

The visitor's attention is drawn to the little domestic out-buildings across the yard. These are in a state of unusual completeness. They include the well with its original leaden bucket, the bread oven, the laundry copper and the bacon roller in the roof.

The pond which lay beside the cross-roads was drained within living memory. Jane Austen wrote to her nephew, James Edward Austen (July 9th, 1816) : "A little change of scene may be good for you, & your Physicians I hope will order you to the Sea, or to a house by the side of a very considerable pond." A little way down the Gosport turnpike on the right hand side is Chawton Rectory, in Jane Austen's day the home of Mr. Papillon, of whom Jane Austen said, in reply to matchmakers in her circle : " I will marry Mr. Papillon, whatever may be his reluctance or my own."

The gates of Chawton Great House are opposite. The drive, the park and the road leading back to the Austens' house are of particular interest from their association with the visits of the Knight family to the Great House and the intercourse of Jane Austen and her favourite niece Fanny Knight ; entries in the latter's diary commemorate one such visit : "Aunt Jane and I had a delicious morning together." " Spent the evening with Aunt Jane." " Had leeches on for a headache, Aunt Jane came and sat with me."

3

THE AUSTENS AND CHAWTON.

SOME DATES AND PARTICULARS

selected by

JOHN SIMPSON, M.A.

PART I. SHORT CHRONOLOGY.

(With special reference to Dr. R. W. Chapman : " Jane Austen. Facts and Problems." Chronology, pages 175-183 and " Austen Papers 1704-1856 " edited by R. A. Austen-Leigh.)

1764 *April* 26   The marriage of George Austen and Cassandra Leigh.

1775 *Dec.* 16   The birth of Jane Austen, at Steventon Rectory.

1801 *May*   The Austen family leaves Steventon.
(1801—1809. The Years of Exile.)

1805 *Jan.* 21   Death of the Rev. George Austen, at Bath.

1808 *Oct.* 24   The plan to live at Chawton, mentioned in a letter of Jane Austen to her sister Cassandra. (" *Jane Austen's Letters.*" *Edition Dr. R. W. Chapman*, pp. 226-227 and 229.)

1809 *July* 26   The first letter (*in verse*) from Chawton, after Mrs. Austen, Cassandra and Jane had taken up residence. (" *Jane Austen's Letters.*" *Edition Dr. R. W. Chapman*, p. 264.)

1811 *May* 29   " *Some of the flower seeds are coming up very well, but your mignonette makes a wretched appearance. . . . Our young piony at the foot of the fir-tree has just blown and looks very handsome, and the whole of the shrubbery border will soon be very gay with pinks and sweet-williams, in addition to the columbines already in bloom. The syringas, too, are coming out. We are likely to have a great crop of Orleans plums, but not many greengages ——.*" (" *Jane Austen's Letters.*" *Edition Dr. R. W. Chapman*, pp. 280-1.)

1811 *Nov.*   First publication of " *Sense and Sensibility,*" the authoress's first book to be published.

1812 *Oct.* 14   Death of Mrs. Thomas Knight. Edward Austen comes into the full inheritance of the Chawton property.

1812   Edward Austen assumes the name of Knight.

1813 *Jan.*   First publication of " *Pride and Prejudice.*"

1814 *May*   First publication of " *Mansfield Park.*"

1815 *Dec.*   First publication of " *Emma.*"

1816 *Dec.*   Henry Austen " *ordained to the curacy of Alton.*"

1817 *Jan.* 27   " *Sanditon,*" the last work, commenced.

Feb. 16   The Rev. Henry Austen preaches at Chawton.

May 24   Jane Austen leaves Chawton for the last time, travelling with Cassandra in Edward Knight's carriage, by the coach-road to Winchester, and attended on horseback by her brother Henry and her nephew, William Knight (later Rector of Steventon, 1823—1873).

CHAWTON STREET AS IT WAS

Reproduced from an old photograph in the possession of Mrs. Archer, showing the former Pond and Jane Austen's House before the rebuilding of the garden wall.

Photo, J. Butler-Kearney

JANE AUSTEN'S HOUSE

Chawton Cottage, in 1949, as restored by The Jane Austen Society.

SHORT CHRONOLOGY (*continued*).

1817	*July* 18	Death of Jane Austen, at Winchester. She is buried in Winchester Cathedral.
1818		Published date of 1st Edition of "*Northanger Abbey : and Persuasion.*"
1818	*April* 3	" *The Chawton Lawsuit* (between Edward Knight and a descendant of the (Martin) Knights) *compromised, Mr. Knight gave £15,000 that all claims on the estate should be for ever relinquished.*" (From the Journal of a neighbour, the Rev. Edmund Yalden White, Gilbert White's great-nephew.)
1818	*May* 12	" *The Inhabitants of Alton sign a petition to the Bishop and Mr. Poulter (Vicar) that Mr. Austen may continue as Curate.*" (Rev. E. Y. White's Journal.) Henry Austen was later Curate of Farnham, Surrey, and Bentley, Hampshire.
1827	*Jan.* 18	" *Mrs. Austen of Chawton, died.*" (Rev. E. Y. White's Journal.)
1837		Jane Austen's nephew, the Rev. James Edward Austen adds " -Leigh " to his name.
1845	*Mar.* 22	Death of Cassandra Austen.
1869	*May* 4	Death of Lord Chief Justice Lefroy (" Tom Lefroy ") at the age of 93 years, more than 70 years after the Steventon days.
1870		First publication of the Rev. James Edward Austen-Leigh's " *Memoir of Jane Austen.*"
1884		The 1st Lord Brabourne's Edition of the " *Letters of Jane Austen.*"
1902		Publication of " *Jane Austen, Her Homes and Her Friends,*" by Constance Hill.
1911		Publication of " *Chawton Manor,*" by William Austen-Leigh and Montague George Knight.
1913		Publication of " *Life and Letters of Jane Austen,*" by W. and R. A. Austen-Leigh.
1917		Jane Austen Centenary and erection of Memorial Tablet, designed by Ellen G. Hill, and subscribed for by Anglo-American friends.
1925		First publication of " *Sanditon.*"
1932		" *Jane Austen's Letters,*" edited by Dr. R. W. Chapman.
1940		Foundation of The Jane Austen Society, on the initiation of Miss Dorothy Darnell, for the purpose of preserving Jane Austen's House.
1945	*Feb.* 2 & 9	" *Chawton House, Hampshire.*" Articles by Christopher Hussey in " *Country Life.*"

| 1948 | *Feb.* 18 | Agreement for Purchase of Jane Austen's House (Chawton Cottage), by Mr. T. Edward Carpenter, B.A., LL.D., J.P., in memory of his son, Philip John Carpenter, of Christ's College, Cambridge, and the Middle Temple, Lieutenant, 1st Battalion The East Surrey Regiment, who fell in battle at Trasimene on June 30th, 1944. |
| 1948 | *May* 26. | Conveyance of Jane Austen's House by Mr. Edward Knight (the 3rd), of Chawton, to Mr. T. Edward Carpenter. |

Pkoto, J. Butler-Kearney

CHAWTON HOUSE AND CHURCH

Chawton House was built at the end of the 16th century and added to in the 17th century. The old Church, which consisted of chancel and nave with a low tower, burnt down in 1871, was rebuilt in flint and Bath stone, to the design of Sir Arthur Blomfield. Mrs. Austen, Cassandra and many members of the Knight family lie buried in the churchyard, the graves of the former having been restored by the donor of Jane Austen's House.

| 1948—1949 | | Restoration of Jane Austen's House, the cost being defrayed out of funds raised by The Jane Austen Society. |
| 1949 | *July* 23. | Date fixed for the formal opening of Jane Austen's House by His Grace the Duke of Wellington, President of The Jane Austen Society. |

This date has been arranged for the final execution of the Conveyance of the property by Mr. T. Edward Carpenter, together with the requisite Declaration of Trust of The Jane Austen Memorial Trust.

The following Trustees have consented to act, jointly with Mr. Carpenter, and have been appointed by him :—

1. Dr. Robert William Chapman, M.A., HON. D.LITT., HON. LL.D.
2. Mr. William Hugh Curtis, F.S.A.
3. Miss Dorothy Gwynnydd Darnell.
4. Miss Mary Madge Lascelles, M.A., B.LITT.
5. Mr. Richard Arthur Austen-Leigh, M.A., F.S.A.

7

PART II. THE "HAMPSHIRE - BORN" AUSTENS.

(See " *Jane Austen's Letters,*" *July* 3, 1813. *Edition Dr. R. W. Chapman, p.* 314.)

The following table is designed to show, as concisely as possible, the relationship of those members of the Austen family who are best known through the letters, and their connection with some of their descendants living to-day, by whose and whose ancestors' kindness the various Austen M.SS. and portraits have been made available to the public, in published works by the 1st Lord Brabourne, three generations of the Austen-Leigh family, Miss Constance Hill, Dr. R. W. Chapman and others.

The Children of the Rev. George Austen (1731 - 1805) and Mrs. Austen (1739 - 1827 were—	They married—	Their children included—	Whose marriages were—	And whose descendants living to-day include—
The Rev. JAMES 1765 - 1819	(1) Anne Mathew - 1795	Anna 1793 - 1872	Rev. Benjamin Lefroy* 1791 - 1829	Miss Louisa Lefroy
	(2) Mary Lloyd - 1843	Rev. James Edward (Austen-Leigh)	Emma Smith (niece of Mrs. William Chute of The Vyne)	E. C. and Richard A. Austen-Leigh Esquires
George 1766 - 1838	Unm. (invalid)			
EDWARD (Knight) 1768 - 1852	Elizabeth Bridges 1773 - 1808	Fanny 1793 - 1882	Sir Edward Knatchbull, Bt.	Lord Brabourne
		Edward (the 2nd) 1794 - 1879	(1) Mary Knatchbull - 1838	Lt.-Col. A. B. Knight, of Pamber
			(2) Adela Portal - 1870	Edward Knight, Esq. (the 3rd), of Chawton
		Rev. William 1798 - 1873	(1) C. Portal (2) M. Northey (3) Jane Hope	
The Rev. HENRY Thomas 1771 - 1850	(1) Eliza de Feuillide 1761 - 1813 (2) Eleanor Jackson	None None		
CASSANDRA Elizabeth 1773 - 1845	Unm.			
Admiral of the Fleet Sir FRANCIS William, R.N., G.C.B. 1774 - 1865	(1) Mary Gibson - 1823	Catherine Anne 1818 - 1877	John Hubback	Miss Helen Brown
	(2) Martha Lloyd 1843	None		
JANE 1775 - 1817	Unm.			
Rear Admiral CHARLES John, R.N., 1779 - 1852	(1) Frances Palmer - 1814	Several		Several
	(2) H. Palmer	None		

*NOTE.—The Rev. Benjamin Lefroy, Rector of Ashe (1823 - 1829), was the younger son of the Rev. Isaac Peter George Lefroy, Rector of Ashe (1783 - 1806), and Madam Lefroy. The Lefroy family, of Itchel Manor, Crondall, are descended from his elder brother, the Rev. Henry George Lefroy, Rector of Ashe (1806 - 1823). Jane Austen's dancing partner, " Tom Lefroy " (Thomas Langlois Lefroy, later Lord Chief Justice of Ireland), was a first cousin of the Lefroy brothers. From him are descended the Lefroy families of Carrig-Glas, Co. Longford, and of Croft House, Botley, in Hampshire.

8

DESIGN FOR A GARDEN
for
JANE AUSTEN'S HOUSE
by
SELWYN DURUZ.

Introduction

IT is not easy to picture the garden in which Jane Austen moved, for hers was an age of great change in garden fashion. At the time when she was writing at Chawton, the early " landscape school " of garden architects was in its heyday, tearing asunder the mellowed, often homely gardens of the well-to-do and famous ; gardens which had grown up within the shelter of yew hedges and stone-topped walls. In their place came the wildly extravagant type of garden of which Sir Walter Scott was later to write " it is not simplicity but affectation labouring to seem simple."

On great estates, like Blenheim, at Gunnersbury, " Claremont " at Esher and Pain's Hill in Surrey, first William Kent and later " Capability Brown " (so called because when asked to give his opinion he could be counted upon to say the subject had " great capabilities ") had set in train a movement which, by 1810, can aptly be described as a major pastime for the landed gentry. Where Kent and Brown, influenced by the natural taste of their customers, created beauty, others in hundreds fancied themselves as experts and wrought untold havoc among simple, lovely, old-fashioned English gardens. Flowers were banished or relegated to hot-houses ; stately avenues of trees were felled ; hedges uprooted—whole stretches of ground torn up, while artificial lakes and streams, hills and dales in miniature were substituted. Where fine effects could be achieved on large and naturally undulating estates, only a flatness and infinitely boring emptiness resulted on the majority of small estates.

At the turn of the 18th century, fantasy reached its height in an outburst of temples, grottos, imitation ruins and other exaggerated expressions of " the picturesque," which Jane Austen satirized in " *Sense and Sensibility* " (Chapter XVIII) and in " *Mansfield Park* " (Chapter VI).

We can be quite sure, however, that simplicity marked the garden at Chawton. A good old-fashioned array of flowers, an arbour (or gazebo) and a well-stocked fruit and kitchen department, were pretty surely there. For material, there was much less choice of plant than would have been available even thirty years later (*i.e.*, 100 years ago). Plants we think of as old-fashioned, such as the rose " Gloire de Dijon," were not yet available. Jane Austen's era coincided, in fact, with the lowest ebb, in English garden history. Despite the genius of Humphrey Repton, mentioned by name in " *Mansfield Park*," other " improvers " were wrecking the old gardens. Nevertheless the seeds of a counter-movement, to restore colour to the garden, were well implanted. Horticultural literature was the medium and never have horticultural publications appeared equal to or more magnificent than the great works of the early 19th century. How well did the universal longing for colour and blossom find expression in the superb if phantasmagorial " *Temple of Flora* " of R. J. Thornton (1805) ; in Redouté and Thory's " *Les Roses* " (1817 - 1824) ; in Conrad Loddiges' " *Botanical Cabinet* " (1818 - 1833) and the still more celebrated " *Botanical Magazine*," begun in 1787 by William Curtis, an ancestor of Mr. W. H. Curtis, Chairman of The Jane Austen Society, and still to this day published—the world's most celebrated botanical work.

What sort of garden, then, can Jane Austen have known ? Probably it will have resembled the type of happy mixture of bettered cottage garden one associates with old rectories and vicarages. Such an one is suggested in the present scheme. It is populated with contemporary plants. The colourings will be soft and the flowering season shorter than in modern show-places. It may, we hope, recapture the calm and rest of those quieter days.

ENVOI.

" *Oft when I've seen some lovely mansion stand*
Fresh from the improver's desolating hand,
'Midst shaven lawns that far around it creep
In one eternal undulating sweep ;
And scatter'd clumps, that nod at one another,
Each stiffly waving to its formal brother :
Tired with the extensive scene, so dull and bare,
To Heaven devoutly I've address'd my prayer ;
Again the moss-grown terraces to raise,
And spread the labyrinth's perplexing maze ;
Replace in even lines the ductile yew,
And plant again the ancient avenue.
Some features then, at least, we should obtain
To mark this flat, insipid, waving plain :
Some vary'd tints and forms would intervene
To break this uniform, eternal green."

from " The Landscape "—
a didactic poem in three Books, addressed by R. P. Knight to Sir Uvedale Price (2nd Ed.
1795), *quoted by Elinour Sinclair Rohde in " The Story of the Garden."*

BIBLIOGRAPHY.

1794-98 Price, Uvedale "*An Essay on the Picturesque, as compared with the Sublime and Beautiful, etc.*" 8vo.

1795 Repton, Humphrey " *Sketches and Hints on Landscape Gardening.*" Ob. fol.

1803 Repton, Humphrey " *Observations on the Theory and Practice of Landscape Gardening.*" 4to.

1806 Repton, Humphrey "*An Enquiry into the Changes of Taste in Landscape Gardening.*" 8vo.

1806 Loudon, J. C. "*A Treatise on Forming, Improving and Managing Country Residences. Illus.*" 4to.

1829 Johnson, G. W. "*A History of English Gardening.*"

1910 Amherst, Hon. Alicia (later Lady Rockley) "*A History of Gardening in England* " (Murray). 8vo.

1932 Rohde, Elinour Sinclair " *The Story of the Garden,*" Col. pls. (Medici Society). 8vo.

1938 Clark, H. " *The English Landscape Garden* " (Pleiades Books). 8vo.

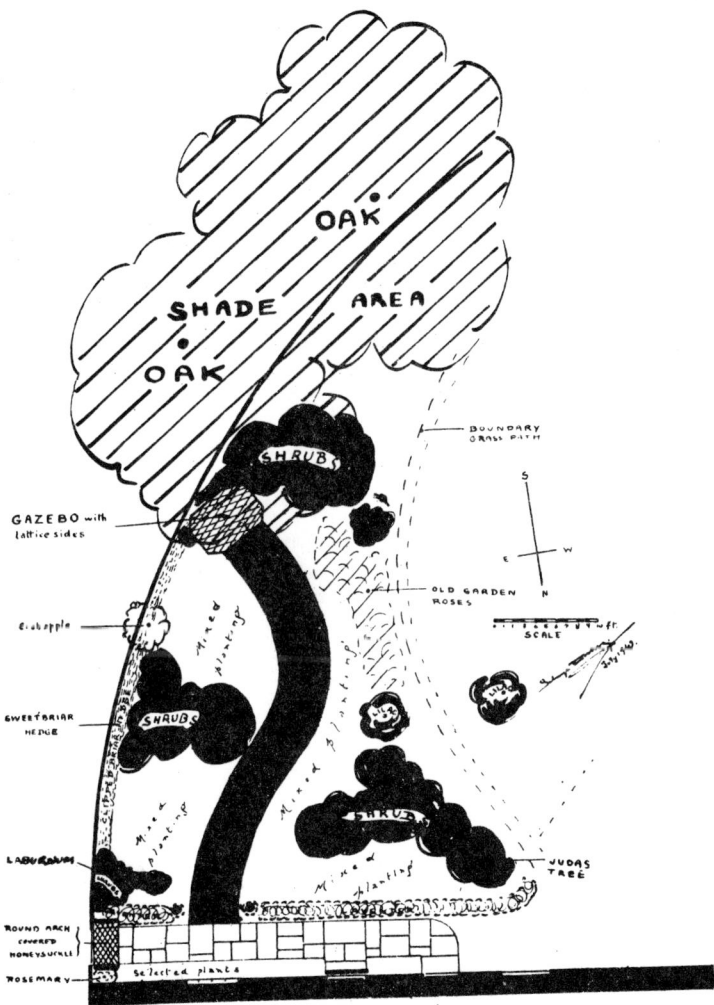

OAK

SHADE AREA

OAK

OAK

SHRUBS

BOUNDARY
GRASS PATH

GAZEBO with
lattice sides

OLD GARDEN
ROSES

Crabapple

SCALE

SWEETBRIAR
HEDGE

SHRUBS

SHRUB

LABURNUM

JUDAS
TREE

ROUND ARCH
COVERED
HONEYSUCKLE

ROSEMARY

Selected plants

PRELIMINARY STUDY,

showing proposed design for the garden of Jane Austen's House (first stage of development).

*In the design a grass path, 5ft. wide, curves from opposite the window to a gazebo, standing
in the shade of the oaks which are now outside the garden wall, as reconstructed.*

11

LIST OF PLANTS, ETC.,
cultivated in English Gardens in the early 19th century.

The list is not exhaustive, but it gives a fair idea of the flowers commonly grown 150 years ago.

GARDEN PLANTS.

Acanthus
Achillaea
Agrostemma
Alyssum
Anchusa
Anemone
Arabis
Auricula
Bergamot
Bocconia
Borage
Bugle
Campanula
Candytuft
Canterbury Bell
Carnation
Chrysanthemum
Colchicum
Columbine
Coreopsis
Crocus
Crown Imperial
Cyclamen
Delphinium (early hybrids)
Dictamnus
Forget-me-not
Foxglove

Galega
Gladwyn Iris
Gypsophila
Hellebore
Hemerocallis
Hollyhock
Houseleek
Hyacinth
Hyssop
Iris (pallida and purple flag)
Jacob's Ladder
Lathyrus
Lily (Madonna, Tiger, martagon)
Lily-of-the-Valley
Love-in-a-Mist
Lupin
Marigold
Mignonette
Monkshood
Mullein
Narcissus
Nasturtium
Paeony (double red)
Pansy
Perrywinkle

Phlox (weak varieties)
Pinks
Polyanthus
Poppy
Primrose
Rose—old garden varieties, including Sweet Briar, alba celestial, centifolia Provence, York and Lancaster, Rosa Mundi, etc.
Snowdrop
Soldiers and Sailors
Solomon's Seal
Southernwood
Spiraea
Stock
Sweet Pea (4 varieties)
Sweet William
Thrift
Tradescantia
Tigridia
Tulip
Valerian
Viola cornuta
Violet
Wallflower

TREES AND SHRUBS.

Ailanthus
Almond
Aucuba
Box
Broom
Buddleia globosa
Cistus
Coronilla emerus
Daphne mezereum
Dogwood
Guelder Rose
Hawthorn

Hypericum androsaemum
    „   calycinum
Irish Yew
Judas Tree
Laburnum
Lavender
Lilac (common)
Magnolia conspicua (denudata)
Philadelphus coronarius
Phlomis fruticosa
Prunus avium ; cerasus ; padus

Pyrus aria ; floribunda ; torminalis ; salicifolia
Rosemary
Rubus odoratus
Ruscus
Santolina chamaecyparissus
Spartium junceum
Syringa (cf. Philadelphus)
Viburnum tinus (laurustinus)
Viburnum opulus
Yucca filamentosa
Yew

CLIMBERS AND WALL SUBJECTS.

Agapanthus
Honeysuckle
Ivy
Japonica (C. japonica) 1815

Jasmine
Kerria Japonica (1700)
Magnolia grandiflora (1737)
Passion Flower (P. caerulea) 1699

Rosa Banksiae (double white) 1809
Wistaria chinensis (1816)

S.D., *July*, 1949

EDITOR'S NOTE.

   This publication is issued by The Jane Austen Society to commemorate the formal opening of Jane Austen's House, to be performed by His Grace The Duke of Wellington, President of the Society, on July 23rd, 1949. This marks the first step in the fulfilment of Miss Dorothy Darnell's original idea which led, with the assistance of Mr. W. H. Curtis and Miss Elizabeth Jenkins, to the formation of the Society. Members are requested kindly to assist in making known the publication which will be on sale at Jane Austen's House and is also obtainable from Messrs. Warren & Son Ltd., 85 High Street, Winchester or the Hon. Sec., Jordans, Alton, Hants. The proceeds will be handed to the Trustees of the Jane Austen Memorial Trust, to be devoted to the improvement and maintenance of the house and garden. The Society wishes to place on record its gratitude to Mr. T. Edward Carpenter for guaranteeing the cost of production, to all those who have contributed, to Miss Louisa Lefroy, Mrs. Archer, Mr. Selwyn Duruz and Mr. J. Butler-Kearney, in connection with the illustrations, to Dr. Chapman and Mr. R. A. Austen-Leigh, for permission to make reference to their works and to Miss Cornelia White for quotations from the Journal, in her possession, of her cousin, the Rev. Edmund Yalden White, son of the Rev. Edmund White, Vicar of Newton Valence. The journalist was for very many years Curate-in-Charge of Crondall, in Hampshire. He used to dine regularly at Chawton House and play cricket with Jane Austen's nephews, the Knights.   The copyright of the various contributions is reserved to the respective contributors.

JOHN SIMPSON.

THE JANE AUSTEN SOCIETY

Report for the period 1st October, 1949—31st December, 1950

The Steventon Furniture

THE JANE AUSTEN SOCIETY

(Founded 1940)

President :

His Grace The Duke of Wellington.

Vice-Presidents :

T. Edward Carpenter, Esq.

Dr. R. W. Chapman, M.A., Hon. D. LITT., Hon.LL.D.

Chairman :

W. Hugh Curtis, Esq., F.S.A.

Vice-Chairman and Joint Honorary Treasurer :

Lt. Col. C. R. Satterthwaite,
Lansdowne House, Alton, Hants.

Committee :

Miss Elizabeth Bowen, C.B.E., LL.D. (Mrs. Alan Cameron).
Mrs. W. Hugh Curtis.
Miss A. B. Darnell.
Mrs. K. A. Robbins.
Miss Ann Sitwell (Mrs. Cubitt).
Lady Smiley.

Joint Honorary Treasurer :

F. H. Foster, Esq., Lloyds' Bank, Ltd. Alton, Hants.

Joint Honorary Secretaries :

Miss Dorothy Darnell, Brook Cottage, Alton, Hants.
Miss Elizabeth Jenkins, 8 Downshire Hill, Hampstead, N.W.3.

Honorary Auditors :

Messrs. Sheen, Stickland and Co., Alton, Hants.

THE JANE AUSTEN SOCIETY

Report for the period 1st Oct., 1949—31st Dec., 1950

The Committee of the Jane Austen Society have the honour to report that His Majesty the King has been graciously pleased, at the suggestion of Mr. T. Edward Carpenter, to give directions to the Librarian at Windsor Castle, Sir Owen Morshead, that the three volumes of "Emma", which were sent by Jane Austen's publisher, Mr. John Murray, at her request to the Prince Regent at the end of 1815, just before the novel's publication, are to be lent to the Trustees during the summer of 1951. It will be remembered that "Emma" was dedicated to the Prince Regent at his own suggestion, and it is hoped that these most valuable volumes will be on view in Jane Austen's house from Easter until the autumn.

The Committee are also greatly pleased, and not a little proud, to be able to report the purchase, in 1950, of a walnut escritoire and two Hepplewhite chairs, which formed part of the furniture of Steventon Rectory when Jane Austen lived there, and were left behind for the use of James Austen, who succeeded his father as Rector of Steventon when the latter moved with his wife and daughters to Bath in 1801. This is the Society's first major purchase, and it was made possible by a most generous gift from the National Art-Collections Fund, which gave £55 in October (and a further £25 in January, 1951) towards the total cost of £210. But the fact that the Society could afford to pay the balance shows how well its membership has been maintained, and how generous its members and well-wishers are.

These lovely pieces of furniture are now to be seen in Jane Austen's house at Chawton, where the visitors' book now lies for the signature of all who enter, on the desk that Jane Austen almost certainly used in her younger days.

Other additions to the contents of the room, made during 1950, include :

A patchwork quilt, made by Mrs. George Austen about 1810, and mentioned in Jane Austen's letters: lent by Mrs. W. J. Knight.

A scarlet postillion's coat, for theatricals, perhaps worn by Eliza de Feuillide: lent by Mrs. Jenkyns.

A watercolour sketch of Marianne Knight (Jane Austen's niece) in old age: presented by Mrs. Bursnall.

A watercolour sketch of Stoneleigh Abbey, where Jane Austen stayed in 1806: presented by Mrs. E. M. Huson.

A photograph of a carriage from Stoneleigh Abbey: presented by The Shakespeare Memorial Trust.

The lock of Jane Austen's hair, beautifully mounted, is now also to be seen, with that of her father. These relics were presented, at the Opening of the house in 1949, by Mrs. Henry G. Burke of Baltimore. The Donkey-cart mentioned in last year's Report is now on view in the old Bake-house at Chawton, and with it is a small brass-studded travelling trunk, traditionally the property of Jane's brother Edward Knight. It was presented by Mrs. Allen.

Nearly 1500 people have seen the house since September, 1949, besides a party from the Dickens Fellowship, and two parties, mainly composed of foreign visitors to England, organised by the British Council. The house is officially open from 11 a.m. to 4 p.m. on Tuesdays. Thursdays, and Saturdays ; but the Caretaker of the main room, Mrs. Newman, is always ready to admit visitors at other times if she is at home—her front door is next to the entrance of the house. Members of the Society enter free, and are asked to sign the Visitors' Book, others pay 1/- (children 6d.)

The Garden has now been laid out as far as possible according to the design of Mr. Selwyn Duruz which was described in the pamphlet printed at the time of the Opening in 1949. All summer, and well into the autumn, it was gay with flowers that Jane Austen would have known, including those mentioned in her letters: syringa, laburnum, peony and mignonette. The Committee have been greatly helped by a generous donation towards the garden expenses from Mrs. J. B. Clark.

A General Meeting of the Society was held in Alton on July 8th, 1950, some 140 members and their friends being present. Mr. W. Hugh Curtis presided, and the business included the unanimous adoption of the draft Constitution of the Society (printed on p. 6); and of the Report and Accounts for 1946-49. The Officers and Committee whose names appear on the first page of this Report were elected, also unanimously. The Meeting then heard a most interesting short speech by Dr. R. W. Chapman, and a brilliant address on Jane Austen's art by Miss Elizabeth Bowen. After the meeting, members went to Chawton and saw the house and garden. The weather was fine, and Chawton looked its best for the occasion.

On the afternoon of Sunday, July 9th, a short Service of commemoration was held in Chawton Parish Church, and attended by many members. The Rector of Chawton, Canon T. C. R. Moore, conducted the Service; Canon R. F. Pechey read the Lessons, and the Sermon was preached by Canon Roger Lloyd, Canon Residentiary of Winchester Cathedral. The anthem, "The Lord is my Shepherd", set to "Brother James's air" was beautifully sung by the choir, and among the hymns were "God moves in a mysterious way", and "O for a closer walk with God", by Cowper, whose poetry Jane Austen loved.

After the General Meeting, letters were written to all members whose subscriptions were in arrear. As a result, many members paid; a few resigned, and they, with those who did not answer, have now been removed from the list of members. The effect has been a reduction in numbers below the figure of membership reported last year; but the Society had, at the end of 1950, a total of 699 members, of whom 135 were Life-members. 144 new members joined in 1950, 26 of them becoming Life-members. These are most satisfactory figures, and much above those of other recent years. 68 of the Society's members, or nearly ten per cent, are citizens of the United States, and if space allowed, the Committee would like to quote many instances of their enthusiasm and generosity. One instance must suffice: the Freshman Class of the Low-Heywood School of Stamford, Connecticut, all joined the Society in 1950, and are planting on the school Campus acorns from Jane Austen's own oak-tree in the Chawton Garden.

The Accounts show that expenditure has exceeded income in the 15 months ending in December, 1950. This was to be expected, as the final instalment of the cost of the major restoration of the house had to be paid in 1950. As the house is now in an excellent structural state, however, its upkeep should cost little for some time to come (though the lighting of the main room must be improved), and the Committee feel confident that they will be able to meet current expenses in 1951. They have already been able to reduce office expenses considerably, and, since August, 1950, to dispense altogether with paid clerical assistance. But the Committee want not only to be able to meet the cost of maintenance. It is essential for the Society's purpose to be able to buy any genuine relics that come on the market. The cost of the Hepplewhite chairs—it amounts to £80—must be met early in 1951, and to cover this, and start the building-up of a substantial fund which can be drawn on without delay whenever some really desirable relic is for sale, and may pass into other hands, the Committee again ask for donations, large or small.

This Report, and the Accounts, will be presented to members at a General Meeting of the Society to be held later in 1951. Members will be given ample notice of the place, date, and time of the Meeting, and the Committee hope that very many will attend.

The Constitution of
THE JANE AUSTEN SOCIETY

(As approved at the General Meeting of the Society held on July 8th, 1950)

1. The Society is to be known as the Jane Austen Society.

2. The annual subscription shall be 5/-, and the Life subscription £5 0s. 0d.

3. The Society shall be administered from year to year from the first day of January in each year.

4. All annual subscriptions shall be due in advance on the 1st January in each year.

5. The affairs of the Society shall be administered by a President, two Vice-Presidents, a Chairman, Vice-Chairman, Honorary Treasurer, Honorary Secretary, one Assistant Secretary, and a Committee of members of the Society consisting of not less than three and not more than ten persons. Each of such officers shall retire annually, and may be re-elected at the Annual Meeting of the Society.

6. The Annual General Meeting shall be held in the month of March in each year, or as soon after as may be convenient. The Committee, which shall be deemed to include the other officers (save the Assistant Secretary, who may attend on the directions of the Committee) mentioned in Clause 5, shall meet at such times as the Chairman or Vice-Chairman may direct.

7. The objects of the Society are of a charitable nature and are:
(a)   to promote or procure the acquisition of the residence of Jane Austen, at Chawton in Hampshire, as a national memorial to the novelist.
(b)   to raise, by public subscription, gifts, grants, or otherwise such monies as may be requisite to restore and maintain from time to time such residence.
(c)   similarly to raise and use money to procure, for the purpose of founding a museum in such residence, any manuscripts, pictures, prints, articles, or other relics likely to prove of interest to the general public visiting such museum.
(d)   to carry out, by direction of the Trustees of the Jane Austen Memorial Trust, all such objects of a charitable nature as are set out in the Deed of Trust executed by such Trustees relative to such residence as a national memorial.
(e)   generally to do all such things as may be incidental and necessary for the carrying out of all the above objects.

8. The society shall keep regular and complete accounts of their receipts and expenditure, which shall be balanced on 31st day of December in every year and examined and audited by a Chartered or Incorporated Accountant appointed by the members at the Annual General Meeting.

THE JANE AUSTEN SOCIETY.

Report for the year 1951

Jane Austen's House.

THE JANE AUSTEN SOCIETY

(Founded 1940)

20

THE JANE AUSTEN SOCIETY
Report for 1951

Review of the Year

The Committee of the Jane Austen Society are glad to be able to report that 1951, the year of the Festival of Britain, was a most successful one for the Society; showing an increased membership, an improved financial position, a larger collection of relics on view, and the highest number of visitors to Jane Austen's House of any year so far recorded.

Membership

At the end of 1951, the Society had 168 Life Members, and 536 members who paid their annual subscriptions for the year. This makes a total of 704, which is slightly higher than that of 1950. Sixty members are citizens of the United States, fifteen live in countries of the British Empire outside the United Kingdom, and five in foreign countries.

Jane Austen's House

1,365 people paid for admission to Jane Austen's House in 1951. The house is open throughout the year from 11 a.m. to 4 p.m. on Tuesdays, Thursdays and Saturdays, when the Museum, in the Austens' drawing room, is shown by the Chief Caretaker, Mrs. Newman, and other rooms, including Jane Austen's bedroom, by their tenant, Miss Stevens. Although the caretakers are not on duty officially at other times, they are always ready to admit visitors whenever they are at home. Members are admitted free, and asked to sign the Visitors' Book; others pay 1/- (children 6d.). A form of concealed strip lighting has now been installed in the Museum room, which gives the light necessary for a Museum without detracting from the appearance of the room by incongruous fixtures.

" The Country of Jane Austen and Gilbert White "

As many overseas visitors were expected in England in 1951 for the Festival of Britain, the Committee decided early in the year to produce a leaflet for free distribution to Travel Agencies, describing Jane Austen's House and other features of the Alton neighbourhood. The Alton Urban District Council generously agreed to assist, and the Rev. W. Sidney Scott, of Selborne, kindly undertook the preparation of the leaflet. Gilbert White's Selborne is barely four miles from Chawton, and Alton has much historical interest and a High Street in which some of the buildings are unchanged since Jane Austen's day; while the Curtis Museum, founded by the son of the Austens' doctor, and the grandfather of the present Chairman of the Committee of this Society, is well-known throughout southern England. The title page of the leaflet, "The Country of Jane Austen and Gilbert White," was designed by Miss M. H. Whitehouse. Nearly 4,500 copies were accepted by Travel Agencies; it is difficult to assess its effect, since the number of those who paid for admission to Jane Austen's House in 1950 (eighty-two fewer than in 1951) undoubtedly included many members of the Society, who, after the Chairman's announcement at the General Meeting in that year, were admitted free; but it is certain that the leaflet produced some new members of the Society, and many visitors to the House.

Relics

No important relics of the Austen family were offered for sale in 1951, and the only purchase made was that of a mahogany Sutherland table, of the Sheraton period, which was traditionally part of the Austens' furniture at Chawton. Some valuable loans and gifts were received. Among the loans were :

The three volumes of " Emma," specially bound by Messrs. John Murray for presentation to the Prince Regent, after the novel had been dedicated to him at his own suggestion. The volumes, graciously lent to the Trustees by His late Majesty King George VI, were returned to Windsor Castle at the end of the Festival Year.

A black and gold lacquered work table, once the property of Jane Austen, lent by Mrs. T. E. Carpenter.

A cabinet of relics of the Austen family, including :
A white India muslin scarf, embroidered in white by Jane Austen.
Two necklaces that belonged to Jane Austen.
Two bead purses of the period.
Silhouettes of the Rev. George Austen and Mrs. Austen and of Mr. and Mrs. Leigh Perrot.
" Poems by Dr. Goldsmith," inscribed " Jane Leigh Perrot." Lent by Mr. Laurence Impey (a descendant of Jane Austen's eldest brother, James).
An Ivory Cup and Ball, one of two still in existence with which Jane Austen played at Chawton or Godmersham (James Edward Austen Leigh, in his " Memoir of Jane Austen," says " Her performance with cup and ball was marvellous.").

The loan of the patchwork quilt worked by Mrs. Austen for which Cassandra and Jane collected materials, and to which Jane refers in her letter of May 31st, 1811, has been kindly renewed by Mr. W. J. Knight for the season of 1952.

Gifts made in 1951 include :
A photograph of Steventon Church, with the 19th Century alterations suppressed, so that the church appears as the Austens knew it.
Photostat copies of Jane Austen's mischievous entries in the Steventon Marriage Register.
Presented by Mr. Henry Henshaw.
" The Trial of Mrs. Leigh Perrot." Pamphlet.
Presented by Dr. R. W. Chapman.
" Charades," written a hundred years ago by Jane Austen and her family, by Mary Austen Leigh.

Two watercolours of Chawton in the Austens' day.
Presented by Miss Beryl Bradford.
" Emma." First Edition.
Presented by Mrs. Richard Williams.
" Pride and Prejudice." First Edition.
Presented by Miss Alice Pechell.
" Pride and Prejudice." Specially bound and presented by Miss
Phyllis Lang.
" Persuasion " in the Finnish language.
Presented by Mr. Rex Littleboy.
A coloured sketch of an officer in the uniform of the Oxfordshire
Militia, as worn by Henry Austen about 1800.
Presented by Miss Joan Corder.

All the new acquisitions mentioned above are on view in Jane
Austen's House, and the thanks of the Trustees and the Society are
due to those who have generously given, and lent them. Labels in
script have been written for the exhibits by Miss G. A. George.

Mr. Ian Henderson, of Carlyle House in Chawton (previously
called Denmead, and at one time the Dower House of Chawton
Manor) has kindly allowed the Society to remove from his garden
the flagstones that formed the floor of the kitchen in the Austens'
house. These were laid in the Dower House garden when the Austens'
house was converted into homes for Chawton villagers after Cassandra
Austen's death in 1845, and they have now been relaid in the pathway
between the Austens' house and the garden.

The need for some means, visible to passers-by, of identifying
Jane Austen's House has long been felt by the Society, and to meet
this need Mr. G. A. Tippett has kindly given the Society a hanging
sign. This has been placed on a low oak post just inside the garden
wall. It consists of a small, black, enamelled board, with the words
" Jane Austen's House " in gold, hung in a wrought iron frame with
scroll work, adapted by Mrs. Joy Tippett from an 18th Century
model design, and made by the Hampshire craftsman, A. C. Thorpe,
of Mattingley. This useful gift is gratefully welcomed.

The Garden

The Garden has been further developed on the lines proposed by
Mr. Selwyn Duruz, and the Committee is again indebted to him for
his help and advice, and to Mrs. J. B. Clark for the gift of a number of
plants and shrubs, and for her personal help in their planting and
arrangement. On the day of the General Meeting, it was generally
agreed that the garden, in its summer glory of flowers that Jane Austen
would have known, was a proper setting for the old red brick of the
house, with its curved grass path leading to the oak seat under the
boundary wall.

23

The Annual General Meeting

The Annual General Meeting was held, in fine weather, on the afternoon of Saturday, July 21st, in a marquee kindly lent by Messrs. Crowley & Co., pitched, as in 1949, in Mr.Clarke's field behind Chawton Village Hall. The Duke of Wellington took the Chair, and there was an attendance of upwards of 300 members and their friends. The Chairman of the Committee, Mr. W. Hugh Curtis, expressed the Society's thanks to the Duke for his leadership as President, and to many other helpers and benefactors. The Report and Accounts for 1950 were presented and accepted, and the officers and Committee, as printed on the first page of this Report, were unanimously elected. After the formal business, members heard a delightul informal address by Lord David Cecil, who, in twenty minutes, was able to communicate to his audience something of his own deep love for Jane Austen's novels, and of his unique understanding of her mind and genius. Dr. R. W. Chapman's address, which followed, seemed all too short. Mr. T. Edward Carpenter spoke of his hopes that teas might be available in the future at the Grey Friar Inn at Chawton, under its new ownership, and the proceedings terminated with votes of thanks, proposed by Miss Elizabeth Bowen and Mr. R. A. Austen Leigh, and a brief reply from the Duke of Wellington.

After the meeting, members were able to visit Jane Austen's House, the gardens of Chawton Manor (by kind permission of Major Edward Knight), the Church and Churchyard, where Mrs. Austen and her daughter, Cassandra, lie buried, and the Rectory garden (by kind permission of Canon and Mrs. Moore).

To all those who helped to make the Meeting a success, and specially to Mr. Clarke, whose field makes such a perfect setting for the Society's meetings, the Committee offer their warm thanks.

" Scenes from Pride and Prejudice "

After the General Meeting more than 150 members attended a performance in the Alton Assembly Rooms of " Scenes from Pride and Prejudice," acted by members of the Alton Business and Professional Women's Club. The producer was Mrs. Cathleen Callender, and the script, written by Miss Dorothy Darnell, was taken word for word from those scenes in the novel in which only women were present, while the whole was knit together by a narrative spoken and acted by a member of the Club who is a direct descendant of Jane Austen's brother, Edward. It was a lovely performance, and the Society is greatly indebted to the Club for specially arranging it.

.The Service of Remembrance

On the afternoon of Sunday, July 22nd, following the General Meeting, a Service of Remembrance was held in Chawton Parish Church. The fine weather broke that morning, and a heavy thunderstorm struck Chawton, cutting off all electricity. Chawton Church needs artificial light, even in daytime, and Major Knight collected some hundreds of candles from Alton stores after the storm, and had them arranged in the fine brass candelabra, so that the lighting at the service must have been much as Jane Austen would have known it— although, apart from the chancel, the present Church is not that in which she worshipped. The service was well attended; it was conducted by the Rector, Canon T. C. R. Moore, assisted by Canon R. F. Pechey; the lessons were read by Colonel C. R. Satterthwaite and Mr. R. L. McAndrew, and the sermon was preached by Archdeacon Chute, of Basingstoke, members of whose family still live at The Vyne as they did in the days when the Austens were at Steventon and the Chutes were their friends, and Tom Chute one of Jane's dancing partners.

Sales of Property in Chawton

In the summer of 1951, a number of buildings in Chawton, including some old cottages, were sold by auction. Many of the cottages were bought by their tenants, who thus became the owners of the homes in which some of them have lived for many years. All who love Chawton as it is will be glad to know that no important changes will follow the sale, though it may be that a small car park will be made.

In the autumn, the pair of very old thatched cottages adjoining the Austens' house to the north came under the hammer. Apart from periodical re-thatching, these cottages, which may in part be 500 years old, cannot have changed in outward appearance since long before Jane Austen's day. One, next to the Forge, is and will remain the home of Mr. and Mrs. Cooper; the other, known as " Clinkers," was empty; and it was the death of old Mrs. Clinker that brought about the sale. It is believed in Chawton that 1951 was the first year since 1540 when no member of the Clinker family was at home in the cottage at Christmas. To this cottage the table bought by the Society, and referred to earlier in this Report, was transferred after 1845. Both these cottages were purchased by Mr. G. A. Faithfull, of Alton, a member of the Society, who is now engaged in restoring " Clinkers " internally so far as possible to its original state, and it is fortunate that the cottages have come into the hands of one who will preserve their character and charm.

Printing of the Memoir by Caroline Austen

In 1949 Mr. Richard Austen Leigh gave the Society the manuscript of the recollections of her aunt Jane Austen, which Caroline Austen had written shortly before her brother James Edward Austen Leigh began his Memoir of Jane Austen, which was published in 1870. Caroline, who was the daughter of Jane's eldest brother James, by his second wife, was twelve years old in the year of Jane Austen's death; she retained a child's memory of a dearly-loved aunt, and her story has always been recognised as of unique value among the first-hand descriptions of Jane Austen. A great deal of it has been published already; for James Edward Austen Leigh used much of it verbatim, and large extracts were quoted by Mary Augusta Austen Leigh in

" Personal Aspects of Jane Austen." But it has never been printed in full, and members will be glad to know that the Committee now feel able to defray the cost of printing it, hoping as they do that many will buy copies. It will be called, " My Aunt Jane Austen," and will have a preface by Dr. R. W. Chapman, a cover designed by Miss Dorothy Darnell, six photographic illustrations, and, as an appendix, the recollections of John White, a Chawton agricultural labourer, who died in 1921 in his hundredth year, and who, although just too young to remember Jane Austen, had clear memories of her family, and of the village in his early youth.

Copies are now available, and the price will be 3/6 a copy. An order form and addressed envelope are enclosed. The book will be on sale in Jane Austen's house, and, it is hoped, in some bookshops.

The Thanks of the Trustees

The Committee were much gratified to receive, in February of this year, the following from the Chairman of the Jane Austen Memorial Trust :—

" I wish to place on record, for the benefit of the Members of the Society and its officers my high appreciation of, and my grateful thanks for, the services they have rendered my Trust in acting jointly with the Managing Committee of the latter in the various activities required in dealing with Jane Austen's House, its many visitors, and its relics. The plan proposed in the Trust Deed has worked admirably and my especial recognition is here recorded on behalf of my fellow Trustees."

(*Signed*) T. EDWARD CARPENTER,
Chairman of Trustees

The Society's Accounts

The Accounts show that, even though the whole cost amounting to £80 of the Heppelwhite chairs from Steventon, which were bought in 1950, was paid in 1951, the Society's position is satisfactory. We began the year with a balance of £135, and ended it with nearly £300 in hand. This good increase is partly due to some very generous donations, notably one of £36 from Mrs. Folwell W. Coan, of Minneapolis and Miss La Monte, of New York, for the purchase of relics, and one of £25, additional to that of £55 in 1950, from the National Art-Collections Fund towards the cost of the Steventon furniture. But it is also due to the large number of Life-members (thirty-five) who joined in 1951, and especially to the punctual payments made by subscribing members—to whom the Honorary Treasurers offer their deep gratitude. Many signed Banker's Orders, and if any others would like to pay their subscriptions in this way the Honorary Treasurer will be glad to send the necessary forms.

The Committee regard the coming year with some confidence, but—apart from the possibility of desirable but costly relics coming on the market—they anticipate heavier expenses in 1952 than in 1951. The House at Chawton, after its complete structural overhaul and repairs in 1948-49, is in sound condition externally; internally, there are indications that money must soon be spent, in the interests both of the tenants and of the preservation of the fabric. Again, therefore, the Committee appeal for donations, large or small, from all those who like to feel that Jane Austen's home is being cared for.

This Report, with the Accounts, will be placed before members at a General Meeting to be held later in the year. Members will be given ample notice of the place, date, and time of the Meeting, and the Committee hope that very many will attend.

Detail of the Quilt (see P.22)

THE JANE AUSTEN SOCIETY

Report for the year 1952

Jane Austen's Music Books

THE JANE AUSTEN SOCIETY

Report for the year 1952

Membership

1952 was a good year for the Society, bringing a considerable increase in membership, and the prospect of more rooms in Jane Austen's house being at the Trustees' disposal. At the end of the year, there were 176 Life Members, and 590 members who paid annual subscriptions, making a total of 766, which is sixty-two more than a year ago. Sixty-eight members were citizens of the United States, twenty-two lived in countries of the British Empire outside the United Kingdom, and seven in foreign countries.

Jane Austen's House and Garden

1,396 people paid for admission to Jane Austen's House in 1952. This is thirty-one more than in 1951. The House is open throughout the year from 11 a.m. to 4 p.m. on Tuesdays, Thursdays, and Saturdays; and although the Caretakers are not officially on duty at other times, they are always ready to admit visitors when they are at home. Members are admitted free, and are asked to sign the Visitors' Book; others pay 1/- (children 6d.).

As was forecast in the Report for 1951, much internal reconstruction of the extensive attics of the house was necessary in 1952, and this has been satisfactorily completed at a cost to the Society of nearly £170.

The Garden has been well cared for during the year, and was looking its best at the time of the Annual Meeting.

New Rooms to be available

In recent years the Austens' Dining Parlour and Jane Austen's bedroom have been shown to visitors by the tenant Miss Stevens, although they were occupied by her and contained her furniture. Now, as members who were at the General Meeting in July heard, arrangements have been made whereby these rooms will be at the Trustees' disposal. It is entirely due to the generosity of Mr. T. Edward Carpenter that the hopes many members have long cherished are to be fulfilled ; he has provided alternative accommodation for the widowed sister of Miss Stevens, who lived with her; and Miss Stevens now forego̱es the use of these rooms. They will provide a proper setting for many of the relics, at present rather crowded in the Drawing Room, and it is hoped that they will be open in their new guise early in 1953. Already the hob grate, which has recently stood in the fireplace opening in the Drawing Room has been replaced in the Dining Parlour, where it stood in the Austens' day. The rooms Miss Stevens retains are being redecorated and improved in convenience by the Society. The aim of the Society and the Trustees is to bring the property into an irreproachable condition.

Structural alterations made to the house in 1845 after Cassandra Austen's death, to provide further accommodation, reduced the size of the Dining Parlour by that of the existing passage to Miss Stevens' front door, and the window opening was reduced in size; but the room is still a pleasant one. Its walls are to be covered with paper of the appropriate period. The Bedroom is believed to be structurally as it was when Caroline Austen visited it for her last interview with her aunt, which she describes in " My Aunt Jane Austen."

" My Aunt Jane Austen "

In the spring of 1952 the Society published, from the manuscript given by Mr. R. A. Austen-Leigh, the memoir of her Aunt Jane written in 1867 by Caroline Austen, who was the daughter of Jane's eldest brother James. The little book was well reviewed, and at the end of 1952, 1,258 copies had been sold. Many were still in the hands of booksellers, and only a few hundreds are left out of the 2,000 printed. The cost of publication has already been covered by sales. Besides Caroline's memoir, the book contains the recollections of John White, a Chawton agricultural labourer who died in 1920 in his hundredth year; it has a preface by Dr. R. W. Chapman, a cover designed by Miss Dorothy Darnell, and six photographic illustrations; and it costs 3/6 post free. It does not seem likely that a reprint will be called for, but while any remain copies will be sent to all members who send 3/6 for each copy ordered to Lt.-Col. Satterthwaite at Lansdowne House, Alton, Hants.

Other publications of interest

The publication by the Oxford University Press of the second edition of Dr. R. W. Chapman's " Letters of Jane Austen " in the autumn of 1952 was an event of great interest to many members; and the success of his small book of Jane Austen's juvenilia, " Volume the Third ", published in 1951, prompted Dr. Chapman to make the Society the fine donation of £90 in 1952. The Committee are deeply grateful to Dr. Chapman, and also to Mr. R. A. Austen-Leigh, without whose loan of the manuscripts this book could not have appeared.

An English edition of " Presenting Miss Jane Austen," by May Lamberton Becker, an American member of the Society, is being published by Messrs. G. G. Harrap & Co. This pleasantly written little book is intended for readers who know little of Jane Austen, and would like to know more.

None of these books can be supplied by the Society, and members wishing for copies should consult their booksellers.

A Broadcast from Chawton

On the afternoon of Friday, October 3rd, listeners to the B.B.C.'s Home Service heard a short broadcast from Chawton. It was one of a series in which Audrey Russell visited the homes of great writers who lived near London. Miss Russell met and talked with Colonel Satterthwaite in the Drawing Room and Garden of Jane Austen's house, with Miss Dorothy Darnell in the outbuildings, and with Miss Stevens in the Dining Parlour; and passages from the novels and letters were read. The Broadcast was repeated in the B.B.C.'s Overseas Service on January 14th, 1953.

Relics

During 1952 nine of Jane Austen's own music books came into the possession of the Trustees. These most interesting and valuable books were the gift of Miss Beryl Bradford (a descendant of Jane's brother Edward), to whom all members of the Society will feel most deeply grateful. Three of them, bound in calf, are in manuscript; two in Jane Austen's own handwriting, and one, of an earlier date, in a hand at present unidentified. The bindings were in a bad state, and they have been carefully repaired by Mr. H. J. Phillips, the Examiner of Binding in the Department of Printed Books at the British Museum, as much as possible of the original covers being retained. These books are on view in Jane Austen's house. The other six books are of printed music, and appear to consist of loose music-sheets specially bound; some of them have manuscript contents-pages, but not in Jane Austen's hand. Three of the books however have Jane Austen's name in her own writing on the title pages.

Miss Bradford also presented a small oil-painting of the house " Prowtings ", as it was in the Austens' time.

Other gifts received during the year include the following books :
From Mr. R. A. Austen-Leigh,
    " Jane Austen, her homes and friends," by Constance Hill,
    " Letters of Jane Austen," edited by Lord Brabourne.
    " Personal Aspects of Jane Austen," by Mary Augusta Austen-Leigh.
    " Letters of Jane Austen," with introduction by R. Brimley Johnson.
    " Memoir of Jane Austen," by J. E. Austen-Leigh.
    " Jane Austen and Bath," by Emma Austen-Leigh.
    " Jane Austen," by F. W. Cornish.

From Miss W. M. Smith,
    " Letters of Jane Austen," edited by Lord Brabourne.

From Miss M. Hope Dodds,
    " Mary Queen of Scots vindicated," by John Whitaker, (1788), 3 vols. (This book is referred to by Jane Austen in " Love and Freindship.").
    " The Holy Ghost Chapel, Basingstoke," by J.J. (1808).

From Dr. R. W. Chapman,
    " Jane Austen's Letters, to her sister Cassandra and others," collected and edited by himself. 2nd Edition, 1952.

From the Ealing Public Library,
    " The Scottish Chiefs," by Jane Porter, on the title page of which it is stated to be " by the author of Pride and Prejudice and Sense and Sensibility " !

From Mrs. May Lamberton Becker,
A copy of her own book, " Presenting Miss Jane Austen " (1952).

From Miss Edith Sparvel-Bayly,
" Jane Austen, a selection from her works," (1930).

From Mrs. Angela Thirkell,
" Lovers' Vows," 7th Edition (1804); the play rehearsed in " Mansfield Park."

Gifts other than books included :—

From Miss Joan Corder,
The Sultan of Turkey's medal commemorating the capture of St. Jean d'Acre, probably that presented to Charles James Austen.
A printed list of the officers of the Oxfordshire Militia in 1800, including the name of Henry Austen.

From Mr. W. Rayner Batty,
A Three-shilling piece of 1815 (the same size as Mrs. Croft's blister in " Persuasion ").

From Mrs. Lonsdale Ragg,
A framed photograph of a painting of the Mathew family, including James Austen's first wife.

From Mrs. Edwin Cohen,
A framed and coloured enlargement of Cassandra's drawing of Jane Austen.

From Mr. Selwyn Duruz,
A copy made in 1840, of the deed of Nov., 1812, under which Edward Austen assumed the name and arms of Knight.

From Mr. G. A. Faithfull,
The baking-oven rake used in the Austens' bakehouse.

Mrs. Horne has generously presented to the Trustees the Ivory Cup and Ball, which has been on loan for two years.

During the year a small bedroom mirror which was among the Austens' furniture at Chawton has been purchased; and a second copy of the " Five Letters to Fanny Knight", published by the Clarendon Press in 1924, has also been acquired.

A most acceptable loan for the year has been the three volumes of the first edition of " Pride and Prejudice " which belonged to Lady Caroline Lamb, who was the wife of Lord Melbourne and the intimate friend of Lord Byron. The title page of the first volume bears her signature. For this loan the Society is indebted to Mr. T. Edward Carpenter.

The Curtis Museum of Alton has made the loan of an oven peel of 18th Century type. This, with the original rake presented by Mr. Faithfull and referred to above, completes the equipment of the Austen's baking oven, which may be seen in the outhouse in which Jane Austen's donkey cart stands.

The Annual General Meeting

The Annual General Meeting was again held in Mr. Clarke's field behind Chawton Village Hall, on Saturday, July 19th. The weather was fine, and in the unavoidable absence of the President, the Duke of Wellington, the chair was taken by Mr. W. Hugh Curtis, who in his opening remarks, after regretting the absence of the President, and, through ill health, of Mr. T. Edward Carpenter, expressed his thanks to all those contributing to the pleasure of members attending the Meeting. The Report and Accounts were presented and accepted, and the Officers and Committee, as printed on the first page of this Report, were unanimously elected. Colonel Satterthwaite outlined the Bypass proposals, and the resolution quoted below was passed; and he referred to the new rooms shortly to be at the Trustees' disposal. Miss Margaret Kennedy (Lady Davies) then gave an address, taking as her subject " Jane Austen's singular freedom from the doubt which besets most novelists—the fear that nobody will believe in their characters." Her address was of absorbing interest, and Miss Kennedy's article " How ought a Novelist . . . ? " in the issue of the " Fortnightly " for November 1952, is based on it. Dr. R. W. Chapman then spoke, and a vote of thanks to the speakers was proposed by Mr. John Gore, seconded by Miss Elizabeth Jenkins, and carried unanimously.

After the Meeting members had tea, and were able to visit Jane Austen's house, the gardens of Chawton House (by kind permission of Major Edward Knight), the Church and churchyard, and the Rectory garden, (by kind permission of Canon and Mrs. Moore). Members were also invited to see " Clinkers ", a 16th Century cottage adjoining Jane Austen's house which has been recently acquired by Mr. G. A. Faithfull, a member of the Society, after occupation by the same Chawton family for many centuries. Mr. Faithfull is engaged in restoring the interior so far as possible to its original state, and members enjoyed their visit to a building that Jane Austen must have known well.

The Service of Remembrance

On the Sunday following the Annual Meeting, July 20th, the Annual Service of Remembrance was held in Chawton Parish Church, and was well attended. It was conducted by the Rector of Chawton, Canon T. C. R. Moore, assisted by Canon R. F. Pechey; and the sermon was preached by the Right Reverend Bishop Lang, Assistant Bishop of Winchester. Mr. R. L. McAndrew and Colonel Satterthwaite read the lessons.

The Alton Bypass Proposals

The question of a bypass road for the town of Alton has been under consideration for many years, and the Society has long known that any such road might have a sad effect on the surroundings of Jane Austen's house, and on the beauty of the village of Chawton. The plans originally prepared showed a bypass to the North-West of Alton, and a road so planned would scarcely touch Chawton at all. In 1952 however this scheme was abandoned by the Hampshire County Council on the score of expense, and plans for a bypass to the South-East of Alton were produced. These plans were strongly objected to by the Alton Rural District Council and the Chawton Parish Council, as well as by the local branch of the Council for the Preservation of Rural England; and the Committee of the Jane Austen Society, whose officials had been allowed to see the plans, agreed that if carried out they would be disastrous to the village of Chawton. Not only would the village be cut into non-communicating blind alleys, with no traffic at all passing Jane Austen's house, but many houses and cottages, some of them old and pleasant in appearance, and all of them lived in, would be demolished. The Committee therefore immediately wrote strongly to the Hampshire County Council on the matter, and the General Meeting of the Society in July unanimously passed the following resolution :

"That the Jane Austen Society lodge a formal objection with the Minister of Housing and Local Government to the plans for an Alton Bypass road, which form part of the County Development Scheme, as they affect the village of Chawton."

This Resolution was sent to the Ministry, and as a result of this and other protests the question was placed on the agenda of the Inquiry into the Hampshire Development Plan which was held in Winchester in December, 1952. Before this Inquiry, the Society's Officials had been allowed to see the plans of an alternative scheme, prepared by the County Engineers, for a bypass for Alton on the South-East but with roads through Chawton which involve no demolitions and would do little to harm the village. Under this plan no fast through traffic would pass Jane Austen's house, but the road past the house would be open to local traffic, and the Committee therefore held that if a North-Westerly route avoiding Chawton altogether was ruled out, this alternative was one that the Society could not object to. Colonel Satterthwaite, who gave evidence at the Inquiry, therefore said that while preferring the North-Westerly route the Society would withdraw its objection if the South-Easterly route with the alternative proposals for Chawton were approved.

The result of the Inquiry has not yet been announced, but those who were present at it feel some confidence that their efforts have not been in vain, and that Chawton will escape the worst evils of an ill-conceived plan. In any event, it is understood that no work on the bypass will be begun for at least five years, and that at the end of that period there will still be opportunity for those interested to lodge objections to the plans.

Sale of pictures from Chawton House

In December, 1952, a number of pictures from Chawton House, the property of Major Edward Knight, were sold at Sotheby's Auction Rooms in London. All but one were 18th Century portraits of members and ancestors of the Knight family, belonging to earlier generations than the Thomas Knight who adopted his distant cousin Edward Austen (Jane's brother) as his heir. These pictures were of little interest from the "Austen" standpoint, and of little artistic value. With them however was the large portrait of Edward Austen which is illustrated in Constance Hill's book, " Jane Austen, her homes and friends," and is there stated to have been painted in Rome while Edward was on the " Grand Tour " at the age of twenty-one (which would have been in the year 1789). This picture has been acquired by the Society, but as it is too large—8 feet high and 5 feet 6 inches wide—to be placed in Jane Austen's house, the Committee have accepted Colonel Satterthwaite's offer to hang it over the stairs at Lansdowne House in Alton High Street. It does not look its best, of course, in a small house, but it can be seen fairly well, and is in Georgian surroundings. Colonel Satterthwaite will always be glad to show it to members who would like to see it after visiting Chawton.

The Thanks of the Trustees

The following letter, addressed to the members of the Society, has been received from the Chairman of the Jane Austen Memorial Trust, and the Committee feel that members will read it with pleasure and renewed gratitude to Mr. T. Edward Carpenter.

Dear Fellow-Members,

The present time is suitable for addressing to you a few remarks to supplement your Committee's Report and again to thank its members, and especially Colonel Satterthwaite the Vice-Chairman and Joint Honorary Treasurer, for the aid they have given the Trustees' Sub-Committee in managing Jane Austen's house. The greater weight of the burden has been shouldered by Colonel Satterthwaite. This merits especial recognition and I have appointed him an additional Trustee of the above Trust. In view of my advancing age I have also appointed my wife, Mrs. Catherine L. M. Carpenter and my surviving son, Mr. Francis E. Carpenter, additional Trustees.

On the 9th December, 1952, on behalf of the Trust, I attended at the Castle in Winchester to give evidence against the plan suggested by the Hampshire County Council for the passage of the Alton Bypass road through Chawton. A full account of the sitting appears in the local paper and I need only add my sincere hope that the interposition of the Trust and the Society may hereafter prove effective.

In September I visited Sir Walter Scott's library at Abbotsford in the hope of arranging for the display during the summer of his copy of the first edition of " Pride and Prejudice." By the courtesy of the Librarian I was able to inspect the bulky catalogue of the Library, but we only discovered records of " Emma " and " Mansfield Park." The present owners explained that they could not see their way to loan the novels. But they gratefully accepted my suggestion that the mis-spelling in the catalogue of "Austin " should be corrected to "Austen." You will recall Sir Walter's reference to " Pride and Prejudice " in his diary on the 14th March, 1826. Meantime the display of the first edition of the book inscribed Caroline Lamb, the wife of William Lamb, subsequently Queen Victoria's trusted Prime Minister Lord Melbourne, is continued.

I am glad the Trust will be able to offer to the public entrance to the two additional rooms in the House. The Trustees have been particularly anxious to accomplish this in the present eventful year. They are giving the set-out of the rooms careful thought, and offer to the Society their grateful thanks for supplying the means of restoration.

In conclusion I thank with gratitude all those, and especially Jane Austen's relatives, who have contributed to the success of our movement by gifts and loans.

Very truly yours,

(*Signed*) T. Edward Carpenter,

January, 1953. *Chairman, Jane Austen Memorial Trust*

The Accounts

The Accounts show that the Society's credit balance has gone up by nearly £70 during the year. The increase in membership is reflected in a £17 rise in the total for subscriptions—and the Honorary Treasurers again thank subscribing members for their punctual payments—while donations, headed by Dr. Chapman's gift already mentioned, were £42 above the figure for 1951. There was a drop in fees from Life Members, only 17 joining, against 35 in 1951. Once again, there were virtually no " office " expenses, and little money was spent on relics. Expenditure on Jane Austen's house was, however, heavy.

The cost of decorating the new rooms, and of the improvements to Miss Stevens' quarters, will fall to be paid in 1953, and it will not be light. With more rooms, moreover, the Trustees will naturally hope for more relics to display. There are relics of the greatest interest to all lovers of Jane Austen that could be purchased if funds were available, and, good though the Society's financial position is at the moment, the Committee feel justified in asking again for donations, large or small.

This Report, with the Accounts, will be laid before members at a General Meeting to be held in the summer. Members will be given ample notice of the time, place and date of the Meeting, and the Committee hope that very many will attend. In the case of overseas members it will be very helpful if those intending to visit England during the summer would inform Colonel Satterthwaite at Lansdowne House, Alton, Hants, of the dates and probable duration of their stay, and, particularly, of an address that will find them during the month of June.

THE JANE AUSTEN SOCIETY

Report for the year 1953

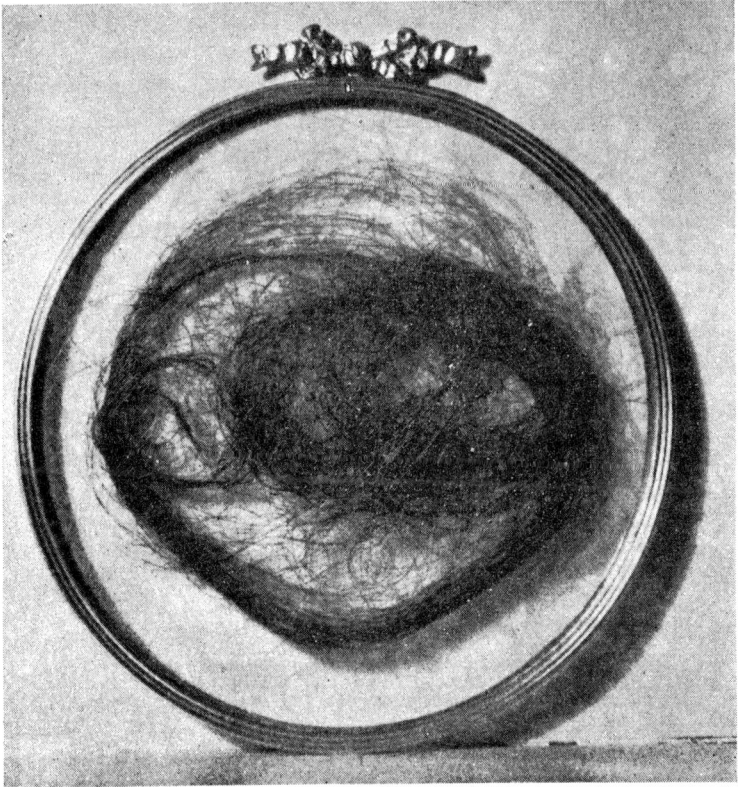

Lock of Jane Austen's hair

Presented in 1949 by Mrs. Henry Burke of Baltimore

THE JANE AUSTEN SOCIETY

(Founded in 1940 by Dorothy G. Darnell)

President:

His Grace The Duke of Wellington, K.G.

Vice-Presidents:

T. Edward Carpenter, Esq., B.A., LL.B., J.P.
R. W. Chapman, Esq., F.B.A.

Chairman:

W. Hugh Curtis, Esq., F.S.A.

Vice-Chairman and Honorary Secretary:

Sir Hugh Smiley, Bt

Committee:

Mrs. A. S. Bates.
Miss Elizabeth Bowen, C.B.E., LL.D.
Mrs. W. Hugh Curtis.
Miss A. B. Darnell.
John Gore, Esq., C.V.O.
Miss Elizabeth Jenkins
Mrs. R. L. McAndrew
Mrs. K. A. Robbins.
Mrs. Jervoise Scott.
Lady Smiley.

Honorary Treasurer:

F. H. Foster, Esq., Lloyds' Bank, Ltd., Alton, Hants.

Honorary Auditors:

Messrs. Sheen, Stickland & Co., Alton, Hants.

Trustees of the Jane Austen Memorial Trust:

T. Edward Carpenter, Esq., B.A., LL.B., J.P. (Chairman).
R. W. Chapman, Esq., F.B.A.
R. A. Austen-Leigh, Esq., M.A., F.S.A.
W. Hugh Curtis, Esq., F.S.A.
Miss Mary Lascelles, M.A., D.Litt.
Mrs. Catherine L. M. Carpenter.
Francis E. Carpenter, Esq.

THE JANE AUSTEN SOCIETY
Report for the year 1953

Membership

At the end of 1953 there were 821 members of the Society, of whom 188 were Life Members. This shows an increase of 55 members over the previous year. Of the total, 82 are citizens of the United States, 27 come from the Commonwealth, and 7 from foreign countries.

One hundred new members were gained during the year, but many members are in arrears with their subscriptions. It would be a tremendous help if all members who are able would pay their subscriptions by Banker's Order, one of which is enclosed.

Opening of Additional Rooms in Jane Austen's House
Visit to Steventon and Manydown

On Thursday, 14th May, some 90 members of the Society foregathered at Chawton, where Mrs. Edward Carpenter opened the newly decorated rooms, which she had made available by the purchase of another cottage for the tenants.

Opening the ceremony, Mr. W. Hugh Curtis, the Chairman, spoke of the sudden death of Colonel Satterthwaite, who had made all the arrangements for that day. He also said how sorry he was that Miss Dorothy Darnell was not well enough to be present.

Mr. T. Edward Carpenter paid similar tributes, and went on to describe the changes that had been made in the house, that the parlour and Jane Austen's bedroom were now open, and had been decorated with wallpapers of contemporary designs. A number of pictures and other relics were now on view in these rooms.

Before declaring the rooms open, Mrs. Carpenter made a charming speech about the importance the dining parlour must have had in the Austens' family life. She also spoke of a patchwork quilt, now in the bedroom, which had been worked by Mrs. Austen and her daughters. It was now 150 years old and was in very good condition. Mrs. Carpenter also mentioned the staircase, with its half-landing and window, through which the Austen family must often have looked.

After a tour of the house and a picnic luncheon, the members drove to Steventon. Here they visited the 13th century church, where Mr. Carpenter gave a talk on associations with the Austen family. The party then, at the invitation of Colonel and Mrs. A. S. Bates, went on to Manydown Park, to see the house where Jane Austen used to visit the Bigg-Wither family, and in particular the ballroom where she used to dance.

Report from the Chairman of the Trust
Jane Austen's House

The Chairman of the Trust furnishes the following information :

" The number of persons paying for admission in 1953 was 2087, an increase of 691 over the attendances in 1952.

This is due to several factors, namely :

(1) Judicious Advertising;
(2) Additional rooms to be seen;
(3) Additions to the relics and a more convenient display of the collection.

The number of visitors might have been greater but for the attraction of the Coronation Festivities.

The number quoted above does not include members of the Jane Austen Society, who enter without fee. It would be appreciated if these would make a point of signing the Visitors' book in the drawing-room, adding the letter ' M ' after their signatures, so that a complete record of their attendances may be compiled. It may be mentioned that a very large number of members visited the House during the year.

In April last Mrs. Edward Carpenter purchased a freehold dwellinghouse in Alton for occupation by Mr. and Mrs. King and their daughter, thus rendering available for the Trust the sittingroom on the ground floor connecting the drawingroom with the passage leading to the front door, the parlour and, of course, the staircase leading to Jane's bedroom. This additional accommodation was opened by her on the 14th May last. The room in question was restored by the Chairman. It is now no longer necessary to go out into the street to reach the other part of the House available for inspection.

The Trustees can now space out their exhibits more effectively. The House is open Tuesdays, Thursdays and Saturdays, and on other days, including Sundays and holidays, on application to the resident caretakers. The hours in each case are from 11 a.m. to 4.30 p.m. The admission fee is one shilling, and for children sixpence.

Various interesting and valuable exhibits have been added during the year just past.

The Chairman of the Trust has presented framed and annotated photographs of the originals of Jane Austen's letters owned by him. These are now hanging in the room recently opened.

He has also obtained from the Prime Minister, Sir Winston Churchill, an autographed extract from his work, ' The Second World War '; this has been framed with two extracts, engrossed by Miss Gertrude A. George, from the Diary of Sir Walter Scott in 1826, and the Essay of Lord Macaulay on Madame D'Arblay. These can be seen in Jane Austen's bedroom.

This latter exhibit is above a little work-table once owned by Mary Jane (afterwards Mrs. Purvis), the eldest daughter of Admiral Sir Francis Austen, G.C.B. This has been generously given by Mrs. Purvis. She has also presented a drawing by Cassandra, now over the bedroom mantelpiece, and a very valuable miniature by John Smart, of the Rev. Geo. Austen's sister, Mrs. Hancock, framed in gold and diamonds. This is not at present on view but a photograph has been presented by the Chairman of the Trust and now hangs over the mantelshelf of the Family parlour with certain other family portraits.

In the Family parlour also hang some original letters of Jane's Father, Mother and Sister, most kindly presented by one of the Trustees, Mr. R. A. Austen-Leigh. Dr. and Mrs. Chapman have, in memory of Miss Dorothy Darnell, with their repeated kindness and continual interest, given a pencil portrait, thought to be by Cassandra, of one of her nieces.

Mrs. Margaret Merewether, of the United States, has sent most generously to the Trust a complete set of the first American edition of the Novels dated 1832.

Various other interesting exhibits have been acquired or bestowed during the Year and to each and all the donors the Trustees tender their very grateful thanks. They appeal to others of the great Novelist's relatives or admirers to remember that the Trust is a National Charity capable of holding the precious relics of L'Aimable Jane in perpetuity and preventing their dispersal from what should be their permanent home in this Country.

The Trustees record their deep sense of loss by the deaths of Miss Dorothy Darnell, the Foundress of the Jane Austen Society, and of Lt.-Col. Satterthwaite, its Hon. Treasurer."

Miss Dorothy Darnell

Dorothy Darnell founded the Jane Austen Society in May, 1940. I was the first member she enrolled after her sisters.

Jane Austen's house at that time was divided into three tenements, each rented at half a crown a week. There was nothing to connect it with Jane Austen in the public mind except the tablet on the wall. Dorothy Darnell wanted passionately to see it made a suitable memorial; she had no money and no influence and did not see how the thing could be done. One day, nevertheless, she decided that it must be done. The cast iron grate from the Austens' dining parlour had been removed to make way for a tenant's gas fire; she found it thrown out on a heap of nettles. She arranged temporary shelter for it in the Curtis Museum at Alton. This was the first work of rescue and preservation accomplished by the Jane Austen Society. Not many months before her death she saw the dining parlour added to the show-place of the Museum, with the grate restored to its original position.

43

Lt. Col. C. R. Satterthwaite, Mrs. Newman, Miss Dorothy Darnell and Mr. T. Edward Carpenter.

What the Jane Austen Society owes to its founder can never be adequately told. Once it had been formed, its object stated and its first band of enthusiastic members enrolled, once the co-operation of the owner, Mr. Edward Knight, had been gained in a long-term policy of acquisition, and a foothold established in the house itself, it was then possible to launch a public appeal which gained distinguished members and eventually the Society's prime benefactor, Mr. T. E. Carpenter who bought the house and vested it in the Jane Austen Memorial Trust. But it was first necessary to create a Society. The war was on, the owner of the property was on active service. We were told on all hands that if such a scheme could ever succeed, it must be postponed indefinitely.

Dorothy Darnell did not think so. The prospect was bleak and her resources meagre, but she had exactly those qualities in herself which made her able to overcome the difficulties which would have staggered anyone else. She combined a deep, inexhaustible enthusiasm for the project with other qualities that do not always go with enthusiasm. Her universal sympathy and friendliness, her ingrained respect for other people's point of view, the experience and tact of a countrywoman in approaching matters of village politics, were invaluable to the Society in its early precarious days. Nor did her value grow less when our original problems were overcome. Her simplicity and unassertiveness never caused one to overlook the authority with which she spoke on matters of aesthetic judgement and taste. Very little local tradition of Jane Austen has survived but that little is extremely valuable, and it was all discovered by Dorothy Darnell and preserved in various reports of the Society. For the last twelve years she made it almost her life's work to discover and trace every relic, association and tradition of Jane Austen in the neighbourhood. The fresh, spontaneous, never-failing interest aroused in her by everything of the kind was the natural outcome of the admiration, gratitude and love she felt for Jane Austen's work. The project of preserving Jane Austen's house could not have taken rise more appropriately than in the mind of such a reader.

ELIZABETH JENKINS

Lieut.-Colonel C. R. Satterthwaite, O.B.E.

Lieut.-Col. Clement Richard Satterthwaite came to live at Lansdowne House, Alton, in May, 1948, and very few can so quickly have taken an active part in the life of the town. It was not very long before he joined the Jane Austen Society and became acquainted with the Darnells. He was soon welcomed as a member of the Committee and became Joint Hon. Treasurer and Vice-Chairman.

He brought to the work of the Society not only boundless enthusiasm and energy, but a considerable organising ability, gained in part, no doubt, from his earlier long association with the Royal National Lifeboat Institution, of which for some years he had acted as secretary. He joined the Jane Austen Society at an opportune moment, when the work of the

Photo J. Butler-Kearney

A pencil drawing, said to be a portrait by Cassandra Austen of one of the daughters of her brother Edward Knight.

Given to the Jane Austen Society by Dr. and Mrs. R. W. Chapman in memory of the Society's founder, the late Dorothy Darnell.

Hon. Secretaries was rapidly increasing, and Dorothy Darnell was delighted to have the benefit of his help and advice. He also undertook the supervision of the house at Chawton, which entailed at least one visit each week.

Many members will remember the broadcast from Jane Austen's home in the autumn of 1952, in which he and Dorothy Darnell took part, and answered in a very able fashion Audrey Russell's questions.

At the time of his death on May 5th, 1953, his plans for the formal opening of two additional rooms on May 14th at Chawton were well advanced, and it was a great grief to everyone that he did not live to see this fulfilled.

Although Dick Satterthwaite took part in several of the town's activities, he was never tired of pointing out that the Jane Austen Society was of National importance, and as far as he was concerned, came first. He must have devoted much time to all matters connected with Chawton and the Austen family, and could converse or correspond with members and others with some authority.

The Annual General Meeting, 1953

The Annual General Meeting was held at the Assembly Rooms, Alton, on Saturday, 18th July. The President, the Duke of Wellington, was in the Chair, and about 220 members and their friends were present.

In presenting the report for 1952, Mr. W. Hugh Curtis paid a tribute to the work done for the Society by the late Lt.-Col. C. R. Satterthwaite. He explained how the duties performed by Col. Satterthwaite would now be carried out by Mr. T. Edward Carpenter as far as Jane Austen's house was concerned, and that Sir Hugh Smiley would do the secretarial work. In regretting the absence through illness of Miss Dorothy Darnell, founder of the Society, Mr. Curtis voiced the affectionate sympathy of everyone present. He also thanked Mrs. Hart, Miss Mussell and Miss Bates for the work they had done to tide over the secretarial work of the Society until a new Hon. Secretary had been appointed. Mr. Curtis said that members would be able to see the newly decorated rooms at Jane Austen's house after the meeting, and mentioned that the portrait of Edward Knight, which had been hanging at Lansdowne House, was for the present being housed at the Alton Urban District Council Offices.

Mr. Curtis described the changes it was proposed to make in the officers; these, having been proposed en bloc by the Duke of Wellington, were elected.

Mr. T. Edward Carpenter spoke about the new rooms, which had been redecorated through the generosity of Mrs. Carpenter. He mentioned that among the new exhibits were photographs of letters relating to Jane Austen's works.

47

An address was given by the President, who recalled that three years before he had taken as the text of his remarks, that there was no author whom it was so difficult to discover in the act of being great. To-day they heard that Jane was very limited. Limitations were imposed upon her by her sex. She seldom described natural scenery, but the Duke maintained that if she had wanted to she could have done it, and illustrated what he had said by extracts from " Emma " and " Mansfield Park ". She did not wish to interrupt the flow of human interest in her narrative, and was concerned with the development of her story. It was no good pretending that she was not limited, but her limitations were imposed by her own judgement, and as Goethe had said, " great mastery is only achieved by self limitation ".

The Duke of Wellington was followed by Dr. R. W. Chapman, who spoke on " Editing and Criticism." He quoted an article in the *Listener*, and said he thought the author meant to say that Jane Austen was the first novelist who really got inside her people and tried to trace their underlying motives and impulses, and particularly their relations with other people.

A vote of thanks to the speakers was proposed by Miss Elizabeth Jenkins and seconded by Mr. John Gore.

The Honorary Secretary announced that Miss Joan Forder had presented to the Society a manuscript book of the genealogy of the Austen family called " Akin to Jane " which she herself had written and made, and that it would be placed in the Museum.

THE JANE AUSTEN SOCIETY

Report for the year 1954

Needle Case made by Jane Austen and given to her niece, Louisa Knight

THE JANE AUSTEN SOCIETY
Report for the year 1954

Membership

Fifty-seven new members joined the Society during the year, of whom twelve became Life Members. Of the total number, twenty-eight are from the Commonwealth, seven from foreign countries and eighty-seven from the United States.

An effort has been made to bring up to date subscriptions which are two years overdue. One hundred and eighty-seven reminders were sent out, bringing in only seventy-three replies. Members are reminded that subscriptions are due on January 1st, and that this Report is the only reminder we normally send out.

Chairman.

The Committee with the greatest regret accepted, in the spring, Mr. W. Hugh Curtis' resignation as the Society's Chairman. He had held the post since the Society was formed, and his work for it has been invaluable. Happily his health so far improved as to enable him to attend the Annual Meeting in July, and he has now rejoined the Committee. The Chairmanship remains at present vacant.

Extract from Report of the Chairman of the Jane Austen Memorial Trust

The number of the Public paying for admission to the House at Chawton in 1954 was 2605, an increase of 518 over the previous total of 2087 for 1953. This is regarded as satisfactory especially as the weather throughout the summer was inclement and many of the visitors come by cycle or on foot. Advertisement is making known to the community at large that there is at Chawton an historic dwelling of great national interest to the sightseer and the student of literature. The four rooms, with the old staircase, the wash-house and garden all now contain interesting exhibits. It is noted with pleasure that many callers repeat their visits.

The number of visitors above quoted does not include those members of the Jane Austen Society who enter free. On the 24th of July last, the day of the Annual General Meeting, a large number of the members came in to view, but the Visitors' book is not sufficiently made use of to enable a precise computation to be made under this heading.

During the year 162 copies of Caroline Austen's " My Aunt Jane Austen," were sold from the house.

The house is now open daily throughout the year including Sundays and holidays from 11 a.m. to 4.30 p.m. at the entrance fee of one shilling or sixpence for children under 14 if accompanied by adults. This involves special arrangements with the Caretakers, but the latter have loyally and enthusiastically co-operated in this extension of the Trust's facilities.

It is regretted that both Mr. W. Hugh Curtis and Miss Lascelles have found it necessary to resign from the trusteeship.

Additional exhibits have become available during the year. The Trustees' heartiest thanks are tendered to the generous donors or lenders.

Mrs. Purvis has presented the Trust with two exquisite copies of the original miniatures of Geo. Purvis, Esq., Secretary to Sir John Jervis at the battle of Cape St. Vincent in 1797, and his wife Renira Charlotte, daughter of David Maitland Esq., respectively the Father-and Mother-in-law of Miss Mary Jane Austen, eldest daughter of Admiral Sir Francis Austen, G.C.B., who married their son, Capt. Geo. Thos. Maitland Purvis, R.N. in 1828. Mrs Purvis also has presented a pencil drawing by Mary Jane Austen with the latter's signature.

Miss Helen Lefroy has lent permanently to the Trust an original drawing in pencil of the front elevation of Steventon Rectory by Anna Lefroy, the Rev. James Austen's elder daughter. Miss Lefroy has two miniatures of this lady and her husband (later the Rev. Ben. Lefroy), and through her courtesy the Chairman has been able to obtain photographs of these miniatures and has presented them to the Trust. Miss Lefroy has also lent a water colour drawing of " Wyards ", the home of this couple.

Sir Hughe Knatchbull-Huguessen has presented to the Society a photograph of a pencil sketch of, it is supposed, Fanny Knight, who in 1820 became Lady Knatchbull. This sketch, reproduced in the present report, may have been by Jane herself or at any rate by her sister, Cassandra.

Mrs. Rosemary Mowll has presented to the Trust a volume of James Beattie's Poems inscribed " M. Lloyd, the gift of her Nephew, P. E. Austen, August 1826," and is considering a loan to the Trust of Martha Lloyd's recipe book.

Miss Corder, the Compiler and Producer of " Akin to Jane " (under frequent consultation by visitors) has presented to the Trust a volume of the Historical Record of the 86th Foot illustrated in colour which records that in 1794 its chaplain was a Charles Austen. It is not known if he was a member of Jane's family. This regiment was that in which Henry Austen was interested in 1796.

The Chairman endeavoured to secure a letter of the Novelist dated 22nd May 1817 to Miss Sharp, the Knights' Governess at Godmersham, together with a letter from Cassandra written to Miss Sharp after her sister was buried, conveying to her some of Jane's trinkets. These letters were auctioned at Sotheby's and bidding rose very high. The successful tender was by an American lady but the Chairman was able to have these letter photographed before transmission to the States. He has presented these photographs to the Trust with an engrossment by Miss Gertrude George of the inscription on Jane's tomb in Winchester Cathedral.

He has also procured and presented to the Trust a photograph of a £1 bank note issued by the bankrupt firm of Austen, Gray and Vincent of Alton, held and endorsed by Edward Knight. Henry Austen went bankrupt in 1816.

Mrs. E. K. Murray has presented to the Trust a curious brass scutcheon in the shape of a heart bearing the embossed inscription " Richard Digweed, Steventon, 1760." This name will be familiar to all readers of Jane Austen's letters but it is not known what the article is nor has it been possible to identify the gentleman in question. Suggestions will be welcomed.

Considerable re-decoration and restoration of the House both externally and internally have been undertaken by the Chairman at a cost of £239 5s. 3d., so that it is now in first class condition.

It is hoped that in the future further rooms in the House may become available for display, but at present the additional cost involved renders this impossible.

The Chairman has bought an additional area of land in the rear of the House to preserve it from building encroachment.

The Duke of Wellington has presented a copy of the score of the " Boulenger " music mentioned in " Pride and Prejudice."

Annual General Meeting 1954

The Annual General Meeting was held at The Assembly Rooms, Alton, on Saturday, 24th July. The Chair was taken by Mr. T. Edward Carpenter, and some 230 members and their friends were present.

In his opening remarks Mr. Carpenter spoke of the retirement from the Chairmanship of the Society of Mr. W. Hugh Curtis, and paid tribute to all he had done for the Society. Mr. Carpenter went on to talk about the extracts published in the *Sunday Times* from Mr. W. Somerset Maugham's " Ten Novels and Their Authors." Although the inclusion of Jane Austen was a compliment, he regretted many inaccuracies which might have been avoided if Mr. Maugham had followed more closely the works of Dr. Chapman, whom he had as an authority. Mr. Carpenter acknowledged the help he always received from Dr. R. W. Chapman.

Speaking of the Society, Mr. Carpenter suggested that a Bi-annual Bulletin be issued to keep members more *au fait* with the work of the Society, and to lead to a wider study of Jane Austen's work. He also thought that the sphere of the Society should be widened, and should not be confined to Chawton and Alton.

The Report for 1953, and the accounts, in the absence of Mr. F. H. Foster the Hon. Treasurer, were presented by the Hon. Secretary. This was seconded by Mr. John Gore and carried.

On the proposition of the Chairman, His Grace The Duke of Wellington, K.G. was re-elected President of the Society. Mrs. Monier-Williams proposed, and Mr. Ralph Dutton seconded, that the remaining officers be re-elected *en bloc*. This was also carried.

Photograph of the drawing of Fanny Knight by Cassandra Austen.
Presented 1954 by Sir Hughe Knatchbull-Hugessen, K.C.M.G.

The meeting then listened to a highly enjoyable talk by Lady Cynthia Asquith who took as her theme the Heroines of Jane Austen—of which a digest reprinted from the Hampshire Herald of 29th July, follows.

Dr. Chapman then made two presentations on behalf of their donors. One was a photograph of a drawing by Cassandra Austen of Fanny Knight, who became Lady Knatchbull. This was presented by her grandson, Sir Hughe Knatchbull-Hugessen, K.C.M.G. The second presentation was a linen table napkin, given by Mr. O. G. S. Crawford, and formerly the property of his grandfather Vice-Admiral Sir Edward J. Foote, K.C.B., R.N. He is quoted in a letter written by Jane Austen to Cassandra on 7th January 1807 as liking only the plainest Christian names for girls, and disliking underdone mutton.

The speakers were thanked by Mr. Dutton, who was seconded by Mrs. Jervoise Scott.

After tea, members were able to visit Jane Austen's house at Chawton, and also, by kind permission of Mr. and Mrs. Hubert Howard, Wyards Farm. This house, a little way out of Alton on the Basingstoke road, is where Jane Austen used to visit her niece, Anna Lefroy. It is only a mile, as the crow flies, from Chawton, and therefore within easy walking distance. Members were delighted by their visit to this house, recently admirably restored by Mr. and Mrs. Howard.

Lady Cynthia Asquith's Address
(quoted from Hampshire Herald of 29th July, 1954)

Lady Cynthia Asquith began her talk by saying that many critics had tempered their praise of Jane Austen by pronouncing her to be limited. Others contended, rightly she thought, that her wisdom in never going outside the range of her own experience was one of her greatest virtues.

" As you know," said Lady Cynthia, " she very seldom depicts any scene she could not herself have witnessed. Not only does she never attempt a conversation between men at which no woman is present, but she gives no ' downstairs ' life. Neither do children figure, except in so far as they impress grown-up people. Even old age is described only as seen through younger eyes. There is no attempt to get inside an old person's mind."

The most memorable indictment of Jane Austen's limitedness was in a letter by Charlotte Brontë. Although as criticism it was as irrelevant as attacking an exquisite example of domestic architecture for not being a Gothic cathedral, it was a superb piece of writing.

" She ruffles her reader by nothing vehement, disturbs him by nothing profound. The passions are perfectly unknown to her; she rejects even a speaking acquaintance with that stormy sisterhood. Even to the feelings she vouchsafes no more than an occasional graceful but distant recognition—too frequent converse with them would ruffle the smooth elegance of her progress. Her business is not half so much with the human heart as with the human eyes, mouth, hands and feet. What sees keenly, speaks aptly, moves flexibly, it suits her to study; but what throbs fast and full though hidden, what the blood rushes through, what is the unseen seat of life and the sentient target of death—this Miss Austen ignores. She no more, with her mind's eye, beholds the heart of her race than each man, with bodily vision, sees the heart in his heaving breast. Jane Austen was a complete and most sensible lady, but a very incomplete and rather insensible woman."

That letter was written long after Jane Austen's death, but Lady Cynthia thought Jan Austen had answered it in advance when in a letter criticising some contemporary novelist, she wrote: " If the warmth of her language could affect the body it might be worth reading in this weather."

When she first read Jane Austen at the age of about 13, the speaker remembered wondering why she enjoyed her so much. The novels did not give what she thought she then sought in books. There was no moonlight, no—what she vaguely called—" ecstasy." Everything seemed to take place under a ceiling rather than under the sky. Yet to read them was sheer delight. She always had to turn the next page. Unconsciously, she was paying tribute to so many things; to the dexterity of those opening paragraphs, that instantly put the reader into a good humour; to the glint of that delicious irony which made the very words smile; to all the amazing artistry which made this mistress of her craft so pre-eminently readable.

Announcing her decision to confine herself to talking about her heroines, Lady Cynthia said she felt it was through these young women that one got closest to Jane Austen. Her other characters—even her heroes—were for the most part shown only fragmentarily as they appeared to those with whom they came in contact. But, as her heroines soliloquized, they were given the freedom of their thoughts. With them only did the reader enjoy a sense of eavesdropping.

Taking the heroines in the order of their creation, she recalled that Jane Austen had given her own opinion of Elizabeth Bennet. " I must confess," she wrote in a letter, " I think Elizabeth as delightful a creature as ever appeared in print."

Lady Cynthia agreed. She had, she said, a charm which never cloyed. Unable to open her mouth without sparkling with effortless wit, she was like one of those natural springs from which it was impossible to procure water without bubbles. Elizabeth's nature was as enchanting as her talk. They loved her sympathetic, loving heart, her sense of fairness, her willingness to acknowledge, and smile at, her own mistakes. Jane Austen never idealised a character. Yet the speaker could think of no respect in which she could wish Elizabeth different.

" To my mind," said Lady Cynthia, " she is one of the great achievements in literature and—staggering thought—Jane Austen, when she created her, was only twenty-one."

With well-chosen quotations, she went on to produce evidence of Elizabeth's charming personality.

Lady Cynthia confessed herself rather humourless about Emma. She could, she said, put up with a fairly high degree of egotism in the young, but not with such insufferable complacency, patronage and cock-sure busy-bodying. Emma, however, was one of the characters whom Jane Austen developed in the course of the narrative. Stripped of self-confidence and brought to mortifying self-knowledge, she improved wonderfully. Her charm and fundamental kindness came triumphantly through, and they could believe, as Jane Austen wished them to believe, that Emma's husband would be a fortunate man.

Annual General Meeting, 1955

This meeting will be held on Saturday 23th July next, when, it is hoped, Sir Arthur Bryant, c.b.e. will give a reading from his books illustrating the times of Jane Austen. Detailed notices will be sent out in due course.

Notice of Somerset Maugham's
Jane Austen in his 10 *novels and their authors.*

Our Society is naturally enough interested in Mr. Maugham's 10 *novels and their authors.* Of the two women in this roll of fame, both are English and one is Jane Austen. The other, Emily Brontë, is much more dangerous ground for critics, and all attempts to assess her nature and genius must evoke the wildest speculations and arouse the fiercest passions. In Jane Austen's case there are still many matters on which we should dearly like more light, but her short and placid life, her character and her art, are very much less obscure and controversial. Our Society has another personal interest in this particular essay. Mr. Maugham relied solely on Dr. Chapman for his biographical details and made (by misquotation and misinterpretation) singularly poor use of his authority and sources here and there; nor has he unearthed any new fact. But in examining some facts for clues to Miss Austen's technique, nature and creative powers, he nevertheless made a number of very shrewd deductions and guesses.

He scouts the notion that any novelist can dispense with personal experience and rely on pure imagination in the creation of character.

The famous letter from Lady Knatchbull to Mrs. Rice is not the only evidence that Cassandra and Jane were " provincial ladies " and acted and reacted as " provincials " did and do in " superior society." It was a fair inference that the patronage Jane accepted on her visits to the Knights in Kent did indeed inspire the creation of Mrs. John Dashwood and Lady Catherine. Mr. Maugham's selected excerpts from Jane's correspondence support rather than deny, if not a charge of cattishness, at least that in love and courtship she was coolheaded and realist rather than passionate, and I would suggest that in her novels perhaps only when Elizabeth meets Darcy at Pemberley and in the revised last chapter of *Persuasion* could a different verdict be proffered.

Mr. Maugham is shrewd also in stressing that whereas Jane adhered in private conversation (though not, conventionally, in her novels) to the frankness of the age of Fielding, that frankness was already bad form in the " superior " society she sometimes met and all the more so to her favourite niece in middle age.

The novel which Mr. Maugham selected was *Pride and Prejudice.* His reasons for preferring it to its chief rivals, *Mansfield Park and Emma*, seem to me valid. It is the best constructed, flowing naturally along to an inexorable conclusion. The " probabilities " are here best safeguarded, if we may swallow the exaggerations of Lady Catherine's constant insolence, Darcy's moments of intolerable pride, Collins' obsequiousness and Mrs. Bennet's heart-breaking vulgarity. Particularly sound is Mr. Maugham's suggestion that Mrs. Bennet might with advantages to probability have been Jane's and Elizabeth's stepmother; but he excuses these exaggerations as not outrageous, and argues that a dash of farce in a dish of comedy is a useful (and justified) seasoning.

Her style was unremarkable but without affectation. She had " all the virtues " and yet escaped being " a paragon no one could put up with." Her dialogue was always true to her characters, if more formalised than contemporary common speech and modern practice in novel-writing. Mr. Maugham sums up: it is not the critics but the sales in posterity which decide what is a classic. Miss Austen had two of the greatest assets a novelist can possess—readability and a humour which pin-points her acute powers of observation. She knew her range and kept within it. Such, in the few words allowed me, are the main points in Mr. Maugham's assessment of Jane Austen.

JOHN GORE

Some banking accounts of the Austen family

Some time ago I was able, by the kindness of the Directors of Hoare's Bank, to examine the ledgers in which the account was kept of the Rev. George Austen, Jane Austen's father. I made a transcript which I gave to Dr. R. W. Chapman, and I have chosen a few entries of obvious interest which, with the countenance of Mr. R. A. Austn Leigh, are published here for the benefit of the Jane Austen Society.

After Mr. Austen's death in 1805 the account was continued in Mrs. Austen's name, and on her death in 1827 it was transferred to that of Cassandra Austen with the same firm. Jane Austen banked with her brother Henry's firm, Austen, Maunde and Tilson; when this failed in March, 1816 she transferred her account to Hoare's Bank, where it was wound up, by Cassandra, her executrix, in 1817. The entries regarding the latter are as follows:

Miss Jane Austen. Account with Hoare's Bank.

July 9th,	1816	By divd. on 600 navy per cents to 5 inst	£15
Jan. 8th	1817	on 600 navy per cents to 5 inst	£15
July 9th	1817	on 600 navy per cents to 5 inst	£15
Sep. 12th	1817	Cassandra Elizabeth Austen, Sptr. Sister, Executrix.	
Sep. 11th		To W. Jebb, Recr. for Probate	— —
12th		To C. E. Austen	£45

Cassandra's own account says:
Paid W. Jebb for Jane Austen's Probate   £22 1s. 0d

The entries in the Rev. George Austen's account concern numbers of persons not at present identified, but some of them confirm what is known of the family history in a very interesting way and some correct mistakes in detail.

A good deal of money passed backwards and forwards among Mr. Austen and his connections. In 1768, his brother-in-law James Leigh Perrot paid £865 into Mr. Austen's account and another £300 in 1772. Mr. Austen paid Mr. Leigh Perrot £20 in 1770, and £12 a year for the years 1777, 1780, 1781 and 1782. In 1783 he managed a payment of £152, and £100 in 1784.

In 1791, £500 was paid into the account by " F. M. Austen." This was presumably Mr. Austen's cousin, Francis Mottey Austen of Sevenoaks, the solicitor who " setting up with £800 and a bundle of pens," became a rich man, and whose second wife was Jane Austen's godmother.

Among Mr. Austen's payments to members of his family, prominent are those made to his sister Philadelphia Hancock, who came back to England from India with her husband and her daughter Betsy in 1764-65. Dr. Hancock's affairs obliged him to return to Calcutta in 1769, and Mr. Austen's payments to his sister begin the next year. Mrs. Hancock's name was rendered by the bank clerks with the following variations: July, 1770, Phil. Hancock, £13. July 1772, Phil. Hancock, £20. May 1774, Philip Hancock, £50. Nov. 1774, Philip Hancock, £50. May 1778, B. Hancock, £17 19s. 0d. Dec. 1778, Mrs. Hancock £17 19s. 0d. May 1780, Philad Hancock, £16 18s. 0d. May 1782, Ph. Hancock £15 17s. 0d.

Mrs. Austen's sister Jane Leigh married Dr. Edward Cooper in 1768, and in that year the Rev. George Austen paid Dr. Cooper £62 in Jan., £40 in April and £43 10s. 0d., in December. He made further payments to Dr. Cooper of £50 in Nov. 1774, £40 in January 1780, £40 in December 1781 and £10 in September 1783. There would seem to be no clue to these transactions but another entry in 1783 confirms the anecdote that in this year Cassandra and Jane and their cousin Jane Cooper were with Dr. Cooper's sister Mrs. Cawley at Southampton when Cassandra and Jane developed typhus, then known as " putrid fever." Mrs. Austen and Mrs. Cooper came to fetch their

Drawing Room at Jane Austen's House, Chawton, 1954

children home, Mrs. Cooper, it is said, contracting the disease and dying the following month, October 1783. This date is confirmed by Mr. Austen's cheque for £10, drawn to Ann Cawley, September 1783.

Considerable interest attaches to three payments made by Mr. Austen to S. La Tournelle, the headmistress of the Abbey School at Reading. A doubt that has been raised whether Cassandra and Jane ever were at the school, is effectively dispelled by evidence of the payment of their fees:—

S. La Tournelle	Aug. 20th, 1785,	..	..	£37 19 0
	Feb. 13th, 1786,	..	..	£36 2 6
	Jan. 2nd, 1787,	..	..	£16 10 0

At the same time, the entries call in question the date hitherto assigned to Jane's leaving the school. The authors of " Life and Letters of Jane Austen " say that she came home for good at nine years old, which would be in 1784. The half year's fees were probably paid in advance, but in any case it seems clear that she did not leave before some time in 1786 at the earliest. The payment in 1787 is difficult to explain; it might be for one girl, returning alone for a last half-year or for both daughters for one quarter. Perhaps the latter is the more likely in view of Jane's passionate anxiety as a child not to be separated from Cassandra. At all events it now seems that 11 rather than 9 should be given as the age at which she began to be educated at home.

Mr. Austen made constant payments to his sons. James, between going up to Oxford in 1779 and his first curacy in 1786, had twice, yearly payments from his father ranging from £10 to £30. Henry, who went up in 1788, received similar sums, except that he drew the unusually large one of £60 in December 1792. There are two payments only recorded to Edward, as one would expect since Edward from his adoption by the Knights was in easier circumstances than his father. Francis when a Lieutenant in the Royal Navy, had £20 in October 1795 and £20 in February 1796, and Charles, who was seventeen in 1796, had £3 3s. 0d., that October and £10 in the following May. Henry, who had already received the largest cheque, also had the last one paid to any of the sons up till 1800. He was given £5 in June 1800. The pocket money of Cassandra and Jane was presumably given to them in cash, but there is an entry of one cheque paid to Cassandra for £12 19s. 6d. on Feb. 23rd, 1799.

The ledgers between 1800 and 1821 were not available with the exception of that for 1817; but it appears that in 1821 Mrs. Austen was receiving half-yearly payments of £50 from her sister-in-law Mrs. Leigh Perrot, a fact which may be of some belated service to Mrs. Leigh Perrot's reputation.

The most grateful thanks of the Society are due to Mr. Ronald Griffin, Director of Hoare's Bank, who told me of these records and spent so much time and trouble in having the ledgers set out for me.

ELIZABETH JENKINS

THE JANE AUSTEN SOCIETY

Report for the year 1955

Chawton House—The panelled room overlooking the porch, known as the Oak Room, and by tradition that in which Jane Austen sat with her nieces when she visited the Great House.

THE JANE AUSTEN SOCIETY

(Founded in 1940 by Dorothy G. Darnell)

THE JANE AUSTEN SOCIETY
Report for the year 1955

Membership

Forty-two new members joined the Society during the year, of whom three became Life Members. This is a drop of about twenty-five per cent on the previous year. The membership now totals 894, of whom twenty live in the Commonwealth, seventy-three in the U.S.A., and seven in other countries.

Members are reminded that subscriptions became due on 1st January, and that this Report is the only reminder they will receive.

Annual General Meeting 1955

The Annual General Meeting was held at the Assembly Rooms, Alton, on Saturday, 23rd July. The Chair was taken by the President of the Society, His Grace the Duke of Wellington, K.G. About 250 members and their friends were present.

The minutes of the previous Annual General meeting, having been circulated with the Annual Report, were taken as read and confirmed. There were no matters arising from them.

The President then addressed the meeting, and discussed Jane Austen's choice of names of both people and places. He showed with point and humour by examples how these choices were, sometimes nationally and sometimes geographically, unsuitable both as regards surnames and the descriptive titles of her country houses.

The Honorary Secretary then gave out the arrangements for the afternoon, and proposed the adoption of the Annual Report. This was seconded by Lady Smiley and carried.

The Honorary Treasurer presented the Balance Sheet for the year, and proposed its adoption. This was seconded by Mrs. Jervoise Scott, and carried.

The election of officers followed. The Hon. Secretary proposed the re-election of the Duke of Wellington as President, and of Mr. T. Edward Carpenter and Dr. R. W. Chapman as Vice-Presidents. This proposal was seconded by Mr. W. Hugh Curtis and carried.

The President proposed the election of Mr. John Gore, C.V.O. as Chairman of the Society. This was carried unanimously.

Mrs. Boys-Ferris proposed, and Mrs. Hart seconded, the re-election of the Committee en bloc. This was carried.

Sir Arthur Bryant, C.B.E., LL.D., was introduced by the President, and gave a reading of extracts from his book "The Age of Elegance," illustrating the time of Jane Austen.

His readings described London during the visit of the Czar of Russia in 1814, the country house of the period, the Englishman's love of boxing, London Society, and finally included a reference to Jane Austen, showing her contribution to the moral virtues of her own and the Victorian age.

Mr. T. Edward Carpenter first thanked Sir Arthur Bryant, and went on to describe some of the newer exhibits at Jane Austen's house, and announced that he had bought a plot of land beyond the garden, with a frontage on the Winchester road.

A vote of thanks to the Duke of Wellington and Mr. Carpenter was proposed by Miss Elizabeth Jenkins, seconded by Mr. John Gore, and carried.

After tea many members and their friends visited Jane Austen's house at Chawton.

" Persuasion "

A footnote

A box of ivory, piqué with gold stars (reproduced twice the actual size) made by Admiral Sir Francis Austen. (Presented by Dr. R. W. Chapman.)

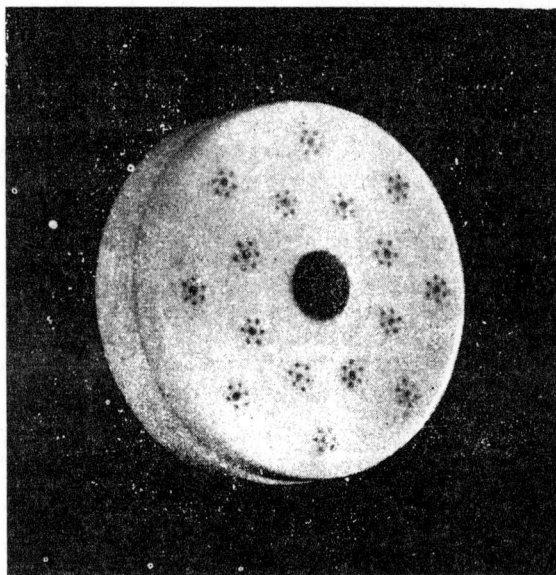

(*a*) Captain Harville's cleverness with his hands is described in " Persuasion," Chapter XI : " He drew, he varnished, he carpentered, he glued, he made toys for the children; he fashioned new netting needles and pins with improvements; and if everything else was done, sat down to his large fishing net at one corner of the room."

(*b*) Francis Austen was similarly gifted. He made toys for his children and Jane wrote of him while he was on shore, February, 1807, as "making very nice fringe for the drawing-room curtains." He said in after years : " I believe that part of Captain Harville's character was suggested by my own."

Annual General Meeting 1956

The Hon. Sir Harold Nicolson, K.C.V.O., C.M.G., has agreed to address the Annual General Meeting, which will be held at Chawton House, by kind invitation of Major and Mrs. Edward Knight, on Saturday, 21st July.

Detailed notices will be sent out later.

The Chairman

Mr. John GORE is known to readers of the SPHERE as *The Old Stager*. He is an authority on the Regency period, as shown by his books *Creevey's Life and Times* and *Creevey* and his *Nelson's Hardy and his Wife*.

He is the author of the official *Personal Memoir* of King George V, for which he was appointed C.V.O. and awarded in 1941 the James Tait Black Memorial Prize for biography.

Jane Austen Memorial Trust
Extract from Chairman's Report

" I have pleasure in sending you a copy of the Trust's accounts for the year 1955, duly certified by our Chartered Accountant, Mr. Edward M. A. Reid.

" The health of the Caretakers has on the whole been satisfactory. But additional help has been given by Mrs. Burgess, Mrs. Newman's daughter, who lives opposite at " Merrivale," a cottage which I bought, enlarged and restored for her occupation. Last October I informed you of the difficult position which arose in regard to Miss Stevens' rooms. The course advocated by the Trust's Solicitor proved effective and the rooms in question are now cleared of the sub-tenants.

" There has been a substantial increase in the number of visitors for 1955. 1954 had already shown an increase of 518 over the attendances for 1953. That of 1955 is 359 over 1954.

" A large party, exceeding fifty, had planned to visit us but found their programme was too extensive and failed to appear. Otherwise our total figures would have exceeded 3,000.

"Gilbert White's House at Selborne was only opened in the late autumn and we have not yet felt the effect of this event. But some visitors have undoubtedly come on from " The Wakes."

" The numbers above do not include those of the Society's members who visit free of charge. I wish the Society could adopt the simple expedient of the National Trust who issue their tickets of membership each year, with the specific date on which each is issued. Such form of ticket could be produced to our caretakers who continue to be handicapped by visitors alleging themselves to be members without furnishing any evidence of a reliable nature.

" The alteration in the garden has much improved the approach to t he House and its surroundings. It has, as I anticipated in my last report, reduced the gardening charges.

" I have carefully watched the condition of the structure. It is in a satisfactory state of repair, allowing however, for annual upkeep, always somewhat heavy on an old building. Certain items under this heading must be undertaken this year. The drawing room has not been decorated since 1949, when cream distemper was used on the walls which are rather rough. I have decided to paper them, having first satisfied myself that the paper closely approaches to the type in use at the period of Jane Austen's residence. The Society are generously supplying the cost of this paper and in fact selected the same for our approbation. This re-decoration should carry us on for the next four years.

" Two modern closets are needed; but, as there is no main drainage in Chawton, it is essential to provide an efficient approved cesspit at a distance of 50 feet from the dwellinghouse. My architect has prepared and lodged the plans. But the cost is likely to be heavy, namely about £250.

" Interesting exhibits have been added in the House.

" The following have been acquired or are on loan :
1. Letter from Geo. Purvis, Esq., Secretary to Sir John Jervis, to his son, afterwards Capt. Geo. Thos. Maitland Purvis, R.N., later the husband of Mary Jane, eldest daughter of Admiral Sir Francis W. Austen, G.C.B. Presented by Mrs. Purvis.

2. Coloured Print, dated 1809, of Messrs. Wedgwood's Show-room at St. James' Street visited by Jane Austen and her brother Edward and her niece Fanny to select china. Presented by Miss Elizabeth Jenkins.

3. Photograph of Sir Walter Scott's edition of ·the Novels now at Abbotsford. Presented by Dr. James E. Corson, the Librarian at Edinburgh University and at Abbotsford.

4. Set of the 1923 limited edition of the Novels in five volumes edited by Dr. Chapman. Presented by a former member of the Society, Miss Ida Pim.

5. Presented by myself :·
Photostat of the Holograph Will of Jane Austen with copy of affidavit filed in support.

6. Photograph of the original of the last composition by Jane Austen on St. Swithin.

7. Photograph of the Oak Room at Chawton Great House.

" Other interesting exhibits are in prospect for the current year.

" In regard to advertising I should appreciate the views of the Trustees. I think that the time has arrived to rely on Jane Austen's fame as the principal attraction for visitors. This item is a heavy one and I favour reducing it to advertisements in the annual issues of "Historical Houses and Castles of Great Britain," and " Museums and Galleries in Great Britain." But these would be supplemented by an annual illustrated advertisement in Country Life Annual and any other well publicised issue. The House is now open daily from 11 a.m. to 4.30 p.m. or at any other hours by appointment.

" Dealing with finance, as already intimated I have received from the Executors of the late Miss Evelyn O'Connor, of New York, her legacy of 1,000 dollars converted into sterling at £357. I have invested this without deduction in the Trustees' names in £441 19s. 8d. three and a half per cent War Stock. The first dividend on which, namely £7 14s. 8d., was received on the 1st December last and appears in the accounts.

" The accountant says :

" The position is that the income of the Trust is just about sufficient
" to meet the wages, rates, electricity and printing, etc. provided the
" expenditure on advertising is reduced. It will not, however, cover
" any special expenditure that may be incurred."

" The indebtedness of the Trust to myself as at 31st December, 1954 was £99 5s. 9d., which has now been liquidated.

" The other items in the account are sufficiently clear, I hope, to require no explanation. Very careful nursing will be required during the next few years if any surplus of profit is to be shown. I may point out that I have this year charged the sum of £46 13s. 8d. for repairs and decorations to those parts of the premises occupied by our caretakers. This I think you will agree is only fair since the Trust draws the rents.

" Permit me to conclude by quoting an illustration of the appreciation expressed by a visitor in regard to the House and its exhibits.

"On the 31st October last Mr. Frank Swinnerton, his wife and daughter visited the house On the following day he wrote to me, inter alia, as follows :

" The whole exhibition is full of charm and taste : a great credit to you
" and an honour to your Son's memory. We were delighted with it.
" The better the house is known, and the more pilgrims it attracts, the
" more appreciated will be your really wonderful work. The care-
" takers were most courteous and helpful. We all greatly enjoyed our
" visit, and felt warm gratitude to you for what you have done to preserve
" the house in such beautiful condition and give it so much the air of
" being a real setting for Jane Austen as she was. I was tremendously
impressed."

He again wrote on the 4th November, 1955 :

" The more I think of the House at Chawton (and I have been re-reading
" Dr. Chapman's edition of Jane Austen's letters with added pleasure),
" the more do I feel that you have entirely succeeded in your aim there.
" One never feels it to be a museum; one has the sense that she really
" has been, and still is, at home there."

THOMAS EDWARD CARPENTER,

Chairman of the Trust

Jane Austen in her Letters

It is good news for members of the Society that a selection from Jane Austen's letters is now available at a very small cost. It has just been published in the World's Classics series (price 5/-). Since it has been edited by Dr. Chapman its excellence goes without saying.

If it is difficult to understand the people who do not care for Jane Austen's novels, it is still less comprehensible that there should be people who admire the novels and have not a good word to say for the letters. Yet there are such, of high authority. I should suppose that they had not time to read the letters carefully enough to find the felicities, were it not that it is actually the characteristic passages to which they take exception. The explanation must be that they exact a much more rigid standard of propriety and caution in the letters of genius than would be acceptable in the private letters of their friends.

Henry Austen, in his memorial notice of his sister, says in her praise that she never uttered a severe expression about anybody. This was certainly not true, though no doubt well meant. Jane Austen wrote, and no doubt spoke, of friends and acquaintances with just the benevolent ruthlessness with which she handled the minor characters in her novels. Phrases from the letters like " more quietly and contentedly silly than anything else," and " his usual nothing-meaning harmless heartless civility " are very obviously by the hand that wrote in " Sense and Sensibility " of the " strong natural sterling insignificance " of Mr. Robert Ferrars.

We can indeed track down in the letters examples of most of the novelist's characteristic turns of style and thought. There is her cool realism—the very antithesis of sentimentality, for example :
" As to pitying a young woman merely because she cannot live in two places at the same time, and at once enjoy the comforts of being married and single, I shall not attempt it."
and
" Single women have a dreadful propensity for being poor—which is one very strong argument in favour of matrimony."
There is the occasional Johnsonian rhythm, used with satirical intent, as when she says of a half-hearted wooer :
" Our indifference will soon be mutual, unless his regard, which appeared to spring from knowing nothing of me at first, is best supported by never seeing me."
There is the happy enjoyment of others' absurdities (so like Elizabeth Bennet's) :
" Whenever I fall into misfortune, how many jokes it ought to furnish to my acquaintance in general, or I shall die dreadfully in their debt for entertainment."
And of course there is the famous irony, with its hint of oblique quotation, which is one of the mainstays of her narrative style as a novelist. There are many examples in the letters; perhaps this light one will serve :
" You know it is not an uncommon circumstance in this parish to have the road from Ibthrop to the Parsonage much dirtier and more

impracticable for walking than the road from the Parsonage to Ibthrop."

These little nuggets of the novelist Jane Austen are embedded in the day to day trivialities of a young lady's life : descriptions of balls (in which we follow her from the days in which she indulged "in everything most profligate and shocking " in the way of flirtation to the time when she rather enjoyed being " a sort of Chaperone "); the new or remade dresses (" I will not be much longer libelled by the possession of my coarse spot "); the maids and housekeeping, the births and deaths. What could be more agreeable than being admitted to this intimacy with the Misses Austen ?

Jane's attitude to her own authorship comes out very clearly in her letters. Above all else it seemed to her *fun*. Fun to be writing novels; fun to await publication; very special fun to hear them read aloud to friends ignorant of the authorship. On finding herself a success her reactions may be summed up in a favourite phrase of hers—"Fancy me! " As to the obligation of her friends to buy the books :

" I shall not mind imagining it a disagreeable duty to them, so as they do it."

The references to particular novels in the letters are well known. Her suggestion that "Pride and Prejudice" seemed to her when read aloud to be " too light and bright and sparkling " is not of course seriously intended. This novel stood with her for "wit" and "Mansfield Park" for ' sense.' She feared that "Emma" would be thought by comparison deficient in wit by some, in sense by others. In connection with ' Mansfield Park,' it is interesting to notice that in writing to Fanny Knight some three years after its publication, she said of heroines in general " Pictures of perfection as you know make me sick and wicked." It is a fair assumption that Fanny Price did not make her creator feel " sick and wicked," whatever she may have done to critics; and it seems to follow that Jane Austen did not regard Fanny as a " picture of perfection." Indeed she did occasionally touch that young lady with her delicate sting, and the only fault I have ever seen in her treatment of the character is that she did not do it more often.

Readers will find in this volume all the important surviving letters about family life and events and authorship; and visitors to Chawton will enjoy the comments made at the time on the garden and the Wedgwood dinner service. It is however a selection of whole letters and not of choice morsels, so naturally some choice morsels are omitted. I will end by quoting a favourite sentence of my own, appearing in a letter for which Dr. Chapman has not found room. It relates to a visitor making too long a stay at her brother's house :

" I cannot imagine how a man can have the impudence to come into a family party for three days, where he is quite a stranger, unless he knows himself to be agreeable on undoubted authority."

That to my mind holds the fine essence of Jane Austen as a correspondent.

MYRA CURTIS

Chawton House in Jane Austen's time. "Mr. Tilson took a sketch of the Great House . . .", from a letter to Cassandra dated June 6th, 1811

Country Life Copyright

Country Life Copyright

Chawton House today

Jane Austen's London Homes

Anne Elliot's views about the advantages of living in the country have generally been held to be Jane Austen's own. But it is evident from her letters that she greatly enjoyed her regular visits to London. By a fortunate chance nearly all the houses she stayed in on these occasions have survived, although they bear no distinguishing mark; and at least two of them have been very much altered outwardly.

In nearly every case the house was the home of her brother Henry, and before her death, of his wife, Jane Austen's much loved cousin, Eliza.

In June of 1808 she paid a visit to Henry and Eliza in what was then the village of Brompton. Dr. Chapman, in his edition of Jane Austen's letters, gives the address as 16 St. Michael's Place, but actually it was called Michael's Place. This was a row of forty-four houses which stood next to Yeoman's Row, on the left-hand side of the main road from London. The little terrace was called Michael's Place after its designer, Michael Novosielski. He was the son of a Polish count, and was born in Rome in 1750. Here he studied architecture, coming to London about 1770. His main achievement was the rebuilding of the Opera House in the Haymarket in 1789, and this is the one which Jane urged Cassandra to visit when she was staying in Upper Berkeley Street in 1801. "I hope you will see everything worthy of notice," she says, " from the Opera house to Henry's office in Cleveland Court."

The ground on which Michael's Place was built was formerly known as " Flounder's Fields " because it was so damp and muddy. This may be the reason that when Novosielski's speculation was pulled down in 1886, many of its houses were still unfinished shells. It may also be the reason why Henry and Eliza moved house in 1811.

Their next home was more ambitious—No. 64 Sloane Street. It is a large house, and still stands, complete and beautiful, inside a cumbrous late-Victorian shell. Now the headquarters of the Family Planning Association, it is being beautifully redecorated. The old panelling, classical reliefs, fireplaces and doorways have all been kept. Perhaps the most interesting feature, from its associations, is the wide landing at the top of the sweeping Georgian staircase. It connects the front and back drawing-rooms, and is the point where Jane Austen placed herself on the night of Eliza's evening party. Thus, as she said, " having all the advantage of the Music at a pleasant distance, as well as that of the first view of every newcomer." The drawing-rooms which on this occasion were " dressed up with flowers, etc., and looked very pretty," have at some time, unfortunately been partitioned into small offices. The secretary of the Association, Mrs. Gabell, kindly showed me over the house, and I gathered from her that these partitions are not necessary, and that the Association, who know of the Jane Austen connection and are interested in it, would welcome their removal, but are not able to undertake it themselves. The one room which is completely unspoiled is a small oak-panelled one at the front of the house on the ground floor. It seems probable that this was Henry Austen's study. Its windows look straight over the grass and trees in the middle of Cadogan Place to the row of

Georgian houses opposite, and if there is a lull in the traffic, the interval of time between his day and ours seems for a moment to be non-existent.

This house is so spacious and beautiful that there seems some excuse for the " unreasonable ideas " which Jane Austen had to abandon, when, after the death of his wife, Henry moved to Hans Place, just round the corner.

But before this move, there was an interval when Henry, whose affairs had begun, perhaps,to be rather involved, very sensibly went to live in the rooms over his bank at 10 Henrietta Street, Covent Garden. In May, 1813, Jane Austen describes the house as " all dirt and confusion, but in a very promising way," and in September she tells her brother Frank: " No. 10 is made very comfortable with cleaning, and Painting and the Sloane St. furniture. The front room upstairs is an excellent Dining and common sitting parlour—and the smaller one behind will sufficiently answer his purpose as a Drawing room.—He has no intention of giving large parties of any kind.—His plans are all for the comfort of his friends and himself. Mde. Bigeon and her daughter have a Lodging in his neighbourhood and come to him as often as he likes or as they like. Mde. B. always markets for him as she used to do; and upon our being in the house, was constantly there to do the work.—She is wonderfully recovered from the severity of her Asthmatic complaint." Does this suggest, Asthma being usually of nervous origin, that Eliza had been rather an exacting mistress ?

No. 10 Henrietta Street still stands. It belongs to the hospital of St. Peter, and having been at some time their Nurses' Home, is now occupied by a Medical Association. It has been robbed in its nurses' home days of nearly every feature of interest or beauty, but the general outline of the house has not been greatly altered.

When you first go into the entrance passage, you are standing on the spot where Jane and her brother Edward's family arrived at a quarter past four on a September afternoon in 1813. They were " warmly welcomed by the coachman and then by his master and then by William, and then by Mrs. Perigord," (Mde. Bigeon's daughter) " who all met us before we had reached the foot of the stairs. Mde. Bigeon was below dressing us a most comfortable dinner of soup, fish, bouillée, partridges, and an apple tart, which we sat down to soon after five, after cleaning and dressing ourselves and feeling that we are most comfortably disposed of. The little adjoining dressing-room to our apartment makes Fanny and myself very well off indeed, and as we have poor Eliza's bed our space is ample every way."

The room with the " little adjoining dressing-room " is unmistakably one at the top of the tall, narrow house; and by a fortunate chance it alone of all the rooms has not been spoilt. The beautiful carved fireplace is still there, and the doctors who use the house as offices have made the room their library. It is decorated in turquoise and white, and but for the water-colours of diseases which hang on the walls, it is easy to realise that this is the room where Jane Austen " went to bed at ten, and slept

75

to a miracle," and where, another time, she left Fanny " fast asleep.—She was doing about last night, when *I* went to sleep, a little after one . . . "

It is not so easy to reconstruct the region below stairs, where Jane had her appointment with " Mde. B " at eight o'clock in the morning, to discuss such domestic details as a " boil'd loaf," (ham ?), and the sad fact that " her master has no raspberry Jam." Unfortunately, the room downstairs which was probably Mde. Bigeon's domain was stripped long ago of any likeness to a kitchen.

In March, 1814, Jane was again staying in Henrietta Street, and she writes : " Here is nothing but Thickness and Sleet, and tho' these two rooms are delightfully warm, I fancy it is very cold abroad." Modern methods of heating have replaced Henry's roaring fires, but these two rooms, which once opened into each other, can be identified as one big room upstairs, lacking any period feature, however, except the sash windows overlooking the street. A very small room, probably a "Sister's " bedroom or office, had been sliced off one side of the front of the big room when I first saw it, and the entrance altered accordingly, which made the geography a little puzzling. It was in this room that Jane "read *The Corsair* and mended her petticoat," and tore through the third volume of *The Heroine*. Henry, meanwhile, was sitting beside her, absorbed in the manuscript of *Mansfield Park*.

In the back part of this long double room, we can imagine in September, 1813, " all four of us young Ladies sitting round the Circular Table in the inner room writing our Letters, while the two Brothers are having a comfortable coze in the room adjoining."

" All four of us young Ladies " meant Jane herself, nearing forty; Fanny—just grown-up; thirteen-year old Lizzy; and poor Marianne, the youngest, whose twelfth birthday the day before seems to have been spent almost entirely at the dentist's.

These letters of Jane's are particularly full and detailed, and we seem to see the party at Henrietta Street in a series of small bright pictures, like those in an old-fashioned magic lantern. Shopping for veils, music and Wedgwood ware, watching the Indian Jugglers, going to the theatre, and driving in the Park. Finally we see Jane, in the Ermine tippet which Cassandra had given her, " bringing Fanny safe home," on foot, through the whirling snow.

Before long, Henry seems to have tired of living in Covent Garden, which cannot have been what is called a good neighbourhood socially. At Midsummer, 1814, he moved to No. 23 Hans Place. This house, like its near neighbour, 64 Sloane Street, seems to be still more or less complete inside a Victorian facade, but its old plan is hard to make out, because a sort of additional wedge has been built all the way up from ground level to the roof, between No. 23 and the adjoining house. No. 23 has been divided into flats, and I doubt if the owner, or owners, had any knowledge of its Jane Austen associations. But the conversion has been well done, and has left unspoilt the remaining Regency features, including the very attractive carved fireplaces, each of a different design. It is a pity that the windows were made hideous when the Victorian shell was added. The alteration is very obvious when the house is compared with the few unspoilt houses still remaining in the square. Jane Austen's final verdict on the house was given in a letter to Martha Lloyd : " I am extremely pleased with this new House of Henry's, it is everything that could be wished for him, and I have only to hope he will continue to like it as well as he does now, and not be looking out for anything better."

There is a large double drawing-room with French windows opening on to a balcony. This is the room where, in the year of Waterloo, Fanny Knight played her harp in the candlelight of a November evening; while Jane listened, and the enthusiastic and talented Mr. Haden offered suggestions for improvement. This young surgeon had been called in on Henry's behalf. He was suffering from an attack which in these days would probably be called appendicitis, and which perhaps was brought on by worry about his financial affairs which were then approaching a crisis.

During his illness, Henry Austen moved down one floor because he fancied it would be warmer, and both rooms, with their lovely fireplaces and arched recesses, saw Jane in placid attendance on her brother.

" You must fancy Henry in the back-room upstairs," wrote Jane to Cassandra, " and I am generally there also, working or writing." Jane Austen's own room was the attic at the top of the house. She calls it the front attic, but, as it occupied all the top floor apart from a little dressing-room now converted into a kitchen, it could with equal truth be called a back attic. Jane considered it " the Bedchamber to be preferred," and, as she had plenty to choose from, it is a little hard to see why, until you actually see the room. One of her reasons might have been that which she gives as a reason for a guest being comfortable in her own room at Chawton—" the maid is most conveniently near."

But the Hans Place attic is really charming—like a country bedroom, with seats in the deep Dormer windows, and a beautiful little Regency fireplace. In Jane Austen's day, anyone sitting on one of the low, wide window seats would have had a lovely view over gardens and fields, and distant heights. Today, gardens and view have both disappeared.

The garden at the back of No. 23 must have extended about as far as the middle of Pont Street, and perhaps the row of skinny trees, now on crazy paving, down the middle are descendants of the trees which bordered the garden in which Jane Austen used to " take a turn " when she was tired of working and wanted refreshment. She speaks of using Henry's room downstairs, (meaning his business room or study) as a living-room, because " it is particularly pleasant from opening on the garden." As all the rooms except the kitchen department are above ground level, it seems probable that there was a balcony to Henry's room, with steps leading down to the garden.* This, according to the account of Letitia Elizabeth Landon, who was at school there, was the case with the corresponding ground floor at No. 22.

*The author has now found a map (London Ordnance Survey 1867-74) which shows these steps, thus identifying Henry's sitting-room.

With its central lawn, and path, and border of flowering shrubs, the garden in the middle of Hans Place does not look so very different today. It is also, judging by the plan in Dr. Chapman's edition of Jane Austen's Letters, very like the garden at the back of No. 23 Hans Place, as it was in the days when Jane Austen called it " quite a love."

Hans Place was Jane Austen's last London home. Henry's illness recovered from, he still had to face his bankruptcy. " Dreams of affluence, nay of competence are closed," he wrote in later years to his rich nephew James Edward; and now the fashionable Henry became a country curate. London knew him no more, and a chapter in Jane Austen's life was ended.

Nearly the last chapter, it had been one of fulfilment and quiet enjoyment. All the business of publishing *Sense and Sensibility* and *Pride and Prejudice* had been arranged from the Sloane Street house; that of *Mansfield Park* from Henrietta Street; while the house in Hans Place had seen the transference to the great Mr. Murray, as publisher of *Emma*. In Hans Place, too, Jane Austen was distinguished by the patronage of the Prince Regent, and his invitation to visit Carlton House.

It seems to me that each of these houses, 64 Sloane Street, 10 Henrietta Street, and 23 Hans Place, should be marked with a tablet giving the dates of Jane Austen's visits there; and that their preservation should be safeguarded by some ruling more dependable than the blind chance which has saved them—more or less—until today.

WINIFRED WATSON

THE JANE AUSTEN SOCIETY

Report for the year 1956

Mrs. Philadelphia Hancock

THE JANE AUSTEN SOCIETY

(Founded in 1940 by Dorothy G. Darnell)

80

THE JANE AUSTEN SOCIETY

Report for the year 1956

MEMBERSHIP

Fifty-seven new members joined the Society during the year, of whom eight became Life Members. In addition, four old members became Life Members. We have lost a number of members who have failed to renew their subscriptions, or who have resigned, and the membership now stands at 829.

Members are reminded that subscriptions became due on 1st January, and that this Report is the only reminder they will receive. The Hon. Secretary would much appreciate prompt payment of the 5/- Annual Subscription, and will gladly provide a Bankers' Order form for anyone who would prefer to pay by that method.

ANNUAL GENERAL MEETING, 1956

The Annual General Meeting was held on Saturday, 21st July, at Chawton House, by kind invitation of Major and Mrs. Edward Knight. It was attended by over four hundred members and their friends. The President of the Society, His Grace the Duke of Wellington, K.G., presided.

The minutes of the previous Annual General Meeting, having been published in the Annual Report, were taken as read. There were no matters arising from them.

The Hon. Secretary gave out the arrangements for the afternoon, and proposed the adoption of the Annual Report. This was seconded by Mrs. Hubert Howard, and carried.

The Hon. Treasurer presented the accounts. Their adoption was proposed by Mr. Noel Blakiston, seconded by Mrs. Leigh-Wood, and carried.

The election of officers followed. Mr. John Gore proposed the re-election of His Grace the Duke of Wellington, K.G. as President, and of Mr. T. Edward Carpenter and Dr. R. W. Chapman as Vice-Presidents. This was seconded by the Hon. Mrs. Cubitt, and carried.

The President proposed the re-election en bloc of the Committee, with the addition of Mrs. Rupert Shervington. This was carried.

The meeting was then addressed by the Hon. Sir Harold Nicolson, K.C.V.O., C.M.G., on the subject of "Jane Austen and her Letters. Sir Harold's address is printed in full at the end of this Report.

A vote of thanks to Sir Harold Nicolson was proposed by Mr. Carpenter, seconded by the Duke of Wellington, and carried. The President then thanked Major and Mrs. Knight for allowing the meeting to be held at Chawton House.

Tea had been provided by individuals in Chawton, and the proceeds of the sale of tickets went towards the Chawton Church Preservation Fund, which, together with a sum collected in a box in the church, amounted to over £50. Members were able to see some of the rooms in the house and visit the gardens and Chawton Church.

Through the generosity of Mrs. Jack Reed, the unworthy wooden plaque on 8 College Street, Winchester, has been replaced by one in a more lasting material. The new plaque of grey slate with white lettering was designed and executed by Mr. Esmond Burton.

ANNUAL GENERAL MEETING, 1957

The Annual General Meeting will be held at Chawton House, on Saturday, 20th July, when the speaker will be Mr. Roger Fulford. Further details will be sent out later.

8 College Street. Winchester

JANE AUSTEN MEMORIAL TRUST

EXTRACT FROM CHAIRMAN'S REPORT

"I have paid during the year 1956, 39 visits to the House so that it has had the necessary close supervision.

"The health of the caretakers has on the whole been satisfactory and I continue to receive from many visitors commendation of the manner in which they are welcomed and the way in which the House and its contents are displayed.

"The weather during the summer was very inclement and undoubtedly had its effect in reducing the number of callers anticipated. Moreover the unfortunate petrol situation added to this circumstance, especially in December and over the Christmas holiday. Nevertheless the total attendances for 1956 shew an increase over the total for 1955 of 229. The actual figure for 1956 was 3193, notwithstanding the reduction in advertisement.

"I am unable to trace that we have had any substantial number of visitors from Gilbert White's House at Selborne.

"I have had a very neat plaque executed in Hopton stone, recording the gift to the Nation by myself of Jane Austen's Home, erected in the front where the original drawing-room window was blocked up by Edward Knight in 1809, and the older tablet has been restored to its old site adjacent to the front door.

"The inscription on the new tablet is as follows—
Jane Austen's Home
Given by Thomas Edward Carpenter, J.P.
in memory of his Son, Lieut. Philip John Carpenter,
East Surrey Regiment,
Killed in action at Lake Trasimene the 30th June, 1944.

Opened 1949 by the Duke of Wellington, K.G.,
President of the Jane Austen Society
Founded 1940 by Dorothy Darnell of Alton

"The Society has not to my regret followed my suggestion made in my report of the 24th January, 1956, as to the issue of membership tickets for the convenience of our caretakers, I have consequently adopted the expedient of a separate membership book for the signatures of members of the Society. But this does not meet the case of members or alleged members who are unwilling to append their signatures.

"The re-arrangement of the garden has proved satisfactory and has been universally commended. The saving on garden charges has been substantial. Mr. Newman living on the spot is always able to expend time in tidying, planting and cutting the grass. I am raising plants at my own home and transferring them to Chawton from time to time.

"In connection with the garden the Trustees will recollect that we have a number of York paving stones originally in the kitchen but transferred to a house the other side of the village street. Miss Dorothy Darnell procured their return and they were laid against the flank wall of the House at the side of entrance. During the wet summer the gravel from the walk outside this flank wall was badly trodden into the drawingroom and elsewhere. I have had these stones removed and laid so as to form a proper paved entrance to both this room and Mrs. Newman's entrance. The appearance is much better than that of the odd original lay-out of these stones. The narrow flanking flower border extending only from the entrance gate to the drawingroom door will now be extended to the north corner of the House as it originally was, I am given to understand, in Jane Austen's time.

"I have also had removed a large yew stump at the corner, assumed to be dead. It was found on careful examination to be not only alive but to be extending its very large roots under this portion of the fabric. There will now be no risk of subsidence especially as this corner has been well 'packed' to avoid this.

"I have now carried out the works mentioned in my report earlier this year. Two modern lavatories have been installed, the one on the first floor in substitution of the large cupboard at the head of the main staircase, and the other on the ground floor against the corner of Mrs. Newman's kitchen. Certain structural alterations became necessary to comply with the requirements of the local authority, including the opening of another window facing the garden. But my architect has carried out such work so as not to interfere with the nature of the wall and in fact such work is an improvement on the blank stretch of brickwork of the main wall.

"There is no main drainage in Chawton and this lack necessitated the provision of an adequate cesspit with the attendant soakaways, and the laying of drains and surface water drains in the rear yard. This has been skilfully done with a resultant tidying-up of the yard which, against the walls of the House, has a solid concrete flanking path of unobtrusive design making for the comfort of those using the House or the yard. This has got rid of the ugly patches of couch grass which has not hitherto lent itself to effective cutting. "The cost of this work will be in excess of £700.

"Another improvement is the cutting through of the wall erected across the landing outside Miss Stevens' bedroom severing the corridor giving on to what have hitherto been known as the Kings' rooms. A door has been substituted at this entrance, and, when open, gives a pleasant outlook to the village street and allows sun and air to enter, thus increasing both lighting and airiness. The question will ultimately have to be decided as to the user of the three extra rooms thus made available. It will be necessary to retain one for clerical and general executive purposes. It is not however a pressing problem until additional exhibits are forthcoming.

"The re-decoration and restoration referred to in my report earlier in 1956 have been skilfully carried out at a cost of £38 8s. 6d., which the funds of the Trust have met. They have also met the cost of certain necessary repairs to roofs and guttering amounting to £4 19s. 2d., and to the front fencing running to £3 16s. 6d. I do not anticipate any heavy expenditure for running repairs during the next two years.

"It will be recollected that the late Miss Evelyn O'Connor of New York, left to the Trust a legacy of one thousand dollars and that this sum was received on the 5th October, 1955, and invested in £441 19s. 8d., three and one half per cent. War Stock. In order to bring this up to a level one thousand pounds nominal I personally provided a further cash sum of £415 9s. 6d. On the 5th May last our generous donor Mrs. Purvis sent me a cheque for £1000, which I invested in toto in the purchase of £1387 8s. of such stock. On the 28th October last I was authorised by the Trustees to sell the excess over £2000 of our total holding to repay the indebtedness to myself of the sum of £270 11s. 2d., the amount I had loaned to the Trust for current expenditure for 1956. So the Trust starts unencumbered by debt in 1957. Moreover the receipts of the Trust for 1956 enabled the Trustees to clear off the indebtedness shewn in the Trust accounts for the year 1955. Until the receipts for entrance fees and the sale of postcards, it will still be necessary for me to make loans from time to time to keep down expenditure of a recurring nature but it is to be hoped that such advances may be repaid as the year advances.

"I am of course still contributing the monthly sum of £2 5s. under covenant which enables the Trust to recover income tax of approximately £22 to add to its annual resources.

"Two interesting exhibits have been acquired during the year just passed, the gifts respectively, of Mr. P. C. Mundy, of Ickleton Manor, and of Miss Cassandra Hardy. The former discovered amongst his papers an original diary of Mrs. or Miss Elizabeth Leigh, the godmother of Jane's sister, and the latter has presented to us an original diary of Edward Knight relating to a tour he made in Germany in 1817. Both are now on display. Mrs. Upjohn, of the United States, has also presented to our library a complete edition of the Novels issued by Macmillan and Co.

"I have compiled two complete catalogues relating to exhibits and books. These catalogues contain a full description of both categories and give the name of donor or lender, with references to any documentary evidence bearing on each subject. Visitors have found both catalogues useful and they appeal especially to students who are visiting us in increasing numbers.

"I feel that there are still a number of interesting relics of a personal nature of the great Novelist principally with relatives. I think an appeal by the Society stressing the permanency of the Home now established for all relics might produce more interesting articles and avoid the regrettable possibility of their being disposed of in the public sale room and leaving the country.

"I have completed the permanent restoration of the grave of Mrs. Austen and Cassandra in Chawton Churchyard, rendering continual tidying, always a difficult task to arrange, now unnecessary.

"The petrol situation will sadly reduce the numbers of our visitors this year, but the moderate endowment of the Trust will help us to face the future."

THOMAS EDWARD CARPENTER,
Chairman

Miniature of Mrs. Philadelphia Hancock

The cover of this report bears a re-production of a photograph of the above mentioned miniature by John Smart, bearing his initials, of Mrs. Philadelphia Hancock (1730-1792) the sister of Jane Austen's father, and therefore her aunt, married to Tysoe Saul Hancock.

Miss Philadelphia Austen sailed for India in the Bombay Castle on 18th January, 1752 and was married on the 22nd February, 1753 to Dr. Hancock. Their only child was Eliza ("Betsy"), who became Comtesse de Feuillide, was widowed on the 22nd February, 1794 through the guillotining of her husband Jean Capotte, the Comte, and subsequently became the first wife of Henry Thomas Austen, Jane's fourth brother in 1797. She died in 1813.

It is of interest to note that Dr. Hancock, writing twenty years after to his wife, and deprecating the proposed trip of his daughter Betsy to India, said, "You know very well that no "girl, though but fourteen years old, can arrive in India with-"out attracting the notice of every coxcomb in the place". Mr. R. A. Austen-Leigh reminds us of the case of Eliza Sclater

(Sterne's 'Eliza') who was married in 1753 to Daniel Draper at the age of fourteen within four months of arriving at Bombay and suggests that Dr. Hancock may have had this case in mind when writing about Betsy to his wife. Betsy was born in 1761 at Calcutta. Mr. Austen-Leigh adds that Hancock's name appears in a list of surgeons' mates in India in 1748, that in 1753 he was serving as surgeon at Fort St. David and in 1758 as one of the surgeons in the Madras Presidency, removing to Bengal in 1759.

John Smart was, according to all authorities, the outstanding realistic miniaturist of the 18th Century. He was born on the 1st May, 1741 and died on his birthday in 1811. He was thus a contemporary of Cosway (1740-1821), who refers to him as "Honest John Smart". A biographer states "His work is entirely "different from that of Cosway, quiet and grey in its colouring "with the flesh tints elaborated with much subtlety and "modelled in exquisite fashion. He possessed a great knowledge "of anatomy and his portraits are drawn with the greatest "anatomical accuracy and possess more distinction than those "of any other miniature painter of his time".

Our miniature bears all the characteristics of the work of this great miniaturist and its value is enhanced by its exquisite framing in gold, silver and diamonds carried out by Smart's friend and a famous French Miniaturist, Toussaint, a jeweller of great taste and ability.

When the miniature was executed is not known, but in his letter to his wife of the 13th March, 1771, Dr. Hancock says "Is it not possible for Smart to prevent your picture in the "ring which I sent home from spoiling in India?"

The miniature is specifically referred to in Dr. Hancock's will executed on the 8th Decemebr, 1774: "To my daughter "Elizabeth I bequeath the miniature picture of her mother "painted by Smart and set in a ring with diamonds around it "which I request she will never part with as I intend it to re- "mind her of her mother's virtues as well as of her person". Betsy fulfilled her father's wish and retained the miniature and on her death in 1813 it passed to her second husband, Henry Thomas Austen. He subsequently remarried, his second wife being Eleanor Jackson, whose mother had been a Papillon. On Henry's death in 1850, the miniature passed to his widow.

Reference must now be made to another branch of the extensive Austen Family. Admiral of the Fleet, Sir Francis William Austen, G.C.B., had a daughter (his eldest child), Mary Jane, who became the wife of Capt. Geo. Thos. Maitland Purvis, R.N. Their daughter, Mary Renira Purvis, lived for many years with Eleanor, Henry Austen's widow and to her the latter bequeathed the miniature. Mary subsequently became Mrs.

Paine and she gave the miniature to Mary Jane Austen Purvis, subsequently Mrs. Way, the only sister of Lieut. Purvis, R.N., whose widow, Mrs. Mary Purvis, has presented the miniature to the Jane Austen Memorial Trust.

It may be permitted to state its intermediate history prior to the gift to the Trust.

Mrs. Mary Purvis had sold the picture and Miss Winifred Watson discovered one day that it was on sale in the shop of Messrs. Mallett in New Bond Street, London. Miss Watson is the authoress of "Jane Austen's London Homes". She informed the Chairman of the Trust, Mr. T. E. Carpenter, of this fact. He immediately visited these dealers and to prevent its going out of the Country, persuaded them to sell it to him at a somewhat high price. He then got into touch with Mrs. Mary Purvis to obtain further information about it. Mrs. Purvis expressed a wish to present it to the Trust, reimbursed the Chairman the price he had paid for it, and then generously presented it to the present holders.

Not only is the Trust indebted to her for this gift but, in providing an endowment of £1,000, she has become the Trust's greatest benefactress. She writes under the nom de plume of "Queen Mary Rose" and is the authoress of charming lyrics.

It is only fair to her to say that the tradition in the Purvis family is that the miniature is that of Betsy, the Comtesse, and indeed mother and daughter possess strong affinity in personal appearance.

But the documentary evidence quoted above does not support this tradition. Moreover the Arts Section of the Victoria and Albert Museum are of the undoubted opinion that it must be of Mrs. Hancock having regard to the style of dress and the arrangement of the hair of the sitter.

T. EDWARD CARPENTER,
Chairman, Jane Austen Memorial Trust

Chief Justice Lefroy, Marble Bust at Trinity College, Dublin

Jane Austen and her Music Books

Jane Austen sometimes went out of her way to disclaim any taste for music. When the singing of Kitty Stephens failed to give her pleasure she wrote to her sister Cassandra that this was "no reflection upon her, nor upon myself, being what Nature "made me on that article"; and of a projected visit to a gala at Sydney Gardens at Bath she said "even the concert will have "more than its usual charm for me, as the Gardens are large "enough for me to get pretty well beyond the reach of its sound". But it seems likely that this kind of remark was made as a protest against the prevailing assumption that a genteel and accomplished young lady must necessarily show, not only some skill as a performer, but a great degree of "sensibility" as a listener, whatever her real feelings. And, on the other hand, we can quote her genuine appreciation of the playing of "Miss H", who had "flowers in her head, and music at her "finger-"ends". We have Mr. Austen-Leigh's word for it that she was very fond of music, and had a sweet voice both in singing and in conversation; "In her youth", he says, "she had received some "instruction upon the pianoforte".

And now we have the evidence of her own music books—the property of the Jane Austen Memorial Trust, and on view at her Home at Chawton.

These show their owner to have taken the time and trouble to collect, copy and, presumably, practise a representative selection of what would have been called "the most admired" vocal and instrumental productions of her day. Some of this music is printed, but much of it is in manuscript, as was usual in days when music was expensive to buy and no one was afraid of infringing copyright.

Jane was not a very expert copyist in her own view, for she wrote to Cassandra that her sister-in-law, Elizabeth Knight, the wife of her brother Edward, was "very cruel about my "writing music and as a punishment for her, I should insist upon "always writing out all hers for her in future, if I were not "punishing myself at the same time."

Practising and performance were possibly more congenial to her when it came to dance music. We know how she loved young people to dance. "Yes, yes, we **will** have a pianoforte as good as "can be got for thirty guineas, and I will practise some country "dances that we may have some amusement for our nephews "and nieces when we have the pleasure of their company", she wrote in 1808. And so we are not surprised to find among her music country dances, including four pages of "Sauvage Dame", beneath the notes of which she has carefully marked the steps: "The first couple set to the second lady . . . " and so on. But there is no evidence that she ever played for the nephews and nieces that "riotous German dance of modern invention", as Burney called the waltz in 1805, although in music book No. 1, together with regimental marches, traditional songs and strathspeys, we certainly find two waltzes.

Of other sorts of music we find in Book 2 a selection which must surely have been made by her parents, since it would have been considered old fashioned by the time Jane was learning her notes. We have songs from Boyce's "The Chaplet", first performed in 1749; songs by Samuel Howard (1710-1782); music by the Rev. W. Felton (1713-1769); and references to the famous tenor, John Beard, whose best days were in the middle of the century. The other music books, and the song sheets, however, reflect the musical taste of Jane Austen's own period.

The keyboard music includes in Book 3 a printed copy of Pleyel's fourteen sonatas for the harpsichord or pianoforte; and in Book 4, also printed, a good anthology of key-board music of the second half of the eighteenth century under the title of a "Selected Collection of Choice Music"; concertos, duetts (sic), and sonatas by Arne, Handel, Schobert, Janowitz, Haydn, Corelli, Corri and others. Book 4 contains some more sonatas by Schobert, various overtures to Italian operas arranged for key-board, and several duets for two performers on harpsichord or pianoforte—single printed copies, bound up together in a volume bearing her signature.

Jane Austen's instrument was, of course, the early square pianoforte, such as we now see in the Austens' drawingroom in her Home at Chawton.

And now let us turn to the songs.

A complete list of these with notes on their composition would involve a lengthy essay on English vocal music of the late eighteenth century, and so we must select.

Glee singing was very popular at the end of the eighteenth, and the beginning of the nineteenth centuries. Glees were sung at the Sloane Street musical party mentioned in Jane's letter to Cassandra of the 25th April, 1811, and the glee "Robin Hood" appears on one of the unbound music sheets. Another vocal fashion well represented in her music books is that for Scottish songs. Book 7 gives us "Thirty Scotch songs for a voice and "harpsichord, the music taken from the most genuine sets ex-"tant"; and a "Second Set of the Same"; and there are others scattered here and there. Allan Ramsay's "Gentle Shepherd" 1725, a ballad opera making use of Scots traditional songs, was largely responsible for launching this fashion, and by the middle of the century "Scots Songs" were being manufactured wholesale south of the Border and sung with "universal Applause". But the genuine article also survived into Jane Austen's period and beyond, as witness the use which both Beethoven and Haydn made of these Scotch tunes.

In the same book as the two collections of Scots songs we have "Twelve canzonets for two Voices" by William Jackson of Exeter (1730-1803), who, although chiefly famous as organist and composer in his native city, wrote an opera, "The Lord of the Manor", with words by General Burgoyne, which was very successfully performed in London in 1777.

Book 5—a varied collection of songs—contains a song from Jackson's "Lord of the Manor" originally sung by Jack Bannister—a very popular and talented singing actor.

Jane Austen herself was no Londoner and therefore did not take her characters to places of London entertainment as did Fanny Burney. But in this book we have songs sung at the Pantheon opened in 1772 and the Hanover Square rooms opened in 1775, as well as at the pleasure gardens and of course the theatres.

There is a song from "Jack of Newbury" by James Hook, one of the most prolific of eighteenth century song writers, first performed in 1795, and there are songs sung at Ranelagh and Vauxhall, at Covent Garden and Drury Lane.

A duet in the "Siege of Belgrade" by Stephen Storace, sung by his famous sister Nancy Storace and Jack Bannister in 1791, has been copied out in manuscript, and on a separate printed music sheet belonging to Jane's mother are airs sung by Nancy Storace in "La Camariera Astuta" in 1788. There are several songs by Charles Dibdin which were introduced in his "one man entertainments"—including a lively piece about "Jolly Dick "the Lamplighter", a London Street character. Jane Austen may never have heard such popular singers as Nancy Storace, Mrs. Crouch, Mrs. Bland, Mrs. Vincent, Miss Brent, Signor Tenducci, and Mrs. Blanchard, but she certainly knew their names and the songs they sang. It is of course possible that she may have heard some of them at Bath. Although we visit a Bath concert in "Persuasion", we are, alas, given no account of performers or programme. But her own recollections of Bath belong to the time when the Italian singer, Rauzzini, was directing the concerts at the Assembly Rooms, and it is reasonably certain she could have heard during that period many famous singers, and possibly Nancy Storace, one of his pupils.

But leaving such conjectures, we can at least claim that she followed the musical taste of the day with intelligence and that her library of music was a very fair one for an amateur.

MOLLIE SANDS

ADDRESS GIVEN BY THE HON. SIR HAROLD NICOLSON, K.C.V.O., C.M.G., AT THE ANNUAL GENERAL MEETING, 1956

It is, I understand, customary for those whom you invite to address you on these occasions to confine their remarks to praising the famous novelist who spent so many years of her life at Chawton. Although I am no uncritical admirer of Miss Austen's works, I should hesitate in such a company and on such an occasion to say anything that might wound the susceptibilities of a single devotee. I shall therefore make but passing reference to Jane Austen's novels and shall concentrate my remarks upon her Letters, which, to my mind, have been too lightly esteemed. I should wish you to feel that my intention is similar to that of Mr. Oscar Adams, her American biographer, who announced that the purpose of his book was "to place her before the world as the winsome, delightful woman that she really was and to dispel the unattractive, not to say forbidding, mental picture that so many have formed of her".

In dwelling on her Letters, as edited with such laudable impartiality by Mr. Chapman, I am aware that I may be causing offence to those who regard them as unworthy of so exquisite a novelist. I have myself encountered some enthusiasts who assert that it is a pity that the letters were ever published and that all loyal devotees should refrain from reading them. This surely is an extreme attitude to adopt. I have noted also that even the most reasonable members of the cult adopt towards the Letters a faintly apologetic tone, contending that it is not fair to judge her talent by the intimate reports she would send to her sister, her brothers, or her nieces, on domestic affairs. Even her niece Caroline Austen remarked that her correspondence was "rather over cautious for excellence". And her nephew and biographer, the Rev. J. E. Austen-Leigh, urges the reader to realize that her letters resemble "the nest which some little bird builds of the material nearest to hand".

Subsequent apologists fall into four different schools. There are those who assert boldly that it is wrong to say that the letters are dull or trivial, since in fact they are sprightly and alive. It is thus unfair to write, as one critic has written, that they provide us with no more than "a desert of trivialities punctuated by occasional cases of clever malice". So far from being trivial, they furnish important documentary evidence of the habits, thoughts and feelings of a distinct class in English society at the outset of the nineteenth century. So far from being heartless or ill-tempered, they give evidence of unflagging, busy, rather bossy, family solicitude. True it is that the Letters abound in what Mr. Chapman has well called "gentle or playful malice". "The author of **Pride and Prejudice**," Mr. Chapman reminds us, "was not insensible to the beauty of candour". "Whatever", he concludes, "may be thought of these asperities, they are not spiteful." It is to this school of apologists that I belong myself. I do not mind the letters being trivial and I certainly do not find them dull. I find them revealing.

The second school of apologists is composed of those who contend that all the more interesting passages, all those passages which divulged Jane Austen's more serious thoughts, emotions or reflections, were expunged by her sister before they were seen by any other eye. Miss Caroline Austen assures us that her Aunt Cassandra, after the death of Jane Austen, "burnt the greater part of the letters". When we calculate for what long periods the two sisters were living in the same house, how continuous and seemingly unbroken was the correspondence between them on the rare occasions that they were separated, how numerous are the letters that survive, it is difficult to believe that Cassandra did in fact destroy "the greater part of them". The gaps, so far as I can see, must be few. Nor are the little bits which Cassandra cut out of the letters with her scissors very numerous; they amount to little more than two or three lines here and there and it is evident from the context that these excisions contained remarks such as references to their sisters-in-law which might have proved wounding to surviving relations. Thus I do not believe that the letters which were destroyed or mutilated can have been so very numerous, that in tone and substance they were so very different from those which have been published, or that we are being unfair to Jane Austen's memory in judging the general level of her correspondence by the very numerous examples that have survived.

A third school of apologists consists of those who remind us that the purpose of the letters was to keep her sister imformed of daily domestic happenings and of the episodes of family or village life. The members of this school point out that postal charges in those days were high and were paid, not by the writer of the letter, but by its recipient. Jane Austen would not have wished to expose her sister to the cost of paying surcharges by increasing the bulk of her letters with reflections on incidental public events, such as the Battles of Trafalgar or Waterloo, or by the indulgence in religious or metaphysical reflections. She restricted herself to telling Cassandra what Cassandra desired most of all to know.

That brings me to the fourth school of apologists, a school who in their mistaken loyalty to Jane Austen have cast a shadow on the memory of her devoted sister. These people suggest that Cassandra was such a stupid woman that Jane Austen felt it necessary to write down to her low intellectual level. The Rev. J. E. Austen-Leigh was perhaps first responsible for suggesting this excuse. I regret that Mr. Chapman has followed his lead. "I must add", the latter writes, "though with reluctance, my impression that Cassandra Austen was not the correspondent who best evoked her sister's powers".

It is, I know a horrible presumption for an amateur such as I am, to question any statement that Mr. Chapman may make. But I do not quite see on what evidence he mastered his reluctance to defame Cassandra. True it is that Jane Austen teased her on one occasion about her "starched notions"; true it is that a surviving letter from Cassandra in which she tells Miss Fanny Knight of Jane Austen's funeral in Winchester Cathedral is couched in stilted terms. Yet, on the other hand, we find Jane Austen asserting again and again that Cassandra was one of the most gifted correspondents that this world had ever seen and Caroline Austen in her memoir records that Aunt Jane really did regard Aunt Cassandra "as the superior to herself". It seems that Cassandra's own letters, to which we only have the replies, were anything but starched in tone. "You are," wrote Jane Austen to her sister, "indeed the finest comic writer of the present age". I really do not see why Mr. Chapman, in the face of such evidence, can dismiss Cassandra as a fool.

The few surviving letters, moreover, which Jane Austen wrote to her sailor brothers or to her nephews, who were presumably unstarched men, are indistinguishable from the Cassandra letters both in tone and form. It may be that the two future admirals, Francis and George, over there with their frigates at Antigua were not deeply interested in the illnesses and misdemeanours of the Chawton villagers. But they **were** interested in how far their exploits and endurances were appreciated at home. It is not apparent from the very few letters which survive whether in writing to her sailor brothers Jane Austen indulged in reflections on world events or the eternal verities. But from such specimens as have come down to us we may assume that her correspondence with her brothers was in the same tone of maidenly sprightliness as that adopted in her letters to poor defamed Cassandra.

I am not, therefore, convinced by the arguments of those who contend that the silliness of Jane Austen's letters is due to adventitious causes, such as that all the more interesting letters were destroyed, or that Jane Austen was afraid of excess postal charges, or that Cassandra was such a dull girl as to be incapable of understanding anything above the level of family or village gossip. I regard the letters as perfectly natural and spontaneous, as valuable social documents, and as providing us with important evidence of the scope and nature of Jane Austen's temperament and mind.

All letters written to a close relation and describing the events of the last two or three days are apt to be quotidian. It is inevitable that much space should be given to the description of recent purchases, to accounts of passing indispositions or to reports on the state of the weather. "I intended", writes Jane Austen to her sister, "to call on the Miss Biggs yesterday had the weather been tolerable." "What dreadful hot weather," she writes again, "we are having! It keeps me in a constant state of inelegance." There are those, I know, who consider that such remarks are scarcely worth printing. To me they seem to add reality, as well as period flavour, to the correspondence.

It may be that the letters do not contain many references to international politics, to strategic problems, the industrial revolution, or the impending religious revival. But it is not true to say that Jane Austen in her novels and her letters makes no mention at all of contemporary events. Thus in **Persuasion** she goes out of her way to state that Admiral Croft had taken part "in the Trafalgar action" and in the letters there are at least two references to the Peninsula War; Napoleon is mentioned at least once in the contemporary guise of "Buonaparte"; and the retreat and death of Sir John Moore is twice referred to. It is legitimate to assume that a passage in a letter of May, 1811 refers to the battle of Fuentes de Onore, news of which had just reached England. "How horrible," she writes, "to have so many people killed! And what a blessing that one cares for none of them". I do not therefore agree that Jane Austen is deserving of blame for not having mentioned in greater detail, or with more apparent sympathy, the ordeals through which her countrymen and her brothers were then passing.

It was her nephew, again, the Rev. J. E. Austen-Leigh, who started the legend that the Miss Austens were dowdy and indifferent to their personal appearance. "Although", he records, "remarkably neat in their dress and all their ways they were scarcely sufficiently regardful of the fashionable or the becoming". I question in any case whether Mr. Austen-Leigh was himself an authority on aesthetics, since we find him referring to Waterhouse's odious reconstruction of the front of Balliol as "the beautiful building in Broad Street". But the letters entirely dispose of any suggestions that Jane Austen and her sister were indifferent to personal adornment or to the changing fashions of the town. On two separate occasions does she denounce flannel, which at that date was the pride and solace of the dowdy, as an ugly cloth. What she really loved was muslin, dimity, ribbons and bombazine. The austere critic might complain even that too much space is given in the correspondence to descriptions or speculations about caps, mantuas and flounces. I do not agree with this criticism and I share with Mr. Oscar Adams a regret that her nephew, and I fear her niece also, should have conveyed to posterity the impression that both the sisters hated clothes and prematurely adopted the drab habiliments of spinsterhood. I enjoy reading about Jane Austen's needle-work, hemming and purchases. "I have been able," she writes to her sister, "to give a considerable improvement of dignity to my cap. I shall venture to retain the narrow silver around it, put twice round without any bow, and instead of the black military feather shall put in the Coquelicot one as being smarter". Evidently this scheme was not successful since a week later she informs her sister that the Coquelicot has been discarded and that the new cap will now take on a Mameluk appearance. The Rev. Austen-Leigh's disregard of this persistent love of finery confirms me in the impression that he was not over-scrupulous in presenting to posterity an accurate portrait of his apple-cheeked and moon-faced aunt.

The correspondence will, it may be added, be of great value to all students of Jane Austen's very personal style, a style in which the firm fine expletives of the eighteenth century fuse gently into the delicacy of the age of refinement. We find in her letters instances of the inconsequent association of disparate concepts which, as in the writing of Virginia Woolf, I find so entrancing. There is a letter to her brother about a Miss Lewis from the West Indies who had married the Rev. Samuel Blackall, who appears to have been the only man to have occasioned even a momentary flutter in Miss Austen's sturdy heart. "I would wish Miss Lewis," she writes, "to be of a silent turn and rather ignorant but naturally intelligent and willing to learn : fond of cold veal pies, green tea in the afternoon, and a green window blind at night". In this we catch the echo of many similar inconsequences in the novels. "Her father," we read in **Northanger Abbey,** "was a clergyman without being neglected or poor and a very respectable man, though his name was Richard and he had never been handsome." "Mr. Jackson," we read in the letters, "is fond of eating and does not much like Mr. or Mrs. P." "However," we read again, "Miss Chapman's name is Laura and she has a double flounce to her gown." I rejoice in this special trick of logic and language. It makes me understand why so many of my most gifted acquaintances enjoy Jane Austen so much.

These are perhaps but secondary subjects and I merely wish to point out that in these small matters the letters reveal qualities in the great novelist which are not mentioned, or are disguised, in the official biographies. I contend also that her correspondence with Cassandra throws a gentle side-light on those aspects of Jane Austen's character which, in the novels and the memorials, are often presented to us in a light that is too harsh and crude. Was Jane Austen really as callous as the novels suggest? Was she in fact as snobbish as we might assume, so intensely preoccupied with shades of class distinction, so deeply aware of, and interested in, the incomes of her family and friends? Was her malice the evidence of a resentful or merely of a playful disposition? Did she really hate children? Was she in fact, as Miss Mitford remembered her, "the prettiest, silliest, most affected husband-hunting butterfly there ever was"? Did she, in later years, stiffen into "the most perpendicular, precise taciturn, piece of single-blessedness" that ever existed? Did she really possess a weakness for militia officers and enjoy glances of flirtation exchanged in the streets of Basingstoke or Alton? Was she, as some have contended, too early influenced by the cult of respectability which was already casting its dark shadow over our pleasant fields? Did she end by becoming an acid and perhaps embittered old maid? And was her peculiar style and range of perception deliberately assumed for purposes of fiction or were they spontaneous and wholly natural? Those are some of the questions which even the most devout admirer of Jane Austen's novels is bound to ask himself. It is my contention that many answers to these questions—many satisfactory answers—are provided by her letters.

It has been said that Jane Austen was a natural blue-stocking who lacked the required education. It has also been said that she would have become a proselytising evangelical had she lived on Clapham Common rather than in rural and therefore eighteenth century Hampshire. A study of her letters disposes of any such illusions. She did, it is true, prefer men to possess a certain level of instruction. Thus when Emma is enquiring about Frank Churchill, her first question is whether he is handsome, her second whether he is agreeable, but her third whether he is well educated. "Does, he", asks Emma, "appear a sensible young man, of information?" Women on the other hand should take pains to conceal such knowledge or intelligence as they may possess. "Imbecility in females," she comments acidly in **Northanger Abbey,** "is a great enhancement to their personal charms." And I admit that there are many admirers of her novels who can discover a certain attraction even in the idiot Harriet or the ninny Fanny Price, or the insufferable Marianne.

The cult of respectability did not, as some have contended, lay its cold hand upon Jane Austen. It may be true that in the second edition of **Sense and Sensibility** she deleted a shocking reference to a bastard son. But she was not in the least as prim as some of her enemies contend. It may be true again that at the end of her life, when her wits were failing, she wrote to her niece wondering whether after all the Evangelicals might not be "happiest and safest". But while her mind retained its vigour she refrained from postures of piety. Like all men and women of good-sense she abominated the works of Madame de Genlis and distrusted those of Hannah More. "Pictures of perfection" she writes to Cassandra, "as you know make me sick and wicked." "I do not like Evangelicals" she writes again. She could often be gloriously indelicate, even by our own tolerant standards. **Lady Susan** is a highly indelicate book and I am sure that her contemporaries were shocked by the conversation about Willoughby which takes place in **Sense and Sensibility** between Elinor and Colonel Brandon. No person who reads the Letters with any attention could ever again regard Jane Austen as squeamish, pretentious or prim.

On the other hand we must, i regret to say, admit that the correspondence confirms the impression conveyed by the novels that Jane Austen was an essentially callous women. At the age of twenty-three, when too old for thoughtlessness and too young for disappointed hopes, she could write to her sister the following phrase of unfeeling sprightliness:—"Mrs. Hall of Sherbourne was brought to bed yesterday of a dead child owing to a fright. I suppose she happened unawares to look at her husband". "Only think," she wrote on another occasion, "of Mrs. Holder's being dead. Poor woman she has done the only thing in the world she could possibly do to make one cease to abuse her." Such sentiments written down in cold blood and in an age of sensibility suggest a heart of pomice-stone. Nor do we derive from the letters the impression that Jane Austen was fond of her parents. Her references to her father are dutiful but devoid of warmth. Her references to her mother suggest that there existed but slight affection between them. "I suppose", she writes from Godmersham, "my mother will like to have me write to her. I shall **try** at least". Referring to a tea-party given by her mother to some of her old cronies when Jane herself was absent she writes—"all of whom my mother was glad to see and I very glad to escape". On the other hand there can be no doubt that she was devoted to her sister, her brothers, her nephews and her nieces. She could not, it is true, abide children who were indisciplined or noisy. But she had a powerful sense of family obligations and was really fond of her schoolboy nephew Edward and of her niece Fanny Knight who became Lady Knatchbull. She had a profound faith in the functions and duties of a maiden aunt and expressed the view that members of a family, even of an enormous family such as her own, should remain affectionate and united. "I like first cousins", she wrote, "to be first cousins and interested in each other". Her sense of obligation was a board beneath the thin plush cushion of her affections.

It is evident also that her malice, or what in **Persuasion** she so excellently calls "pleased contempt", was not assumed for literary purposes but came to her quite naturally. How many passages in her novels are, in quality and intention, reflected in this single phrase of a letter describing some local dance. "I looked at Sir Thomas Champneys and thought of poor Rosalie:

I looked at his daughter and thought her a queer animal with a white neck." Remarks such as this, and they are frequent both in the novels and the letters, make one realise why she was described by an acquaintance as "a poker of whom everybody was afraid". The modern psychologist would, I presume, attribute these outbursts of "pleased contempt" to the need felt by a proud and sensitive woman to compensate herself for being obliged to live in an environment far inferior to her own taste and intelligence. The letters help us to realise that it was a similar desire for compensation which underlay what many critics have regarded as her exaggerated preoccupations with social and financial status, or with what she would herself have called "rank and connection" and "degrees of consequence".

Her novels, it will generally be agreed, are almost inconceivably snobbish. I find it painful to read the warnings given to Harriet by the abominable Emma on the social status of Bob Martin, even as I blush to be told of the fluttering of Emma Watson's heart at being noticed by Lord Osborne. I am disturbed by her contempt of those who are connected with trade or commerce and I rejoice when Frank Churchill, who is the only one of her young males who is in any way tolerable, is blamed because "his indifference to a confusion of rank bordered too much on inelegance of mind". The Rev. J. E. Austen-Leigh contends that his aunt failed to finish **The Watsons** because she feared that the heroine had been caste in too low a rank. His comment is worth quoting:—"My own idea is, but it is only a guess, that the author became aware of the evil of having placed her heroine too low, in such a position of poverty and obscurity, as though not necessarily connected with vulgarity, has a sad tendency to degenerate into it . . . It was an error of which she was likely to become more sensible as she grew older and saw more of society. Certainly she never repeated it by placing the heroine of any subsequent work under circumstances likely to be unfavourable to the refinement of a lady". This comment becomes even more perplexing when he recalls that Emma Watson's father was a perfectly respectable clergyman.

The impression conveyed by the novels that Jane Austen must have been a most snobbish and mercenary woman is mitigated by the few comments upon money or social status that the letters contain. It was rather that she was fully conscious of the status of her own family and the condition of her own limited fortunes and would have regarded it as ridiculous and undignified to indulge in extravagance beyond the family means or to adopt stylish airs. Throughout her correspondence her attitude in such matters is controlled by her infallible sense of human values. Thus when she called on Mrs. Lance at Southampton she evidently felt both proud and shy. "They live," she writes to Cassandra, "in a handsome style, are rich, and she seemed to like being rich and we gave her to understand that we were far from being so. She will soon feel therefore that we are not worth her acquaintance." I call that an excellent example of "pleased contempt". In her novels, as I have said, the characters disconcert us by being disturbingly aware of the exact figure of each other's incomes. The letters show a far healthier attitude towards money. "People", she writes to Cassandra about the sale of her novels, "are more ready to borrow and praise than to buy. But though I like praise as well as anybody I like what Edward calls **pewter** too!" She took a sensible pride in not wishing to consort with her social superiors and refused an invitation to meet Madame de Stael, not because she had heard that the baroness had sneered at her novels as being trivial, but because she rightly foresaw that she could never compete in conversation with that formidable ventriloquist.

There were moments, of course, when she realised that her own circle was culturally restricted. "There was a whist table for the gentlemen", she informs Cassandra after a dinner with county neighbours, "a grown-up musical lady to play backgammon with Fanny and engravings of the Colleges at Cambridge for me." In general however she enjoyed her own narrow circle and was perfectly aware that it provided her with the very material most suited to her talent. "Three or four families," she wrote to her niece, "in a country village is the very thing to work on". She enjoyed the small fortnightly dances held in what is now known as the hay-loft of the Angel Inn at Basingstoke just as much as she enjoyed the assemblies at Bath, Southampton or Lyme Regis. She had no ambition at all to move in more brilliant society. "I do not," she wrote, "want people to be very agreeable as it saves me the trouble of liking them a great deal".

I suspect that, as most writers of creative gifts, Jane Austen was fundamentally unsocial. She enjoyed sipping tea in the octagon room and watching Bath society revolve around her. "I cannot," she wrote after an evening in the Assembly Rooms, "continue to find people agreeable. I respect Mrs. Chamberlayne for doing her hair well but cannot feel a more tender sentiment —Miss Langley is like any other short girl with a broad nose and a wide mouth, fashionable dress and exposed bosom. Admiral Stanhope is a gentlemanlike man, but then his legs are too short and his tail too long—Mrs. Stanhope could not come . . ." What Jane Austen really enjoyed was cosy company, when she could sit watching silently and without effort. "To sit in idleness", she writes, "over a good fire in a well-proportioned room is a luxurious sensation." "Bye the Bye", she writes to Cassandra, "as I must leave off being young, I find many douceurs in being a kind of Chaperone, for I am put on the sofa near the fire and can drink as much wine as I like."

Surely this reveals a Jane Austen much more likeable than the cynical or foolish figures whom she depicts in her novels?

My contention is, therefore, that the correspondence, far from being trivial or dull, introduces us to a more placid, less worldly, and more sensible woman than the student of her novels might suppose. What we admire above all is her inflexible resolve not to be diverted by the suggestions of her admirers, such as the Prince Regent's Librarian, into attempting themes which she knew to be outside her scope. There is a letter to Cassandra written after listening to her mother reading **Pride and Prejudice** aloud in the parlour at Chawton. "The work," she writes, "is rather too light and bright and sparkling; it wants shade: it wants to be stretched out here and there with a long chapter of sense, if it could be had: if not, of solemn specious nonsense about something unconnected with the story:—an essay on writing, a critique of Walter Scott, or the history of Buonaparte, or anything that would form a contrast and bring the reader with increasing delight to the playfulness and epigrammatism of the general style". She was aware that the romantic or the grandiose were beyond her even as she was aware of the danger, in her own special manner, of becoming what she called "foolishly minute". And finally we have the famous letter, written to her nephew Edward on December 16th, 1816, seven months exactly before her death, about "the little bit (two inches wide) of ivory on which I work with so fine a brush as produces little effect after much labour".

I deeply respect such literary integrity and it is for this reason, apart from others, that I urge the admirers of Jane Austen to devote time and trouble to the Letters which Mr. Chapman has edited with such scholarship and which reveal so much of what was most honest and most admirable in her character and mind.

THE JANE AUSTEN SOCIETY

Report for the year 1957

ELIZA HANCOCK, Comtesse de Feuillide

THE JANE AUSTEN SOCIETY

(Founded in 1940 by Dorothy G. Darnell)

THE JANE AUSTEN SOCIETY
Report for the year 1957

Membership

Forty-eight new members joined the Society during the year, of whom nine became Life Members. In addition, eight existing members became Life Members.

A considerable number have failed to renew their subscriptions, and membership now stands at 776.

Members are reminded that subscriptions became due on 1st January, and that this report is the only reminder that they will receive. The Hon. Secretary would much appreciate prompt payment of the 5/- Annual Subscription, and will gladly provide a Banker's Order form for anyone who would prefer to pay by that method.

Annual General Meeting, 1957

The Annual General Meeting was held again at Chawton House, kindly lent by Major and Mrs. Edward Knight, and some 300 members and their friends attended.

The President of the Society, His Grace the Duke of Wellington, K.G., presided, and opened the meeting by lamenting the absence, through illness, of Miss Beatrix Darnell. He asked members to take the minutes of the previous Annual Meeting as read. There were no matters arising.

The Hon. Secretary proposed the adoption of the Annual Report. This was seconded by Miss Helen Lefroy, and carried.

The Hon. Treasurer presented the Accounts. Their adoption was proposed by Lt.-Col. Sir William Makins, Bt., seconded by Mr. Hubert Howard, and carried.

The election of officers followed. The Hon. Secretary proposed the re-election of the Duke of Wellington as president. Dr. R. W. Chapman and Mr. T. Edward Carpenter as Vice-Presidents, and Mr. John Gore as Chairman of the Society. This was seconded by Mrs. Jervoise Scott, and carried.

Before proposing the re-election of the Committee, the President announced that Mr. W. Hugh Curtis, the first Chairman of the Society, had resigned from the Committee owing to ill health, and paid tribute to his work for the Society since its foundation. The President then proposed the re-election of the remainder of the Committee en bloc, and this was carried.

The meeting was then addressed by Mr. Roger Fulford, who, in a witty and scholarly talk, took as his theme the justification of the dedication of *Emma* to the Prince Regent. Mr. Fulford's address is printed in full in this Report.

A vote of thanks to Mr. Fulford was proposed by Lady Cynthia Asquith, seconded by Mr. John Gore, and carried.

Mr. T. Edward Carpenter gave members details of new arrangements and acquisitions at Jane Austen's House.

Lady Cynthia Asquith, who had recently won a prize, on questions about Jane Austen on Television, then answered some further questions put by members present.

A vote of thanks to the President for taking the Chair, to Mr. Carpenter and to Major and Mrs. Knight for lending Chawton House for the meeting was proposed by Miss Elizabeth Jenkins, seconded by Mr. R. L. McAndrew, and carried.

The meeting then closed, and members and their friends had tea, which had been provided by many people in Chawton, in aid of Chawton Church Funds.

JANE AUSTEN MEMORIAL TRUST

Extract from Chairman's Report

"Close supervision has been maintained.

Of the two caretakers, Miss Stevens has had good health. Mrs. Newman had during the course of the summer a fall on her stairs with consequent severe straining of the right shoulder. During her enforced absences her place was taken by her daughter, Mrs. Elsie Burgess. The latter lives in a cottage which I bought, restored and enlarged. The control and cleaning of the House, the reception of visitors and sales of literature have not suffered and I am glad to say that Mrs. Newman has resumed her duties.

Mr. Newman has most conscientiously, with myself, undertaken the garden work. Areas of the surrounding land, including about half an acre I bought myself, now present a tidy and attractive appearance, and I am engaged on planning a suitable permanent layout with trees and shrubs to enhance the beauty of the rear of the House.

At the end of my report for 1956 I predicted that we might have to face a drop in the number of our visitors.

1957 saw a prolongation of the difficult petrol situation, a cold and wet late summer and a provincial bus strike. So the prospect seemed bleak. But the reverse has proved to be the case. The total number of paying visitors was 3,485, an advance of 289 on 1956 year's total. This calculation does not include visits from members of the Jane Austen Society who enter free. The entrances recorded total sixty-nine.

Early in the summer I discovered activity by furniture beetle and woodworm, chiefly in the attics occupied by Miss Stevens, the large cellar beneath the parlour, in the newly opened rooms on the first floor and desultorily about the House.

I called in Messrs. Richardson and Starling Ltd. of Winchester, they made an exhaustive inspection and fully reported in confirmation of my views. The work on the House itself was thoroughly done and my wife and I have paid the account amounting to £122 12s 6d. and hold the firm's guarantee of the complete eradication of the pests. I was advised to have certain beams removed in the main cellar. Steel supports were substituted on brick pillars and other incidental work has been done including some exterior pointing and the removal and replacement of defective brickwork.

I have raised Mr. Ford's rent from £2 10s 0d. per annum to £17. The rents of Miss Stevens and Mrs. Newman have not been raised under the new act of 1957. They give unremitting faithful service without asking for any rise in the standing weekly cleaning charges.

I have opened an additional first storey window in the blank stretch of wall flanking the garden to admit of the greater flow of light and air. The design of this new window follows that of another over the drawing-room entrance. It distinctly improves the appearance of the House on the south side.

I have had erected on the flank (east) wall overlooking the yard gate a simple fascia board carrying the name ' Jane Austen's Home.' This faces up the road to Alton and can easily be seen by passing foot-passengers and motorists. This board is painted white with scarlet lettering. I have also had painted the board attached to the oak trees on the Winchester Road recording their having been planted by Jane Austen.

A number of interesting fresh exhibits have been acquired by loan or gift during 1957, a list of these appears in the appendix to this report

It has been thought not advisable to raise the entrance fee of one shilling, but the Jane Austen Society has been asked to allow us an increase of sixpence above the commission of one shilling payable to the Trust on the sale of each copy of ' My Aunt Jane Austen.'

In conclusion I may express a hope that the many relatives of the great Novelist may come to realise that the House is a permanent re-pository for relics for the Nation and that the Trust may in the future be the most desirable purchaser or recipient of such treasures. It is a matter of regret to all the Trustees that many of Jane's precious letters are held in the United States of America. They ought to be with us."

I have the honour to be,

very truly yours,

Thomas Edward Carpenter,

Chairman

APPENDIX

The following books :—
Presented by Mrs. Estelle Upjohn.
Jane Austen's Novels, in five volumes, published by Macmillan and Co. Ltd.
Jane Austen : Facts and Problems : The Clark Lectures by Dr. R. W. Chapman.
Jane Austen : by Goldwin Smith.
The Story of Jane Austen's Life : by Oscar Fay Adams.
Speaking of Jane Austen : by Sheila Kaye-Smith and G. B. Stern.
More of Jane Austen : by Sheila Kaye-Smith and G. B. Stern.
Jane Austen : a Biography : by Elizabeth Jenkins.
Essays by Divers Hands : Introduction by Sir Francis Younghusband.
Jane Austen, Her Contemporaries and Herself : by Walter Herries Pollock.
Hampshire Pilgrimages : by Kathleen E. Innes.
My Aunt Jane Austen : a Memoir by Caroline Austen.
Jane Austen in Bath : by Louisa H. Ragg.
Jane Austen and Her Art : by Mary Lascelles.
Jane Austen : by Margaret Kennedy.
Jane Austen and Steventon : by Emma Austen-Leigh.
Northanger Abbey in the Scholar's Library presented by Guy Boas, Esq., M.A.
Jane Austen's Novels in two volumes : presented by Mrs. Dobson. T. Nelson and Sons Limited.

Exhibits

Four Volumes of Diaries by the Hon. Mrs. William John Gore dated 1788–1789, 1799 and 1800. Presented by John Gore, Esq. C.V.O.
Photograph of Jane Austen's Spool case and two bead purses used by her; also photograph of verses written by her relating to Maria Beckford. Both presented by Frank Cottrill, Esq., M.A., Curator of the Winchester City Museums.

Six Original pen and ink drawings by Ellen G. Hill sister of Constance Hill, authoress of " Jane Austen: Her Homes and Friends " forming as to five of them illustrations of this book as follows :
    Jane Austen's Tomb in Winchester Cathedral.
    No. 8 College Street, Winchester.
    A Section of Chawton Cottage Garden.
    Tail piece to a chapter of the said book.
    Portrait of the donor, viz, Mrs. Alcock, representing Elizabeth Bennet, and Ashe Rectory.

All these exhibits (6) presented by Mrs. Alcock.

Two Original Playbills announcing two performances of " Lovers Vows " on the 26th October and 27th December, 1799 at the Theatre Royal, Covent Garden, presented by George Chadwick, Esq.

Photographs (3) of accounts in an old ledger dated 1792 of John Ring of Basingstoke. These accounts are of Purchasers namely, the Rev. James Austen, William John Chute and the Prince of Wales (spelt in the ledger " Whales ").

Presented by the Chairman.

GIFTS TO THE SOCIETY

By his will, the late Lord Stanmore, P.C., G.C.V.O. bequeathed to the Jane Austen Society his first editions of *Persuasion, Northanger Abbey* and *Mansfield Park,* and his second edition of *Sense and Sensibility.*

Brigadier B. C. Bradford, D.S.O., M.B.E., M.C., has given to the Jane Austen Society a small tripod table, to which is attached this note in the handwriting of his great-uncle, the late Montague G. Knight of Chawton.

" This table was bought by Montague G. Knight of Chawton House, from a grandson of James Goodchild, who lived in Chawton village in Jane Austen's time. His brother-in-law, William Littleworth, was footman to Mrs. George Austen, Jane's mother, and when he was too old for work she furnished a cottage near the pond for him. Amongst the furniture was this table, at which Littleworth often saw Jane Austen writing. Only the top is original."

"MANY A GOOD LAUGH "

8 College Street, where Jane Austen died in 1817, was, in the 1890's the Winchester tuck shop; it was kept by an old Frenchman, called Octavius La Croix, and known as " Octo's." Sometime before 1899, Octo went to the Second Master's wife, Mrs. George Richardson, whose familiar name was Mrs. " Dick," and said to her : " Will you put up a notice board outside my shop to say that Jane Austen died there? " Mrs. " Dick " replied : " Why, Octo? " Octo said : " Because Americans come in and want to know if she died there; they never buy anything and they waste my time." Mrs. " Dick " accordingly put up the oak tablet, now replaced by the slate plaque presented by Mrs. Jack Reed, and illustrated in the Annual Report for 1956.

Six months later, Octo came again and said : " Will you take please that notice board down? " Mrs. Dick " said : " Why, Octo? " And Octo said : " Because English people come in to know who Jane Austen was."

This anecdote, recounted by Sir Frank Watney, Mrs. Richardson's son-in-law, (The Wykehamist, 1936) is in keeping with another, told, about the turn of the century, of the visitor to Winchester Cathedral, who asked the verger where to find the slab marking Jane Austen's grave. " I'm often asked to show that," said the verger. " Can you tell me if there was anything special about that lady? "

The nuisance of Jane Austen's fame shows no signs of abating.

Some years before she founded the Jane Austen Society, Dorothy Darnell, then a stranger to the neighbourhood, was driving through Chawton. She caught sight of a familiar looking building at the cross-roads, and asked the busy A.A. guide on duty, if that were Jane Austen's house? " Yes," said the man, adding passionately :—" She's the plague of my life! "

Each of these stories, one believes, would have been particularly delightful to Jane Austen herself. Octo, the verger and the A.A. guide would all have joined the company of Lady Saye and Sele, who stayed in a house party with Mrs. Austen and her daughters at Stoneleigh Abbey in 1806, and who, Mrs. Austen said " afforded Jane many a good laugh."

Elizabeth Jenkins

A JANE AUSTEN T.V. QUIZ

Lady Cynthia Asquith took part in 1957 in a television programme, in which she answered questions on Jane Austen, the subject she had chosen. Having won a substantial prize, she most generously gave a donation to the funds of the Society. Below are some of the questions put to her.

Examples from Jane Austen Quiz.

Where did Fanny Price's cousin Edmund Bertram find her crying?

Mrs. Norris told Lady Bertram that she ' always had a bed for a friend ' but in actual fact what did she use the spare room at The White House for?

What did the gardener give Mrs. Norris after she had promised him a charm to cure his grandson of an ague?

Emma's very good opinion of Frank Churchill was a little shaken when she heard of a trip to London of sixteen miles and back which he made for one sole purpose. Tell me the purpose of Frank Churchill's trip to London.

Fanny Price, as you know, was sent as a little girl to stay with her fine relations, Sir Thomas and Lady Bertram. But Fanny was very unhappy at first. Tell me briefly how Lady Bertram tries to cheer up little Fanny on the day she arrives.

Some years later, Fanny returns home to Portsmouth. Describe briefly what her father did as he noisily entered the house.

Tell me why Mrs. Norris was red with anger when she cried : " My dear Sir Thomas, Fanny can walk."

Mr. Bennet, in a stern mood, won't hear of Kitty going to Brighton at all. Her father promises to take her to see something ' if you are a good girl for the next ten years '. What would Kitty be taken to see?

What little event helped to reconcile Mr. Woodhouse to Emma's marriage?

How did Captain Harville pass his time?

He was ' a heavy young man with not more than common sense.' Who was he?

Who lodged in Westgate Buildings, and in what town are they?

" Yes, pretty well; but are they all horrid, are you sure they are all horrid? " Who said this, to whom, and about what?

" He was a stout young man of middling height, who, with a plain face and ungraceful form, seemed fearful of being too handsome unless he wore the dress of a groom, and too much like a gentleman unless he were easy where he ought to be civil, and impudent where he might be allowed to be easy." Who was he?

" The woody varieties of the cheerful village of——and, above all, Pinny, with its green chasms between romantic rocks, where the scattered forest trees and orchards of luxuriant growth declare that many a generation must have passed away since the first partial falling of the cliff prepared the ground for such a state." In which book does this description come?

" They come from Birmingham, which is not a place to promise much, you know." Who said this, of whom?

W. HUGH CURTIS

THE death of Mr. Curtis, our first Chairman, is a great sorrow to everyone who remembers him. The afternoon that Dorothy Darnell first spoke to me of her idea of founding a Jane Austen Society, with a view of making the house at Chawton available to the public, she said: "We must get hold of Mr. Curtis." I was a stranger and did not then associate anything with Mr. Curtis' name, but I saw that it was taken for granted, by some-one who lived in the neighbourhood, that nothing of the kind we wanted to do could be undertaken without his help. When I was introduced to him I saw why.

Mr. Curtis had so much to give to the project that without him in those early days of 1942, we should scarcely have been able to translate our ideas into action. He had a very wide experience of work on societies; he knew exactly what to do, what to avoid, whom to approach. We had, in those days, to write numerous letters asking for co-operation, or information or support, and we never felt confident in sending them unless Mr. Curtis had seen the draft. His knowledge, and tact, and humour, made him invaluable as a chairman who not only conducted meetings but was consulted on the smallest detail as a friend and a fellow-enthusiast.

Anyone who examines his life-work, the Curtis Museum at Alton, and sees there that wonderful demonstration of life as it was in a small country town before the Industrial Revolution—the beauty and the vigour and the ingenuity that country people put into the work of their hands even though they could not read or write—will realize how well he understood the spirit of English life when it was still inspired by imagination. His interest in Jane Austen was scarcely the engrossing one felt by some of us, but he accepted her, I believe, as a great, but natural product of the age he so thoroughly understood. When one sat in his beautiful house, where he and Mrs. Curtis used to entertain the Committee, surrounded by his fine furniture, with the portrait of his ancestor William Curtis, who was Jane Austen's apothecary, in the hall, one felt a sense of continuity: that some of the best elements of life 150 years ago had been carried on into the present age. The Jane Austen Society has met with many pieces of good fortune in the sixteen years of its existence, and that we were able to "get hold of Mr. Curtis" was one of the best of them.

ELIZABETH JENKINS

Eliza Hancock, 1761—1813, first cousin of Jane Austen

m. 1781, Comte de Feuillide.

m. 1797, Henry Austen.

Eliza Hancock was said by a tradition in the Austen family to have suggested some of the characteristics of *Mary Crawford* in *Mansfield Park*. See the article by J. H. Hubback in *The Cornhill Magazine* 1928. Dr. R. W. Chapman cautious against falling into the error of saying that *Mary Crawford* " was " Eliza Hancock (" Jane Austen, Facts and Problems," R. W. Chapman.); but the slight figure, dark eyes, fascinating liveliness and fondness for private theatricals attributed to Eliza, and her having refused her serious-minded cousin James Austen who was going to be a clergyman, evoke, for the impetuous reader of " Mansfield Park ," a suggestion that makes this portrait of very great interest.

———o———

On July 9th, 1816, Jane Austen wrote to her nephew Edward Austen. (afterwards Austen-Leigh) :

" You will not pay us a visit yet of course, we must not think of it. Your Mother must get well first, and you must go to Oxford and *not* be elected; after that, a little change of scene may be good for you, and your Physicians I hope will order you to the Sea, or to a house by the side of a very considerable pond."

The pond, now drained, that lay at the cross-roads outside the Austens' house.

Jane Austen's House 1957

Address given by Mr. Roger Fulford
at the Annual General Meeting 1957

This afternoon I do not propose to follow the advice of that strange soldier in Bernard Shaw's play " Arms and the Man " who, after outrageous behaviour, is made to say " I never apologise ". For I certainly owe the company an apology for standing up here—since I have nothing to offer them in that delightful field of Jane Austen studies of which they are the worthy custodians. I have no specialised knowledge, no new discoveries to offer, no critical observations and I have not even anything to ridicule. I can only couple with that apology the excuse that my inadequacy is tempered by devoted admiration for Jane Austen—yes, even for her gifts as a letter writer.

To many people it must seem slightly incongruous that Jane Austen should have dedicated *Emma* to the Prince Regent. To such people this conjunction of *Emma* and the Regent must seem like imagining " Misunderstood " to be dedicated to the Tichborne claimant or the Daisy Chain to Jack the Ripper. Although I greatly revere the memory of King George IV do not pretend that that incongruity does not exist. I would not attempt to resolve it for you by saying that he was perfection, or by endorsing the verdict of his sister that he was an angel; you may remember that after this *interesting comparison*, his sister went on to say that his countless good deeds were safely registered in the filing system of heaven. I do however allow myself to say this by way of preamble and caution. To-day through the cloudy glass of political passions we see the character and personality of the king darkly. Though I have to be careful in what I am saying because I speak under the shadow of one who cherishes the Whig tradition, who has edited the delightful chronicler of those times—Thomas Creevey—but I think that we should be wrong in taking our ideas of what the king was like from the pages of Creevey—just as wrong as if we were to take our idea of the character of, say, Ld. Mountbatten from the papers controlled by Lord B, or of George V from the brilliant cartoons of that king which appeared some twenty years ago in the *Daily Worker* I would venture to remind you of some words of Lord Holland—the fairest and most astute of the Whig leaders of those days ; he said, " We all incurred the *guilt* (if not the *odium*) of charging His Royal Highness with ingratitude. We all encouraged every species of satire against him." And I would also remind you of this *obiter dictum* of a learned contemporary historian, " The Age was too brilliant to possess a very strict regard for truth." And unluckily it is satire rather than truth which has formed the verdict of history on the man to whom *Emma* is dedicated.

Possibly some of the members of the Society will have noticed that in Victorian times when the feeling against the king was running at its height the dedication of *Emma* was discreetly dropped. I was given a charming set of the novels published in 1856 by Bentley from which all traces of the dedication have been expunged. No doubt while Thackeray's fairy tales about the Four Georges—written of

117

course for a republican audience in America—were enjoying a great vogue in this country, the association of Jane Austen with one of them was thought best forgotten.

Perhaps you would allow me at this point to say something in general about royal dedications. I do not think that we want to regard such things with exaggerated veneration—we don't want to drag down the genteel profession of authorship to the level of the butcher who might regard his finest hour as the provision of scrag end of mutton to the Royal Household at Buckingham Palace. I think I notice a trace of that sort of feeling in an interesting article lately published by the distinguished American critic, Lionel Trilling, in that noisy but wholly admirable publication *Encounter*. He argues that the dedication of *Emma* proves that this novel is—as he puts it—" touched by national feeling " and he goes on, " she thought of herself as having a relation to the national ethic.

> Crowned before all the world
> Flushed with triumph
> Puzzled in her glass box or padded cell."

I am not quite sure that I know what those words mean. But so far as the dedication affected the character of the book you will see at once that this was impossible. The book was in fact written and in the press before any question of the dedication arose. With that innocent and sanguine nature, which is a constant and becoming characteristic of authors in dealings with their publishers, you may recollect that Jane Austen wrote to her publisher John Murray and asked " Is it likely that the printers will be influenced to greater dispatch by knowing that the work is to be dedicated by permission to the Prince Regent? " I am afraid that they were not.

The possible explanation for this is that a royal dedication was not the rarity that it might be to-day. Through the eighteenth century such dedications had been awarded to many works of outstanding scholarship. Certainly both Queen Anne's husband and King George I were not above paying money to the author in return for having their illustrious names recorded in a dedication. Later in the century you had those flowery dedications—several of which were written by Johnson. One of them, done by Johnson for George III's brother the Duke of York, contained the remarkable statement " It is superfluous to tell your Royal Highness that geometry is the primary and fundamental art of life ". By the end of the eighteenth century these formal dedications were somewhat on the wane. By Queen Victoria's time they had really become a matter demanding ministerial advice. Though here I must apologise for trusting to my shaky memory I recall Lord Melbourne, after a cursory reading of a long novel, advising the young Queen not to accept its dedication. And the point I want to make here is that surely the number of novels dedicated to the Royal Family could be counted on one hand. I am very much obliged to Sir Owen Morshead for reminding me that Fanny Burney dedicated one of her novels *Camilla* to Queen Charlotte—to which incidentally Jane Austen was one of the subscribers. Imagination shudders at the tact which Sir Owen would have to exercise if a modern novelist—perhaps some realistic writer about life in a red-brick university—were to ask him to use his influence for a royal dedication. The point I am making here is that by the Prince Regent's time a royal dedication was a mark of personal favour, and, accorded to a novel, was a rare proof of both esteem and genius.

And now a word as to the circumstances in which it came about. I do not intend to weary you with an account of Jane Austen's correspondence with Clarke, the Regent's librarian. I feel sure that as it includes the resounding definition of her own talents and capabilities, it will be familiar to you all and will have engaged the notice of scholars far better equipped than myself. There are however four points which I should like to emphasise.

I think you would possibly agree with me that this small episode reveals how infinitely rewarding to royalty is occasional and spontaneous civility to members of the writing profession. Although no precise account of Jane Austen's reception in the Library at Carlton House has survived, she was plainly gratified and delighted by the attention. Only two years before she had been writing of George IV's terrible wife, " Poor woman I shall support her as long as I can, because she *is* a woman, and because I hate her husband." How easily such ardent feminite loyalties can be soothed by a little attention we may think as we turn to the title page of *Emma*:

To his Royal Highness I. Prince Regent this work is, By his Royal Highness's permission most respectfully dedicated by His Royal Highness's dutiful and obedient humble servant The Author.

First it is generally admitted that Jane Austen owed her visit to Carlton House to one of the Prince's doctors. Now, I have very little doubt that this was Sir William Knighton. You will remember that Henry Austen was ill in the autumn of 1815 and it is possible that Knighton visited him professionally—or he may have known the family through his connexions with the Royal Navy—his wife was a Miss Hawker who belonged to a well-known naval family. Although Knighton has been vilely traduced—he started life as an *accoucheur*— like Stockmar, a medical man, he was not only a devoted servant of the Royal Family but a man of culture and intelligence. He was very well versed in Pope and the eighteenth-century writers and I suspect that such accomplishments helped to endear him to the Prince. Knighton owed his start in life to the Duke of Wellington's brother. I hope I may tell you—for it emphasises the essential respectability of the house of which you, sir, are the head that when the two men were staying together at Petersfield, they discussed the great historian Gibbon and after their talk Knighton, with sorrow, notes, " I could discover Lord Wellesley thought him too loose to be admired."

The second point. People often say on being reminded that *Emma* is dedicated to George IV, " Oh yes and did he not ask her to write a

119

romance about the illustrious house of Coburg? " But of course that was not the prince but his librarian and Chaplain, J. S. Clarke. Unhappy the sovereign who is to be credited with all the *obiter dicta* of his attendants—even down to the rag tag and bobtail of royal chaplains. You will remember that Clarke–a strange, ebullient canon of Windsor–also urged Jane Austen to write a novel about a clergyman and advised her to carry her clergyman to sea. Here I interrupt my narrative to give you an anecdote about Clarke—partly because it illustrates his tremulous character and also because it reminds all students of history of their debt to the Regent. The prince bought for the royal collections the Stuart papers which he acquired through an English Dominican at Rome who had in turn bought them from the bastard daughter of the Young Pretender. Sir James Mackintosh—an historian of note—applied to the Prince for permission to study these papers. In forwarding this application Clarke says, " At the beginning of the French Revolution Sir James Mackintosh printed his celebrated pamphlet styled ' Vindicio Gallicae ' in answer to Mr. Burke, and this work, sir, was so tainted and poisoned with the venom of democracy that I can not sleep until I am well assured of the present principles of Sir James in his intended history. It is for your great and superior mind, sir, to decide respecting this." Though the answer of the great and superior mind to this effusion has not survived we can see the sequel from a letter of Mackintosh. To a friend he writes, " The reason for my being at the levee was to thank the Prince for having granted me access to a very valuable collection of papers which he has lately procured. The Prince spoke to me about them yesterday, so long and graciously as to make the whole circle stare."

The third point. You will recall that in a letter to Cassandra, Jane Austen writes, " It strikes me that I have no business to give the Prince Regent a binding ". She means of course she is uncertain whether to give him the three volumes in ordinary boards or whether she should have them specially bound. It is clear from the correspondence that they were specially bound since Clarke thanks her on behalf of the Prince for " the handsome copy ". Here I would offer my deep gratitude to Clarke's distinguished successor—the present librarian at Windsor—who spent a sultry afternoon in generously hunting up all the copies of Jane Austen's novels in the Royal Library. We found what is indubitably the book in question, beautifully bound in scarlet, with the Prince of Wales's feathers in the panel on the top of the spine and the Carlton House bookplate inside. In Queen Victoria's time—as a rather vulgar book-plate revealed—the copy had been relegated to the library of the royal servants. Here in passing we may be thankful that John Brown's tastes were more for the cupboard than the bookshelf—the whiskey bottle rather than the novel—for the book seems to have passed unscathed or rather unopened through its ordeal.

And now my last point on the correspondence. In conveying the Prince's thanks for the book Clarke, writing from Brighton, adds, " Lord St. Helens and many of the nobility who have been staying here paid you the just tribute of their praise ". Too readily we picture life at the Pavilion as a riot of gaiety or to use the exact words of a Victorian lady writer, " Riot and unrestrained festivity were the order of the day—and it may be added also of the night ". Clarke just offers a corrective to that absurd picture, for St. Helens—perhaps better known as Alleyne Fitzherbert—was a man of outstanding intelligence, gifts and quality, admired by Johnson, and the last survivor into the nineteenth century of those who had known the poet Gray. If all at the Pavilion (as some who should know better still imagine) was booze and ladies, Alleyne Fitzherbert would certainly not have bothered to go. And that brings me on to the general remarks I want to make about the king and his literary tastes.

I want to give you some proof that George IV—on his own account and not just because he was a prince or king—was not unworthy of that solitary and conspicuous position, the only person to receive what we might call the accolade of a dedication from Jane Austen. But first a note of caution—obvious enough but necessary. How easy to attribute too much to kings and princes! How easy to suppose that the possessor of a fine library is necessarily at home with what rests on his shelves. As always, Horace Walpole has something salutary to say on this subject in his rewarding book—*Royal and Noble Authors*. He tells us that two musical compositions of King Henry VIII were still performed in his day at Christ Church Oxford. And then he quotes one of those alarming men of learning who writes " Of the two productions ascribed to the finger of this monarch—the one from its mediocrity is supposed to be genuine while the other is supposed to exceed the capacity of a royal musician." But tempering our judgement with the recollection of that cautionary tale, we have some grounds—in addition to his having distinguished Jane Austen—for holding that George IV was not only generously gifted with a capacity for enjoying literature but particularly enjoyed the company of writers—always as we know a rather perilous adventure.

First his admiration for Scott and Byron. This is Byron writing to Scott, " Let me talk to you of the Prince Regent. He ordered me to be presented to him at a ball; and after some sayings peculiarly pleasing from royal lips, as to my own attempts, he talked to me of you and of your immortalities; he preferred you to every other bard past and present. He spoke alternately of Homer and yourself, and seemed well acquainted with both. All this was conveyed in language which would only suffer by my attempting to transcribe it and with a tone and taste which gave me a very high idea of his abilities and accomplishments, which I had hitherto considered as confined to manners."

Now we know from other sources that what Byron says is perfectly correct. From Scott's letters and journals and from Sir Wm. Knighton's memoirs we know that Scott for the rest of the King's life corresponded with him on literary matters and almost invariably sent advance copies of his works to lie on the library table at the Royal Lodge. We also know that the King certainly had some command of the classics. In the course of a political letter to your relative Lord Wellesley, he puts this p.s., " You will understand me I am sure when I stop at these few words of our old friend ", and then he quotes from one of Horace's Epistles adding " *verb. sap.* "

A study of his correspondence or of his reported conversation shows that he was a reading man.

Secondly I would remind you of his important services to classical learning over what are known as the Herculanean mss. In the middle of the eighteenth century during excavations at Herculaneum there were found a number of blackened rolls, at first thought to be nothing more exciting than lumps of charcoal. On examination they were found to be classical mss., but the difficulty was to open them without spoiling them. Half a century after their discovery—that is to say in 1800—George IV undertook at his own expense to have the papyri unrolled and copied. He put one of his chaplains in charge of this work—the Rev. John Hayter, Etonian, Kingsman and Suffolk rector. What learning in all its branches owes to those roomy Suffolk rectories has yet to be estimated. After adventures which included fighting, this gallant divine got back to England with pencilled copies of some of the mss. The Neapolitan Government presented George IV with eighteen unopened rolls. Four of these unopened rolls together with Hayter's transcripts were presented by George IV to the University of Oxford. (After a sojourn in the Royal Library the remainder drifted to the British Museum.) The King accompanied his gift to Oxford with the advice that the University should not be in any undue haste to open the rolls for fear of damage. I do not think they can be accused of disregarding that advice since the dons did not seriously attack them till the 1880's.

When I mentioned to you just now about the dangers inherent in the society of authors and men of learning I think I can illustrate my point here. A Fleet Street scribbler, Sir Richard Phillips, taking advantage of his friendship with this Suffolk rector, wrote to the King's secretary as follows: " I was well acquainted with the late ingenious Mary Robinson (that is of course Perdita, with whom the King had been in love); as a security for a loan she put into my possession various articles of curiosity, and among others that beautiful lock of hair which His present Majesty sent to her from his box at the theatre, in an envelope on which in his own hand is written the words " to be redeemed ". I have always highly prized it as the memento of a royal passion as well as from profound respect and homage for His Majesty but having had the misfortune to lose two considerable properties by the stoppage of bankers. . . ." He goes on also to offer the bridle of the horse on which William Rufus was riding in the New Forest when he was killed together with Shakespeare's walking stick. I doubt, sir, if even the archives of Stratfieldsaye could reveal a worse example of being exposed to authors, of a more blatant disregard for the private feelings of a prominent personage.

And in conclusion I would remind you of the King's more particular services to literature in helping to found the Royal Society of Literature.

The idea of such a society seems to have started in the fertile brain of that great Bishop of Salisbury—Burgess—whose publications cover fifteen pages in the catalogue of the British Museum. The Society was founded under the special patronage of the King—in fact he seems to have suggested it to the Bishop soon after he came to the throne. The Society came into being two or three years later and the King gave an annual subscription of £1,000 and a further £100 to pay for two gold medals. This enabled the society in its early years to pay annuities of £100 to ten needy writers—one of whom was Coleridge. How personal this was to the King is suggested by the fact that his successors on the throne reduced his benefaction to £100. I think it is possible—but here I am merely hazarding a guess—that when the King sold George III's great library to the nation he saved some hundreds of pounds in the salaries of librarians and assistants, and that he diverted this money instead to the Society. The dates would certainly fit such a proposition.

And finally I offer you this reflection. The tastes of kings and princes deserve well of those who share them. That is to say—to give some random examples—agriculturalists should be grateful to George III, horologists to Louis XVI and philatelists to George V. Similarly I think that those who enjoy the pursuits of literature should not forget King George IV. And I hope you will agree with me that in dedicating *Emma* to His Royal Highness the Prince Regent, Jane Austen made no unworthy choice.

THE JANE AUSTEN SOCIETY

Report for the year 1958

Steventon Parsonage

THE JANE AUSTEN SOCIETY

(Founded in 1940 by Dorothy G. Darnell)

THE JANE AUSTEN SOCIETY
Report for the year 1958

Membership

Forty-eight new members joined the Society during the year, of whom five became Life Members. In addition three existing members became Life Members.

Membership now stands at 830, of whom eighteen live in the Commonwealth, eighty live in the U.S.A., and eight in other countries abroad.

Members are reminded that subscriptions are due on 1st January, and that this report is the only reminder that they will receive. The Hon. Secretary would much appreciate prompt payment of the 5/- Annual Subscription, and will gladly provide a Bankers' Order form.

Annual General Meeting, 1958

The Annual General Meeting was held on Saturday 19th July at Chawton House, by kind permission of Major and Mrs. Edward Knight, when some 300 members and their friends were present.

The President of the Society, His Grace the Duke of Wellington, K.G., presided, and in opening the meeting asked that the minutes of the previous Annual Meeting be taken as read. There were no matters arising.

The Hon. Secretary presented the Annual Report, and, in the absence of the Hon. Treasurer, the Accounts. The motion was seconded by Mr. Hugh Austen, and carried.

The election of officers followed. The Hon. Secretary proposed the re-election of the Duke of Wellington as President, Dr. R. W. Chapman and Mr. T. Edward Carpenter as Vice-Presidents, and Mr. John Gore as Chairman of the Society. This was seconded by Commander Frank Austen, and carried.

The President proposed the re-election, en bloc, of the remainder of the Committee. The resignation of Mrs. W. Hugh Curtis had been received, with much regret, earlier in the year.

The meeting was addressed by Monsieur René Varin, C.B.E., Conseiller Culturel at the French Embassy, who with great wit and a masterly command of the English language, discussed the French attitude towards Jane Austen's works. Monsieur Varin's address is printed in full in this Report.

A vote of thanks to Monsieur Varin was proposed by the Hon. Mrs. Cubitt, seconded by Mrs. Henry Burke, and carried.

Mr. T. Edward Carpenter gave an account of work done at Jane Austen's home, and other matters.

A vote of thanks to the President, to Mr. Carpenter, to Major and Mrs. Edward Knight and to the Hon. Secretary was proposed by Mr. Gore, seconded by Mrs. Shervington, and carried.

The meeting then closed, and was followed by tea, provided by many people in Chawton, in aid of Church Funds.

Annual General Meeting, 1959

The Annual General Meeting will be held at Chawton House on Saturday, July 11th 1959. This is a week earlier than usual, and it is hoped that Members will be caused no inconvenience by this deviation from the normal. The speaker will be the Very Rev. Dr. E. G. Selwyn, sometime Dean of Winchester, who will speak on the clergymen of the novels.

A Letter from Mr. Fulford

Sir,

Members of the Society may perhaps have noticed some allusion in the newspapers to a supposed indiscretion of mine in the paper which I was privileged to read to the annual meeting in 1957. I am grateful to the committee for allowing me to explain how this arose. In commenting on the impression of George IV to be derived from Creevey I said that we should be wrong in taking our impression of the King from those delightful chronicles—" just as wrong as if we were to take our idea of the character of the Leader of the Opposition from the pages of the *Daily Telegraph* or of King George V from the brilliant cartoons in the *Daily Worker*." I seemingly added an impromptu aside—" or our impression of Lord Mountbatten from the papers owned by Lord Beaverbrook." I had of course no intention of being offensive to anyone. And I greatly regret that this last aside, removed from its context and from the friendly atmosphere of Chawton, should have been used as a weapon to attack Lord Beaverbrook.

Yours faithfully,

ROGER FULFORD

LONGBOURN IN NEW YORK—Last autumn the firm of Lord and Taylor of Fifth Avenue, New York City, staged a British Fortnight, when they displayed in their windows scenes from the works of British writers. Among them was the drawing-room at Longbourn, showing Mrs. Bennet and three of her daughters. We are indebted to Messrs. Lord and Taylor for their co-operation, and permission to reproduce this photograph.

Jane Austen and Wyards

Wyards is a house of Hampshire, red brick, of mediaeval foundations with Tudor additions; it received its present appearance in the 1680's except that in the XVIII century, sash windows were added though the leaded casements were retained. Beautifully restored by its present owners, Mr. and Mrs. Hubert Howard, Wyards has the particular interest that it was a house well known to Jane Austen during the last two years of her life. In 1815, it was a farm-house, and part of it was rented by young Mr. and Mrs. Ben Lefroy.

The latter had been Anna Austen, the daughter of Jane's eldest brother James by his first wife. Anna's connection with her Aunt was extremely close. When she was left motherless at two years old, she was sent to Steventon Rectory where she was the special care of her aunts Cassandra and Jane, then twenty-one and nineteen. Here the child had a remarkable experience; upstairs with her aunts in their dressing room she heard the younger read aloud to the elder the story that was afterwards re-written as *Pride and Prejudice*. She had to be cautioned when she began talking about the characters by name downstairs.

When her father married his second wife Mary Lloyd, the little girl went home; she grew up an attractive, volatile young miss whose vagaries caused her serious father and even her more light-hearted aunt, some anxiety. Anna figured frequently in Jane Austen's letters with her dancing, and her catching cold, her unguarded encouragement of Mr. Terry, and her misguided enthusiasm for the fashionable hair-styling of 1809—" that sad cropt head " as Jane described it. At eighteen she was still flighty. " She is quite an Anna with variations," said Jane, employing a musical term; she noted that " miscellaneous, unsettled happiness " was the kind that suited Anna best.

The early connection with Jane Austen and novel-writing Anna maintained by writing, or beginning to write, a novel of her own called *Which is the Heroine*. This she sent to Jane by instalments, thus eliciting those famous letters in which the sympathetic, enthusiastic response to a child's work is mixed with unassuming, straightforward advice on novel-writing from the author of *Pride and Prejudice* and *Emma*.

Jane Austen's two favourite nieces, Anna and her cousin Fanny Knight were born the same year, but their temperaments were so different that while Anna was written to as a beloved niece, Fanny received almost the confidence of a sister, and letters to her contain candid comments on Anna's weaknesses. Anna married Ben Lefroy in 1814 and the young pair first set up at Hendon, where Jane visited them and was pleased with Anna's demeanour as a young married lady, though she confided to Fanny that the purchase of a pianoforte was a silly one : Anna's playing would never amount to anything, and, said Jane, they would " wish the 24 guineas in the shape of sheets and towels 6 months hence." By September 1815, the young couple were established at Wyards, within walking distance of Chawton.

Wyards Farm 1958

Anna, who had married at 21, had her first baby on October 20, 1815, her second on September 27, 1816, and in March 1817, her aunt feared that she was pregnant again. The fear was confirmed in a letter from Jane Austen to Fanny Knight of March 23 : " Anna has not a chance of escape; her husband called here the other day and said she was pretty well but not equal to so long a walk; she must come in her donkey carriage. Poor animal, she will be worn out before she is thirty. I am very sorry for her."

Jane Austen's last illness had begun by the following month; Anna's eleven year old half-sister Caroline had been coming to stay at Chawton, but because of her aunt's illness she went to her sister at Wyards instead. The day after her arrival, Anna brought her over to Chawton Cottage, where they saw Jane in her bedroom, sitting in her dressing-gown, and Caroline heard the last words she remembered hearing Jane say : " There is a chair for the married lady and a little stool for you, Caroline."

Fanny Knight who had been on such intimate terms with Jane Austen, loving and beloved, suffered a sea-change later in life. As Lady Knatchbull, she seemed anxious to dwell as little as possible on her connection with the family at Chawton Cottage; her aunts, she was able to see on looking back, had been decidedly provincial. Anna's warm, unchanging affection in remembrance is the more charming by contrast. Speaking in her own middle-age she said of her aunt : "As I grew older, when the original 17 years between our ages seemed to shrink to 7 or to nothing, it comes back to me how strangely I missed her. It had become so much a habit with me to put by things in my mind with reference to her and say to myself, I shall keep this for Aunt Jane."

Mrs. Tillotson a few years ago published in *The Times Literary Supplement* a letter of 1832 written by Mrs. Mozley who had stayed with the Rev. Fulmar William Fowle, Rector of Allington in Wiltshire. Mr. Fowle was the son of Eliza Lloyd, the sister of the second Mrs. James Austen. Of the Austen family he said : " being his cousins he never considered much about them." Mrs. Mozley was an ardent admirer of the novels and in reply to her eager questioning about Jane Austen, he said : "she was pretty—certainly pretty—bright, and a good deal of colour in her face—like a doll—no, that would not give at all the idea, for she had so much expression—she was like a child, quite a child, very lively and full of humour—most amiable, most beloved." As to his step-cousin Anna, Mr. Fowle said that she used to be staying weeks and weeks at his mother's when single, and he wondered " how it was he did not fall in love with her—so charming was she in every respect."

Anna burned the manuscript of *Which is the Heroine*, telling her child who saw her do it that she could not bear to go on with it, it reminded her so much of her aunt's loss. Mrs. Mozley summed up Mr. Fowle's description of Anna by saying : " She seems to have inherited all her aunt's charms." The words enclose their images like the frame of a pair of miniatures, though one, her children about her, burned up a useless manuscript and the other was lying under the aisle of Winchester Cathedral with *Pride and Prejudice* to her name.

Elizabeth Jenkins

A ground-floor window in Wyards, the home of of Jane Austen's niece, Anna Lefroy.

Pride and Prejudice and Miss Eden

References to Jane Austen's novels in those written by other authors between 1817 and 1837 are not very many, and it is not therefore easy to accumulate proofs that her plots, settings and (inimitable) technique were cribbed by more or less contemporary writers of fiction. One such instance is perhaps worth recalling—Emily Eden's *Semi-Attached Couple*.

In 1834 she wrote to her friend, Mrs. Lister (afterwards Lady Theresa Lewis) : " I wish I could write like Mrs. Hannah More and have money enough to buy myself a Barley Wood." The *Semi-attached* resulted, being substantially written before 1837 but laid away for nearly a quarter of a century and published, after the success of her *Semi-detached House* in 1859, as what she admitted had become a dated period piece. It had a considerable success at the time and when in 1926 Elkin Mathews and Marrot were looking out for ' forgotten ' novels for their " Rescue Series," I recommended them to consider Miss Eden's two novels. This they did, and the *Semi-attached* soon ran into three or four impressions. The *Rescue Series* included more than half a dozen readable forgotten novels and one Victorian masterpiece, *From Generation to Generation* by Lady Augusta Noel. The series came to an unworthy end with the publication of a lamentable " completion " of Jane Austen's *The Watsons*. Recently, an American firm republished successfully *The Semi-detached House*, introduced in 1928 by Sir Anthony Eden. It is hard to pick up a copy today of some of that *Rescue Series*, and the second disappearance of *From Generation to Generation* is a tragedy, for, in the opinion of that good critic, Sir Edward Marsh, it stands among the greatest of Victorian novels.

It is quite reasonable to suggest that in its opening scene the *Semi-attached* was influenced by *Pride and Prejudice*, and perhaps it was Miss Austen and not Hannah More who stimulated Miss Eden to try her hand. No reader is likely fundamentally to confuse the Bennets, père et mère, or their daughters with the Douglas family, but many with frail memories for fictional names might well confuse Longbourn with Thornbank, so close are the parallels in the opening chapter between the two humbler manors, depending for a taste of high life on their neighbouring great houses, and between the characters of the two sarcastic squires, bored with the ill-natured gossip or vulgarity of their wives (" Mrs. Douglas had been an heiress which perhaps accounts for Mr. Douglas having married her . . . He let her have a reasonable share of her own way . . . but kept his own opinion.")

There is a special reference to *Pride and Prejudice* in *The Semi-attached*, among the " tempting novels " on the book table at " *Eskdale Castle* " which certainly owed something of its Whiggish ease to Miss Eden's beloved Bowood. One wonders if the pages had been cut. Certainly Lord Lansdowne, Foreign Secretary of the *Entente Cordiale*, once confessed in my hearing that he had never read an Austen novel. Many novel-reading Victorians did not much care for her. As Margaret

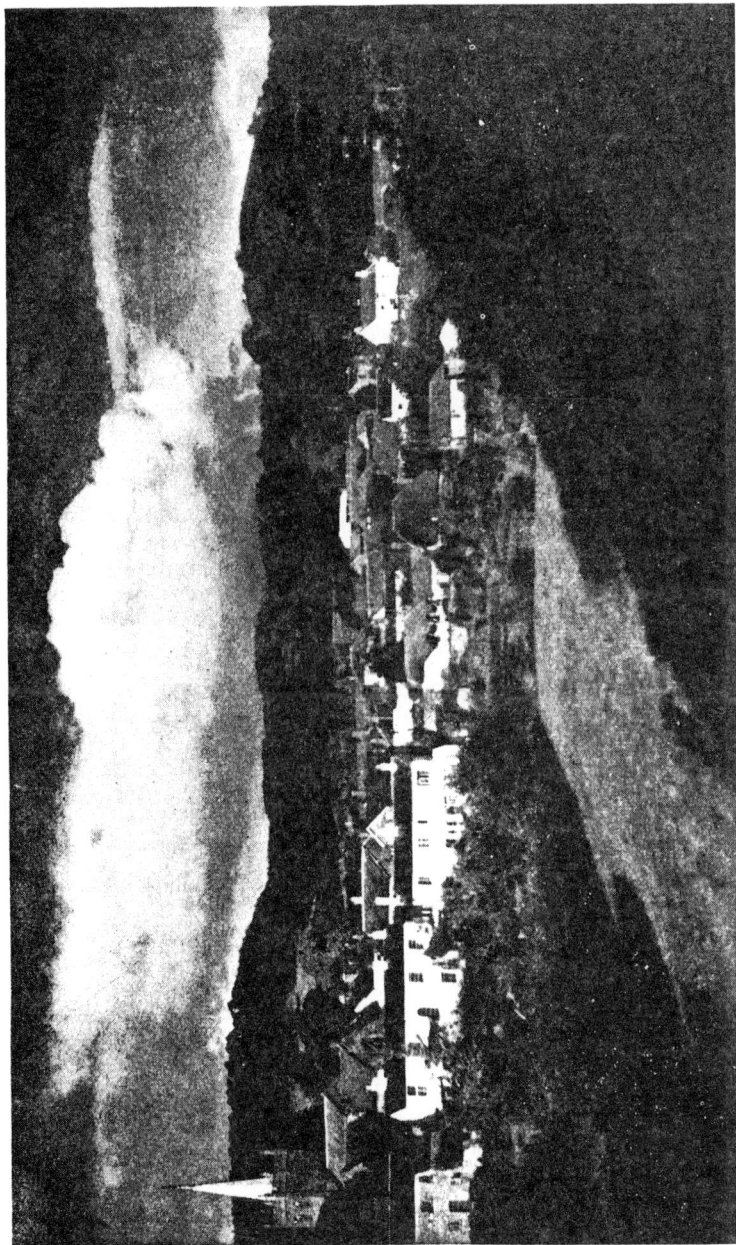

SIDBURY A photograph from Buckley Road in 1958. The cottage, Rose Hill, is on the right side, and is very little changed. The church is placed in the middle of the village, the right half only being in the photograph. Sidbury Manor Park is seen beyond the village. A good general idea of the scenery is given. The larger houses between the church and river would have been groups of thatched cottages in 1801

135

Kennedy wrote, she belonged to an age from which the Victorians had too recently escaped.

I think it certain that Miss Eden cut those pages to good purpose. She was no Miss Gabblegoose, as novelist or woman of the world, and if she took an initial hint from *Pride and Prejudice*, with perhaps a borrowed touch of Darcy for her hero, Teviot. ("You know how I hate those London sort of men with their chains and offensive waistcoats, and Lord Teviot is one of the worst specimens"), it was a sincere form of flattery from a competent novelist to a woman of genius.

John Gore

Sidmouth and Jane Austen

When the Austens were living in Bath, it was their habit to visit some of the Devonshire watering places for holidays. In 1801 they stayed at Sidmouth. Doctor Chapman in his *Jane Austen : Facts and Problems*, devotes a page or two to examining the legend of Jane's attachment at this period to a young man to whom she might have given her heart. That was the legend which grew up out of Caroline Austen's report of some words vaguely let drop by her Aunt Cassandra in old age. In his edition of the letters, in mentioning the visit to Sidmouth in 1801, he added that Sidmouth " may have been the scene of the love-story." There are, of course, no definite proofs to raise it above the status of legend.

Jane Austen's experience of Devon scenery was limited and local. No doubt she crossed the borders from Lyme Regis and certainly she stayed at Sidmouth and Dawlish. Of these proven points, Sidmouth lies towards the centre and it is not very unreasonable to suppose that, when she was needing Devon scenery for her description of Barton Cottage and Park in *Sense and Sensibility*, she may have drawn on what she remembered of the country round Sidmouth.

Finding " originals " for works of art has always been an enchanting pastime, albeit apt to disappoint when applied to the work of a creative artist. Two residents in that area have pleasantly employed their time in seeing how the Sidbury country would " fit " that of Barton. Each of them (Mr. John Frye Bourne and Mr. W. E. Edwards) is, or has been, a resident in Sidbury, a mile or two inland from Sidmouth, where each at different times lived or lives in an enchanting cottage, now called Rose Hill, which was standing in 1801.

Perhaps they were encouraged to probe further by the fact that Rose Hill very admirably fills the bill in the description which Miss Austen supplies of Barton Cottage, its dimensions, room-capacity, views, place-names and setting, and several features of geography round Sidbury certainly give it a claim to attention as the sort of setting which Barton Park and Cottage would have had and of the kind of scenery which would have surrounded them.

SIDMOUTH. A view from the sea, dated 1826. In 1801 the place would have been considerably smaller. Some of the hills of the Sid valley are seen beyond. The open commons, or 'downs', as the Austens would more naturally call them, form the tops of most of these hills. Today many of these are planted with trees. The river Sid meets the sea behind the sailing vessel towards the right of the print.

These gentlemen, at the time of writing, have made no progress in probing the legend of the lost lover or towards establishing it at Sidmouth. It is hoped that they will pursue their researches and that we may hear from them again. Meanwhile the photographs of Sidmouth much as Jane Austen must have seen it and of modern Sidbury, are pleasant illustrations by no means irrelevent.

J.G.

Address given by Monsieur René Varin
at the Annual General Meeting

Ladies and Gentlemen,

When I was invited to speak, in English, before a distinguished audience on so eminently English a writer as Jane Austen, my feeling can be described as one of gratified dismay! There is no need, indeed, to explain why I felt gratified, but my dismay can be easily accounted for by the fact that I am using a tongue which is foreign to me, to speak to experts, whom I hope to find not over-critical, about a novelist worthy of a far better homage.

In fact, having lived in Great Britain on and off since a year before the First World War, I have been in a position to notice how greatly admiration for Jane Austen has increased in this country over the past forty years. This is due to all the Literary Societies, yours in particular, and also no doubt to the influence of writers like Virginia Woolf, who have found this 19th century authoress worthy of comparison with the greatest of the world's writers. Those of you who have read the recently published collection of Virginia Woolf's critical articles and essays, *Granite and Rainbow*, will probably have been struck, as I was, by the way in which, in this volume even more than in the *Common Reader*, Virginia Woolf uses Jane Austen as a yardstick in judging the work of other novelists.

In France the situation, even now, is somewhat different. First of all, we lack a good biography of Jane Austen in French. In England, many excellent works have been published about her : memoirs of members of her family, letters which still provide matter for discussion, all sorts of biographical notes which enable the reader of 1958 to form a clear picture of the charming and witty authoress.

You might object that a book has its own value independently of its author—well, for the French, that is not entirely true, at least for some authors. Indeed, in spite of careful research, we are still somewhat ignorant of the personality of Shakespeare, but this is a problem of its own, and the production of this mighty figure is such as to be of universal interest, even if our knowledge of his life and character be sketchy. But, among other things, a French reader would, for instance, be interested to know whether Jane Austen did, in fact, disapprove as strongly of the stage as would appear from scenes in *Mansfield Park*.

138

I believe that the fact that we have in France good biographies of the Brontë sisters has greatly encouraged the reading public of my country to try and get to know their novels. All the books that have been published in England on the life and character of Jane Austen are naturally known in France to a public of specialists, in particular to the professors of English literature and of comparative literature in our Universities and to their students, but the public at large is not familiar with them. The elegant biography of Shelley, published by Monsieur André Maurois, under the title of *Ariel*, immediately after the First World War, might be described, with some justification, as " Hamlet without the Prince of Denmark," and yet I can testify that the interest aroused by this delightful book has attracted numbers of ordinary Frenchmen to read Shelley's works, in translation and even in the original text.

Another barrier for French people is the great difficulty of making a satisfactory translation of Jane Austen's writing. And I can bear witness to the fact that it is extremely hard to capture the subtleties of her style in French. When you read one of her books, it seems easy enough, but when you come to attempt a faithful rendering in French, you are faced with quite a problem. The very titles of some of her novels present pitfalls. It is perfectly normal for you who know Jane Austen so well, and for all English readers, to delight in such abstract titles as " Pride and Prejudice " and " Persuasion." But " Orgueil et Préjugé " sounds ridiculous to a French ear. " Sense and Sensibility " had to be extended to make in French a double title : " Raison et Sensibilité ou les deux manières d'aimer." Even the translator of " Northanger Abbey " had to resort for a title to the name of one of the characters, Catherine Morland.

I should, however, follow up this catalogue of the reasons why interest in Jane Austen has not increased as rapidly in France as in England by saying that her reputation with us is indeed growing.

The translation of *Mansfield Park*, which I used when a student at the Sorbonne, had been published by Dentu, as early as 1816, that of *Sense and Sensibility* having appeared a year earlier. Now, if we consider the progress made since the last war, we see that a successful translation of *Persuasion* was published in 1945, of *Emma* in 1946, and of *Northanger Abbey* in 1946 also. And if, as a University man, I look at the list of proscribed authors in our various universities, I notice with the pleasure that you can imagine, that since 1940, no year has passed without Jane Austen appearing in the syllabus of at least one of our sixteen universities, to say nothing of the special studies devoted to her by a number of post-graduate and specialist students of the English departments of these institutions. In fact it may not be long before we see a Frenchman swell the ranks of that small army of British writers who attempt, every ten years or so, to complete Jane Austen's unfinished novel *The Watsons* !

If I question my compatriots about her, their answers reveal both interest and surprise. Their main source of astonishment is naturally that the troubled life of Europe at the time when Jane was composing her novels, is never reflected in her books. The French Revolution, Robespierre's terrible reign, the Napoleonic wars, are not even alluded to in the books I have read, in spite of the fact that two of her brothers were, at the time, serving with distinction in the British navy and were directly involved in the fighting. This has obviously struck English readers also, who explain the fact by saying that she was living " far from the madding crowd," and that it would probably have been bad manners for a lady—young or otherwise—to show any interest in politics. But to the Frenchman it seems very strange that when the future of England was at stake, there should be no inkling of this in novels almost solely related to the life, loves and marriages of upper middle-class English people.

Another minor obstacle to the success of these novels abroad is without doubt their length. When a book is sustained throughout by the quality and charm of the language, the reader is held captive, but even in a good translation (and, as I said earlier, good translations of Jane Austen are very difficult to come by), books of four hundred or more pages seem rather lengthy to readers of today, who are invariably in somewhat of a hurry!

But once these obstacles have been enumerated, what a wealth of interest there is for a reader in France, or indeed in any country of the world, in the novels of Jane Austen. Admittedly, the boundaries of her picture of England are those of a limited upper middle-class society. We do not find any study of the work of a gardener or of a labourer, but as she herself points out on several occasions, she did not want to compose an encyclopaedia of England under George III, and what she tells us is, if we read it attentively enough, most informative. We see life as it unfolds itself in the towns—Bath and Southampton for instance, as well as London; while we share the whole round of existence of the people who live in country houses. Their world she depicts very well, and we have a slow-motion film of their activities, talks, discussions, long, somewhat dull evenings, of their parties, balls, invitations, and journeys. We are given numerous illustrations of their prejudices against certain professions or in favour of certain members of their society. A solicitor, for example, was then considered a second-class man for a girl who wished to marry. Jane Austen's portrayal of Ministers of the Church is clearly based upon close observation. All the dogmas and rules of the Anglican Church were hardly questioned in these upper middle-class circles, but Jane Austen has obviously given much thought to the position of the Minister in Society, and in several of her books, particularly in *Mansfield Park*, where Edmund takes Holy Orders, the problem of the duties and the possible influence of the clergy is studied with deep insight and keen perception. But even in England the opinion is divided about the merits of Jane Austen. In considering the picture she gives of her society, for instance, here is a rather strange judgement of D. H. Lawrence :

" In the old England, the curious blood-connection held the classes together. The squires might be arrogant, violent, bullying and unjust, yet in some ways they were *at one* with the people, part of the same blood-stream. We feel it in Defoe or Fielding. And then, in the mean Jane Austen, it is gone. Already this old maid typifies " personality " instead of " character," the sharp knowing in apartness, instead of knowing in togetherness, and she is, to my feeling, thoroughly unpleasant, English in the bad, mean, snobbish sense of the word, just as Fielding is English in the good generous sense."

Most of the French people whom I have questioned share my view that this statement is unjust and unfounded. Indeed, I think that D. H. Lawrence was too definite and full-blooded a personality to judge properly the niceties of Jane Austen's humour, and also to understand the social evolution of her epoch. As to the opposition between *personality* and *character*, this brings us to those abstract terms which are so difficult to define, and which are sometimes sources of misunderstanding between the French and the English; expressions of this kind have shades of meaning which are not easily analysed, even by those who are experts in both languages.

One aspect of Jane Austen's milieu, that of the family, is, of course, peculiar to her era, and obviously different from that of today. The authority wielded by the father, the part played by the mother—whether it be intervention or neglect—(I am thinking of Lady Bertram), seems to be typical of many of the families surrounding her. Today we have other views on the subject, and I would beg permission to quote T. S. Eliot on what he thinks a family should be :

" Now the family is an institution of which nearly everybody speaks well : but it is advisable to remember that this is a term that may vary in extension. What is held up for admiration is not devotion to a family but personal affection between the members of it...Unless reverence *for past and future* is cultivated in the home, it can never be more than a verbal convention in the community. Such an interest in the past is different from the vanities and pretentions of genealogy; such a responsibility for the future is different from that of the builder of social programmes." (*Notes towards the definition of culture, 1948.*)

The problem of the education of daughters is also one that preoccupies Jane Austen very much, and her novels are, to my mind, all the more interesting for it. A passage like the following, taken from the first pages of *Mansfield Park*, provides matter for reflection :

" Such were the councils by which Mrs. Norris assisted to form her nieces' minds; and it is not very wonderful that, with all their promising talents and early information, they should be entirely deficient in the less common acquirements of self-knowledge, generosity, and humility. In everything but disposition they were admirably taught. Sir Thomas did not know what was wanting, because, though a truly anxious father, he was not outwardly affectionate, and the reserve of his manner repressed all the flow of their spirits before him."

141

In fact, Jane Austen is something of a moralist, who depicted and judged a certain kind of society without illusions but also without bitterness.

Her humour has a flavour all its own. I will not use this talk as a pretext to return to the much discussed nature of English humour and wit as compared with " L'esprit français," but the humour of Jane Austen can, fortunately, be transposed fairly easily into French, and indeed into the modern idiom. The main reason is probably that she is very classical in style, and that she hardly ever makes a pun or a play on words. Her playful comment : " What! five daughters brought up at home without a governess!" has only gained in humour for the reader of our time. We can appreciate, too, such a vignette as the scene depicted in the drawing-room with Lady Catherine, that haughty and autocratic lady : " The party gathered round the fire to hear Lady Catherine determine what weather they were to have on the morrow." Again, she speaks of Lady Catherine's having scolded the poor into "harmony and plenty," a turn of phrase which is easily translatable into French.

It is not for me to underline her special gifts as novelist, her talent for unravelling emotions, her art of achieving a delicate balance between passages of pure analysis, descriptions of feelings, the meditations of the characters, conversations and letters. Not only does she delineate finely each character, but, like a true novelist, she blends them together in a way which shows their inter-influences and their inter-reactions.

So far as I am concerned, what I admire most is her supreme art of depicting certain scenes at the most apt moment. Let me give you just one example to illustrate what I mean : Mary Crawford, who is enraptured with Edmund, has received the news that the young clergyman has decided to delay his return to Mansfield Park, which means that she will depart before seeing him again. Her sentiments are such as to make her violently desire to know why he has changed his mind about the date of his return, and *that* she can only learn from Fanny, who is also in love with Edmund! The brief scene where Miss Crawford questions Fanny is, for me, a model of subtle analysis and of Jane Austen's supreme genius for dialogue.

Virginia Woolf has said that Jane Austen is probably, " of all great writers, the most difficult to catch in the act of greatness." This is very true, and yet there are moments when one can put one's finger on passages which mark her as a supreme novelist. I will, if I may, take one more example from *Mansfield Park*—the ball arranged by Sir Thomas Bertram to compensate for his blunt rejection of the plan to act a play in his house. The scene reaches its climax when Edmund comes to dance with Fanny, and here are the few sentences of Edmund that sum up both his own feelings and those of Fanny in what I think is the apex of art in a novel :

" I am worn out with civility," said he, " I have been talking incessantly all night, and with nothing to say. But with *you*, Fanny, there may be peace, you will not want to be talked to. Let us have the luxury of silence."

For French people at least, appreciation of Jane Austen is not so much a question of being swept away by personal enthusiasm or antipathy, as it is the fruit of careful reading and comparison with other writers.

One of our most exacting authors and critics, André Gide, has judged Jane Austen with complete impartiality in the following terms :

" Son ciel est un peu bas, un peu vide, mais quelle délicatesse dans la peinture des sentiments. Si nul démon majeur n'habite Jane Austen, en revanche, une compréhension d'autrui jamais en défaut, jamais défaillante. La part de satire est excellente et des plus finement nuancées. Tout se joue en dialogues, et ceux-ci sont aussi bons qu'il se puisse. Certains chapitres sont d'un art parfait."

" Her horizon is a little limited, a little empty, but what delicacy in her delineation of feelings. Jane Austen may not be animated by any mighty demon, but on the other hand, what unfailing, what sure understanding of others. How excellent is her use of satire, in the most subtle light and shade. The whole story is played out in dialogue, as good as one could wish. Some chapters are art in its perfection."

If I dared, in turn, make a comparison between women writers, I should say, thinking of the contribution of English women novelists to world literature, that without George Eliot we should be deprived of a rare combination of acuteness and generous feeling which is, to my mind, one of her main characteristics. Without the Brontës, we should lack a passionate intuition of a quality which is scarcely to be found anywhere else. If Jane Austen had not written, we should have to forfeit a freshness of approach, a vivacious yet classical limpidity of rendering, that is the delight of all those who read her over and over again. In fact, she has given the world an almost perfect example of a certain English charm which can be described in one word, for once common to French and English : I mean, " enchantment."

René Varin

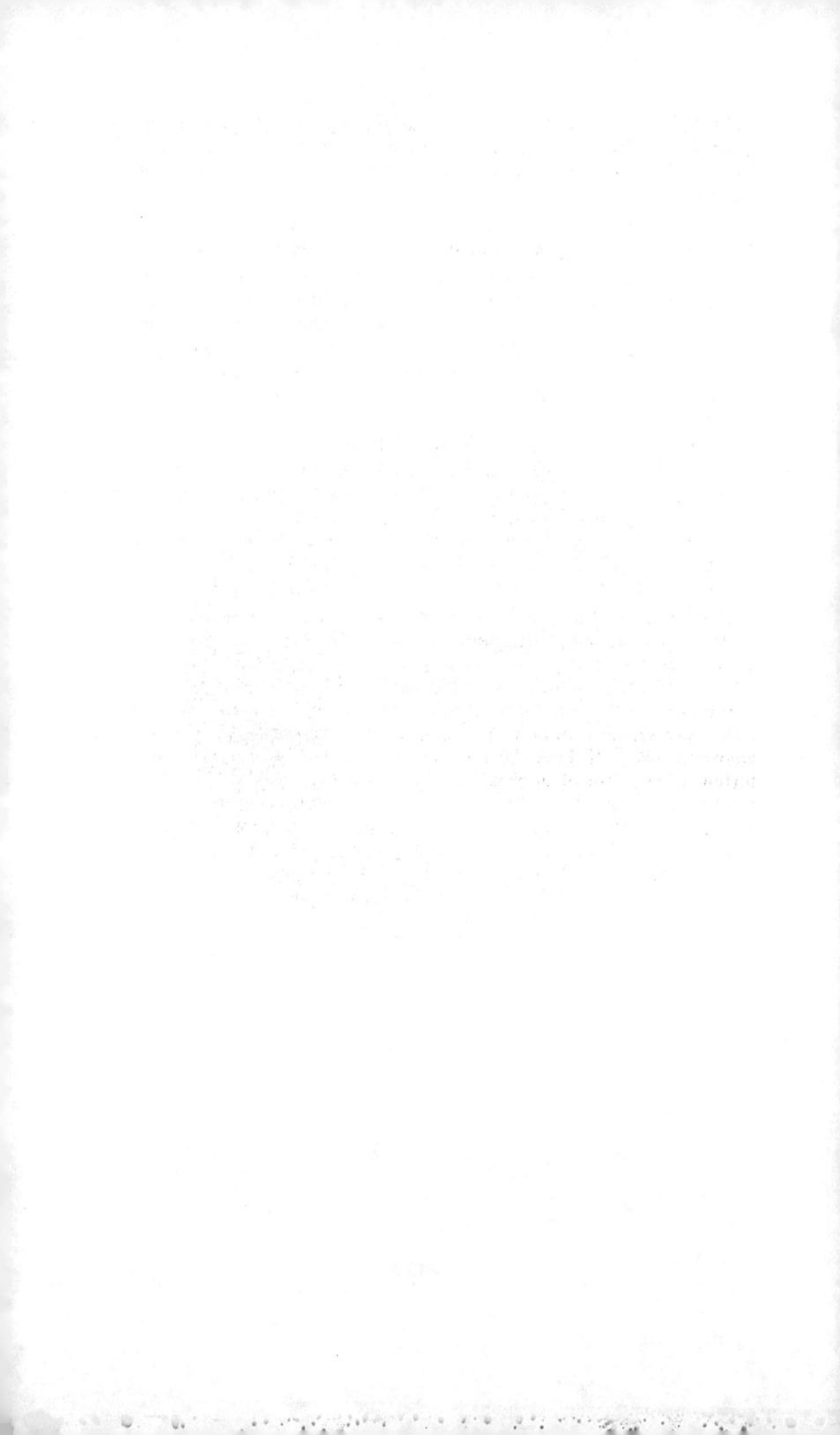

THE JANE AUSTEN SOCIETY

Report for the year 1959

Sagittarius

THE JANE AUSTEN SOCIETY
Report for the year 1959

Membership

Seventy new members joined the Society during the year, of whom twelve became Life Members. Two existing members also became Life Members. The membership now stands at 844.

Members are reminded that subscriptions are due on 1st January, and that this report is the only reminder that they will receive. The Hon. Secretary would much appreciate prompt payment of the 5/- subscription, and will gladly provide a Bankers' Order form.

Annual General Meeting, 1959

The Annual General Meeting was held on Saturday, 11th July at Chawton House, by kind permission of Major and Mrs. Edward Knight, when nearly 300 members and their friends were present.

The President, His Grace the Duke of Wellington, K.G., presided. In his opening remarks he referred to the retirement of the Hon. Treasurer, Mr. F. H. Foster, who was leaving the district after holding office since 1950, and of Mrs. A. S. Bates of Manydown Park, who had served on the Committee since 1953, and he expressed the gratitude of the Society for their services. He asked that the minutes of the last Annual General Meeting be taken as read. There were no matters arising.

The Hon. Secretary presented the Annual Report. This was seconded by Mrs. K. A. Robbins, and carried.

The Hon. Treasurer presented the Accounts. This was proposed by Mr. Walshaw, seconded by Mr. Brooker, and carried.

Mr. T. Edward Carpenter gave a review of his activities in connection with the Jane Austen Memorial Trust, this day being the tenth anniversary of its formation.

The Election of Officers followed. The Hon. Secretary proposed the re-election of the Duke of Wellington as President, of Dr. R. W. Chapman and Mr. T. Edward Carpenter as Vice-Presidents, and Mr. John Gore as Chairman of the Society. This was seconded by Lady Bonham-Carter, who added the name of Sir Hugh Smiley as Hon. Secretary, and was carried.

The President proposed the re-election, en bloc of the Committee. This was carried.

The Very Rev. Dr. E. G. Selwyn, D.D., sometime Dean of Winchester had agreed to address the meeting, and had written to the Hon. Secretary in May to say that his paper on "The Clergyman of the Novels" was finished. He had been ill during the early part of the year, but hoped to be well by the date of the meeting. But he did not get better, and died on 11th June. On that day Mrs. Selwyn wrote to the Hon. Secretary, saying how disappointed the Dr. Selwyn was when he knew that he would be unable to read his paper, and that his last wish was that Mrs. Richard Morgan who had helped him with its preparations, might read it. Mrs. Morgan therefore read the paper, and delighted everyone present.

A vote of thanks was proposed by the Rev. William Jarvis, seconded by Mrs. Reed, and carried.

A vote of thanks to the President and to Major and Mrs. Knight was proposed by Lady Smiley, seconded by Mrs. Gadban, and carried.

A collection was made towards the cost of a pew to be erected in Chawton Church in memory of Jane Austen and of Miss Dorothy Darnell, founder of the Society.

The meeting then closed, and was followed by tea, provided in aid of Chawton Church funds.

Annual General Meeting, 1960

The Annual General Meeting will be held at Chawton House on Saturday, 16th July. The Speakers will be His Grace the Duke of Wellington, K.G., President of the Society, and Mr. John Gore, the Chairman.

Jane Austen in London

The Society will shortly publish "Jane Austen in London", an illustrated pamphlet by Miss Winifred Watson. This can be obtained from the Hon. Secretary, price 3/9 postage free.

Three Footnotes on Literary Sources

Steventon gossip in Miss Mitford's "Belford Regis".

In addition to the famous reports of Jane Austen as "a husband-hunting butterfly" and later, "a poker", another shred of Hampshire gossip seems to have lodged in Miss Mitford's head. The reader of her *"Belford Regis", (1835)* is startled to come upon the name Earl Harwood which also occurs a number of times in Jane Austen's letters. Miss Mitford's Earl Harwood is a clergyman, cold, supercilious, "a prig of the slower and graver order". *("Belford Regis", Chapter Five).* The real Earle Harwood (1773-1811) was, as the invaluable index to Dr. Chapman's edition of Jane Austen's letters tells us, the second son of John Harwood of Deane House. An officer in the Royal Marines, he appears in Jane Austen's letters in 1798, as marrying in such a

148

way as to be obliged to live in the most private manner possible. If his wife behaves well for a year, Jane Austen tells her correspondent, his family will consent to receive her. In 1800, he is again "giving uneasiness to his family and talk to the neighbourhood", this time by accidentally shooting himself in the thigh and narrowly escaping the loss of a leg. In 1808 he appears again, amiably, as speaking in "extravagant terms of praise" of Charles Austen, whom he has left at Bermuda.

The real Earle Harwood was evidently anything but a prig, and I do not suppose that Miss Mitford while writing Chapter Five of *"Belford Regis"* was in the least conscious that she was using the name of an actual person. The name is, however, so distinctive that it seems clear enough that on one or more of the occasions when poor Earle Harwood was the talk of the neighbourhood, something of that talk reached Miss Mitford. (Her mother till she was thirty-three had lived at Ashe, two miles from Steventon, and at Alresford, ten or twelve miles away for the next nine years; she probably continued to have news of the district in letters till her death in 1830.) Many years later when Miss Mitford was writing *"Belford Regis"* the striking name came back to her, to be used for an invented character. Miss Mitford's latest biographer, Vera Watson, mentions that *"Belford Regis"* was written in conditions of stress and anxiety unusual even for Miss Mitford: perhaps she hardly knew what she was doing.

The oddity of the Christian name, which might be a title of nobility, is important in the story; Miss Mitford produces not only an Earl Harwood, but a brother, King Harwood, who gives his name to the tale. The Harwoods are the sons of an upstart clergyman with social ambitions who has christened his sons after friends "of good parliamentary interest". The picture of the whole Harwood family is highly unfavourable, but so unlike the real Harwoods of Deane House that if Earle Harwood's relations (in 1835 he himself had long been dead) ever looked into *"Belford Regis"* they must have realized that only a treacherous upsurge of unconscious memory had led Miss Mitford into making free with Captain Harwood's name.

ii *Two literary references in Jane Austen's Letters.*

1. In her letters to Cassandra of 14th January, 1801, Jane Austen writes: "I am rather surprised at the Revival of the London visit—but Mr. Doricourt has travelled; he knows best". Jane Austen here depends on her sister's knowledge of Mrs. Hannah Cowley's play *"The Belle's Stratagem"*, *(1780)*.

MRS. RACKETT: Well, now 'tis over, I confess to you, Mr. Doricourt, I think it was a most ridiculous piece of Quixotism to give up the happiness of a whole life to a man who perhaps has but a few moments to be sensible of the sacrifice.

149

The Rev. George Austen presenting his son Edward to Mr. and Mrs. Thomas Knight

FLUTTER: So it appeared to me. But, thought I, Mr. Doricourt has travelled—he knows best!

Mrs. Cowley seems to have been a favourite with the Austens; they had acted her play "*Which is the Man*" at Christmas 1787. "Mr. Doricourt" in Jane Austen's letter is, I think, Cassandra, who soon after left Godmersham for three weeks in town.

2. In another letter to Cassandra, (24th January, 1809) Jane Austen writes: "Take care of your precious self, do not work too hard, remember that Aunt Cassandras are quite as scarce as Miss Beverleys".

The scarcity of Miss Beverleys is forcibly stated by the hero of Miss Burney's "*Cecilia*" in a scene which exemplifies Elizabeth Bennet's maxim that general incivility is the essence of love. Delvile is walking in the park with two young ladies, Miss Cecilia Beverley and Lady Honoria Pemberton. They are overtaken by a thunderstorm and Lady Honoria with characteristic folly persists in sheltering under a large tree. Delvile proposes to take Cecilia back to the house and then return for Lady Honoria. Cecilia refuses.

' "By no means," cried she, "My life is not more precious than either of yours and therefor it may run the same risk." "It is more precious," cried he with vehemence "than the air I breathe!" and seizing her hand he drew it under his arm, and without waiting her consent, almost forced her away with him, saying as they ran: "How could a thousand Lady Honorias recompense the world for the loss of one Miss Beverley? We may indeed find many such as Lady Honoria, but such as Miss Beverley, where shall we ever find another?" '

Cecilia, Bk. VI, Ch. III

iii *Mr. B's proposal and Mr. Darcy's.*

The hero of Richardson's novel began the honourable phase of his courtship of Pamela by a letter in which she "found the following agreeable contents: In vain, my Pamela, do I struggle against my affection for you"*. Pamela's humility allowed her to find nothing objectionable in this rather unflattering opening. It is likely that Jane Austen who knew Richardson's works with a minuteness that surprises the modern reader†, was fully alive to the implications of Mr. B's turn of phrase; and that she remembered it when composing Mr. Darcy's markedly uncivil declaration to Elizabeth Bennet: "In vain have I struggled. It will not do. My feelings will not be suppressed‡."

* *Pamela*. Everyman Edition, 1950. i.p. 222.
† "Her knowledge of Richardson's works was such as no one is likely again to acquire." *Memoir of Jane Austen*. ed: J. E. Austen-Leigh, 1871, p. 84.
‡ *Pride and Prejudice*. O.U.P. 1946, p. 189.

E. E. DUNCAN-JONES

Memorial to Anne, wife of the Rev. James Austen, in Steventon Church

16th December. Sagittarius

Astrologers say that certain traits of character and even certain turns of events are common to all people born under the same sign: i.e. during the span occupied by the second half of one month and the first half of the next, when one of the twelve signs of the Zodiac is in the ascendant. The general character associated with each sign is not of course a completely accurate picture of any one person, as the time of birth will modify some of the characteristics; while the sun is in one sign, the moon will be passing through twelve signs. and each of the twelve solar-lunar combinations will exert a slightly different influence on the basic characteristics, emphasising some and reducing the force of others. Nevertheless the outlines of character as based on the "rising sign" are often strikingly recognisable in a person born under that sign's influence.

Jane Austen, born on 16th December, was a subject of the sign Sagittarius, and delineations of the Sagittarian character strike one as reflecting very accurately what we know of her. The main outlines of what I am reproducing here will be found in any book on Astrology; while monthly periodicals, English and American, devoted to the subject, frequently supply psychological details compiled by modern astrologers from their observation of the subjects of the twelve Zodiacal signs. I was drawn to make this brief study by an article in one of these magazines, about the courtship of women governed by the different signs. The writer warned any man courting a Sagittarian woman not to be surprised if, having accepted his proposal, she changed her mind with disconcerting suddenness! Jane Austen's precipitate flight from Manydown on Friday, 3rd December, 1802, having withdrawn the consent she had given to Mr. Bigg-Wither's proposal the day before, rises to the mind immediately.

The symbol of the constellation Sagittarius is a centaur, half horse, half man, shooting with a bow and arrow at the stars, and a certain duality is a basic trait of those born while it is in the ascendant. In them, the qualities of head and heart are equally balanced the passions are ardent but controlled by reason. The typical Sagittarian frame has long, slender limbs, is active and light-footed and has a small head on a long throat. The characteristic colouring is of dark brown eyes and hair.

The Sagittarian temperament is said to be self-confident and independent, highly sensitive, impressionable and reticent. The temper is joyous and optimistic but liable to spells of agitation and capable of great unhappiness. However the normal condition is cheerful, and these people find their happiness in domestic life and take great pride in their relations. Their instinct is to be kind and just, but they are able to wound deeply, as their intuition leads them to detect unerringly the weakness of others. They express themselves with great clearness and decision. The principles by which they appear to be governed are liberty, order and harmony. These generalizations will strike many readers as singularly true of Jane Austen, and it is not, one ventures to think, far fetched, to read an oddly penetrating comment on her work into the statement of one astrologer, who says of the subjects of this sign: "They have exchanged the parochial for the universal".

When the writers descend to minutiae of personality or events they produce several which are applicable to Jane Austen's life. The most startling I have come across is the one I have already quoted. It is also said of Sagittarians that they are liable to encounter misfortune or serious loss in their thirtieth year. In 1804 when Jane Austen was 29, her friend Mrs. Lefroy of Ashe was killed in a road-accident: the deep grief this caused Jane she showed in the verses she wrote about Mrs. Lefroy four years later on the anniversary of her death.

The Sagittarians' motto is said to be: One thing at a time. We are reminded by this of Jane's letter to Cassandra of 8th September, 1816, in which she says: "I often wonder how you can find time for what you do in addition to the cares of the House ... Composition seems to me impossible with a head full of Joints of Mutton and doses of rhubarb".

The Sagittarians' attitude to money is neither extravagant nor mean, but they value it keenly because it provides security. Within three months of her own death Jane Austen learned that her rich uncle, Mr. Leigh-Perrott had left nothing to Mrs. Austen and bequests to his nephews and nieces that would take effect only after his wife's death. Already in her last illness she wrote to her brother Charles on 6th April, 1817, "I am ashamed to say that the shock of my uncle's will brought on a relapse . . . I am the only one of the legatees who has been so silly but a weak body must excuse weak nerves".

Sagittarians love going about and travel for pleasure. Jane Austen's animated descriptions of her journeys, and her enterprising attitude to visiting, come to mind, and she is still more vividly evoked by the statement that Sagittarians are very fond of walking: it suits their health and gives them great enjoyment. Jane Austen had this trait herself and bestowed it sympathetically on her heroines. Catherine Morland declared she did not need botany to get her out of doors: "The pleasure of walking and breathing fresh air is enough for me". "Is there a felicity in the world superior to this?" cried Marianne Dashwood, walking on Barton hills in the face of a high, south-westerly wind.

When Edmund and Fanny, in the eleventh chapter of *Mansfield Park* were looking out on "the brilliancy of an unclouded night" and detecting Arcturus "looking very bright," the cousins, in their conversation about the stars, did not touch upon astrology. One cannot think of it as a study likely to commend itself to Jane Austen; nevertheless two gems are said to be governed by Sagittarius, the carbuncle and the turquoise, and she possessed both of them, each set in a ring: that with the red stone is now in the possession of Mrs. Shervington, the one bearing the turquoise is in that of the Austen-Leigh family.

ELIZABETH JENKINS

Jane Austen's Clergymen

I should like to say, Mr. President, how grateful I am to those who have asked me to address this Annual Meeting today and have given me so interesting a subject. It has given me some winter work of a most agreeable kind, and at a time when I have had leisure, has compelled me to read all Jane Austen's novels again— or rather five of them again and one for the first time. That, I need hardly say, meant several weeks of pleasure. But they were also weeks of instruction: for I am bound to say that, until I read them carefully and continuously in this way, I had never realised how Miss Austen's clergymen permeate her books. The main reason was, no doubt, that the men themselves seem to have so little connexion with any kind of pastoral or parochial work, as we know it today. In certain cases, too, we are dealing not with parsons but with parsons-designate—at any rate I am including these in my survey. But of these things more anon. Meanwhile let us remember that Miss Austen knew her facts. As the daughter of a clergyman and the sister of two others and devoted to all three, she was not likely to criticise the cloth unfairly; but when they do provoke mirth or hostility, then we may surmise that they represent a type which she had herself met with; and they cannot be understood without reference to the social and ecclesiastical system to which they belonged.

Socially, our authoress and her characters belong to what Sir Arthur Bryant has called "The Age of Elegance". Not only is elegance the outstanding feature of her own style; but it is a moral quality of high importance. Delicacy, considerateness, reserve, good taste, good manners—all these are part of it. It is desirable also in a man's or a woman's figure, and in the cut of his coat and of her gown. Yet character and appearance are not on the same footing: Mrs. Elton's gown might be "very elegant"; but as to character, "ease, but not elegance" was Emma's verdict. There appear also—or I am dreaming?—certain faults of grammar which betoken the lack of elegance "Neither Mr. Suckling nor me had ever any patience with them" is the voice of Mrs. Elton. "My

Jane Austen's Tomb in Winchester Cathedral
Copyright Photograph by courtesy of A. W. Kerr, F.I.B.P., F.R.P.S

sister and me was often staying with my uncle", says Lucy Steele to Elinor Dashwood; "Anne and me are to go the latter end of January to some relatives"; "Kitty and me" writes Lydia Bennett several times when she has become thoroughly vulgarized. And there are other examples. I hesitate to generalize; but this solecism—(or should I say, modernism, for it has become quite fashionable with the present younger generation?)—struck me often enough to make me wonder whether Jane Austen used it deliberately as a mark of those of her characters who were deficient in elegance. At the same time elegance had its other side; and our authoress speaks without hesitation of "the elegant stupidity of private parties" providing the Elliotts—those perfect snobs—with their sole evening amusements; and of "the heartless elegance" of Anne's father and sister.

The title of this paper suggests to many minds one name above all other. "Oh, Yes," they say, "of course, Mr. Collins." True. Mr. Collins has become in a unique sense amongst Jane Austen's characters, a household word. Yet, in fact, he is not of great importance for our purpose; indeed he is not even essential to the story of *Pride and Prejudice*. Rather, he stands as a kind of grotesque monolith at the entrance to the garden which Jane Austen has laid out for us. Pompous, selfish and determined to marry, he comes charging like a bull into the Bennets' house, feeling sure that the chance he offers of keeping the entail in the family will make his claims irresistible; and in this frame of mind makes any one of the attractive daughters his target and writes without delay his first famous letter. But like every object of ridicule, he is entitled if not to sympathy at least to justice. As a parson he seems to have had a very poor notion of his parish duties. But he did marry and marry well. Charolotte Lucas was a knight's daughter, and there is nothing to suggest that he did not make her content—and we know that she regarded marriage as a woman's pleasantest preservative from want. That of course, is only negative evidence. But such as it is, he is entitled to it. Let us leave him at that—a clown, a figure of fun. Long ago Aristotle had written the truth about such men. "Comedy (he wrote) is an imitation of characters of a lower type—not, however, in the full sense of the word bad, the Ludicrous being merely a sub-division of the ugly. It consists in some defect or ugliness which is not painful or destructive."

The Church system in Jane Austen's lifetime was indeed extraordinary. There is no indication of any previous theological or pastoral training being required, other than perhaps a University degree, nor of any plan for testing a man's suitability for the Ministry, before he was ordained and even appointed to a benefice. Edmund Bertram had to go to Peterborough for a day before his Ordination there, but the visit is regarded not so much as one of preparation but a tiresome interruption in the course of other and more disturbing claims on his time. All that was needed was to "find a bishop" who would ordain and institute to the living. James Morland was not yet through his Schools at Oxford when he wished to marry; and if I understand *Northanger Abbey* aright, his father's promise to appoint him to succeed him at Fullerton was part of the marriage settlement into which he entered with Isabella Thorpe. I understand that today this might be regarded as simony. Moreover, the abuse of non-residence was rife. You will remember the fierce discussion of this subject between Mary Crawford and Fanny in *Mansfield Park*—a discussion in which the novelist seems herself to be joining with passionate conviction. Mr. Collins and Charles Hayter accepted the necessity of providing for their Sunday services and certain others if they themselves were absent. But they need not live in their parishes. Pluralism was common (though perhaps not so successfully managed as in the days of William of Wykeham); and a large number of Church people regarded a "living" as just that— a house and income to live on rather than as a sphere of duty. We do not often realise how much we owe to the reforming movements which revolutionized the Church in the 1830s; to the later Evangelical Movement under the guidance of Charles Simeon, whose watchword was "seriousness" rather than "enthusiam"; to the administrative gift of Bishop Blomfield, also a Cambridge man, and the foundation of the Ecclesiastical Commission; and to the Oxford Movement which is commonly dated from Keble's Assize Sermon in 1833.

Mention of Simeon brings me back to Jane Austen. Curiously enough, this great man was himself an example of the system prevailing during her life. He was ordained on the title of his Fellowship at King's, as anyone might be today; but he had not in fact reached the canonical age; and he was appointed by the Bishop of Ely to the perpetual curacy of Trinity Church, Cambridge, before he was in full orders. One may respect the bishop's desire to encourage a man of unquestioned vocation to the Ministry and of great learning; but Jane Austen's novels shew that the results of breaking the Church's rules in such matters were unfortunately widespread. *Quis custodiet ipsos custodes?* However, that is a digression. The question I want to ask is how far Jane Austen may have come in touch with the Evangelical movement of her day and what influence this may have had upon her portrayal of the office and the characters of some of her clergy. The late Miss Sheila Kaye-Smith, no mean judge in a matter of this kind, was so much impressed by the contrast between *Mansfield Park* and the other novels that she thought Jane Austen must have come under some strong outside influence shortly before writing it, and that this was the Evangelical movement. It is probable that many of the Bath churches were then, as in fact they still are, associated with the Evangelical tradition; as indeed if we include Lyncombe and also

Walcot, where Jane Austen worshipped and where her father was buried, the number of benefices in Bath which are today in the hands of Simeon's Trustees is quite exceptional. It is worth remembering also the guiding principle which Simeon laid down for the Trustees' guidance: "Judge how far any parson possesses the qualifications suitable to the particular parish, and by that consideration alone must they be determined in their appointment of him."

I think, however, that Miss Kaye-Smith's conjecture is too narrow. Bath and London gave Jane Austen ample opportunities of hearing and perhaps knowing, some of the best clergymen of her time; more than once she writes of going to church twice on a Sunday, morning and afternoon; and the "seriousness" which marked the Evangelical clergymen in particular seems to me to underlie her own portrayals of the clergy in her novels, not least when they are toadies like Mr. Collins or egregious like Mr. Elton (who was unlucky enough "to be in the same room at once with the woman he had just married, the woman he had wanted to marry, and the woman he had been expected to marry".) A more complex case is that of Edward Ferrers in *Sense and Sensibility*. Here was an acute case of conscience arising from the fact that he had let himself get engaged at the age of 19 to the designing Lucy Steele. The dilemma was resolved by the fickle girl being carried off by Edward's brother. But Edward is not only a serious but a tortured man. "Gaiety was never a part of *my* character", he said to Elinor. Yet at the end we find him offered a good living by Colonel Brandon, promised £250 a year by his mother, ordained as he had always wished to be, and happily married in his parsonage at Delaford to Elinor Dashwood. "If Edward might be judged from the ready discharge of his duties in every particular, from an increasing attachment to his wife and his home, and from the regular cheerfulness of his spirits, he might be supposed" to be wholly contented with his lot. Notice the order of the symptoms: his work comes first.

In this her earliest novel, published in 1811 though begun in 1797 when she was only 22, Jane Austen shewed herself a real adept at what is called "Moral Theology"—though I suspect she would have shrunk from the term. She knew, as Shakespeare knew, that comedy could be the vehicle of moral truths; indeed, I could wish that her novels might be added to those more learned tomes which candidates for the Ministry have to read. I cannot find any contrast, so far as this element of "seriousness" is concerned, between *Sense and Sensibility*, and *Mansfield Park*. What we do find is two features which distinguish the later book. First of all, there is the unique concentration upon the lives and manners of certain clergymen, especially upon Edmund Bertram. From the moment when Edmund, home from Eton for the holidays, then aged 16, found his little 10-year old cousin, Fanny

159

Price, "sitting crying on the stairs", and shewed her an understanding, a kindness and an affection, to which she had been a stranger since she left her Portsmouth home—from that moment until the end of the book when he had been ordained and he and Fanny were married, Edmund is the unquestioned hero of the story. That, I imagine, is what Jane Austen meant when she wrote to Cassandra on 29th January, 1813, "Now I will try to write of something else, and it shall be a complete change of subject—ordination." She is contrasting it with what she calls "my own darling child", namely *Pride and Prejudice*, a copy of which had reached her only two days before. And the theme of the book is completely different.

But so, too, is its scope and its dramatic power; and perhaps that is why Cassandra preferred it to both *Emma* and *Pride and Prejudice*. In no other book does the authoress give us such insight into the doings of the Navy; of one long out-pouring by Fanny Price's father, Jane Austen's two sailor brothers said that her "seamanship was faultless". Equally striking, and reminding one of Dickens himself, are the chapters which describe the Prices' house in Portsmouth—its squalor, its disorder, its incessant noise. The only redeeming feature was Sunday, when the whole family put on its Sunday best to go to the Garrison Church and afterwards to the ramparts to see what was afoot on the water. This description of how the poor lived reads as though it were based on first-hand knowledge. One wonders how and where our authoress acquired it.

Dramatically, too, Mansfield Park stands alone. There is the play within the play, for example—*Lovers' Vows*. Edmund's objection to this taking place has been adduced as an argument in favour of the notion that Jane Austen had passed under some "outside influence", before she wrote this book, for many Evangelical leaders were opposed to the theatre. But we know that the Austen family much enjoyed private theatricals, and that she herself was a keen play-goer when in London. But I agree with Miss Jenkins that *Lovers' Vows*, however much it may have been bowdlerized by its English translator, was an unpleasant play. And it was Edmund who put his finger on the point when he distinguished between "good, hardened acting" (that is, the professional stage) and the self-conscious efforts of a party engaged in private theatricals.

But why did Jane Austen introduce this episode of the play? I suggest that her purpose was purely dramatic; Shakespeare had done likewise, when he made Hamlet say:

> The play's the thing
> Wherein I'll catch the conscience of the king.

So in the play in *Mansfield Park* most of the leading characters in the story stand out in vivid light, and not least Edmund Bertram. And his conscience is indeed "caught". For, in fact, his character had a tragic flaw—indecision. He opposed the idea of a play in the house altogether; he was sure that his father would not approve of it; he objected to the play selected. Yet, when the time came, he yielded against his better judgement, and against Fanny's too, and consented to take an important part. This flaw in his character occurs again later, when the charms of Mary Crawford nearly carry him away. Thus early does our authoress give us a kind of preview of what is to follow.

Jane Austen's novels are commonly reckoned as comedies; but in this case the comedy is heavily streaked with tragedy. The dividing line between tragedy and comedy in a play is often not easy to decipher. Shakespeare's *Pericles*, for example, is commonly listed among his tragedies. Yet why? The Prince of Tyre, and his wife Thaisa, and their daughter, Marina, pass through incredible sufferings and separations and disasters; but in fact they are always rescued, and at the last they are re-united again in happiness and all the villains come to a bad end. Pericles, again, is strictly speaking, not a tragic hero, because he is without any fatal flaw in character such as in Otheilo, Hamlet and Lear. I reckon that *Mansfield Park* is much nearer to tragedy than Shakespeare's *Pericles*. On any showing, Henry Crawford's seduction of Mrs. Rushworth was an offence against morality, a plain breach of the Seventh Commandment; and Julia's simultaneous elopement with Mr. Yates was an offence against manners, or in other words, conventon. All those who were concerned with the private theatricals appear again, though now in misery, humiliation and disgrace. But they are not all smitten in the same way nor look at things in the same light. Sir Thomas Bertram felt "the guilt and infamy" of Maria Rushworth's adultery, and, upright man as he was, could distinguish between the sin and vice (the words are his own) of her conduct, and the folly of her sister Julia's; and he blamed himself for not having given more attention to the upbringing and education of his daughters. Mrs. Norris, at first quieted and stupefied by the news, quickly discovered the scapegoat: "Had Fanny accepted Mr. Crawford this could not have happened." Mary Crawford on the other hand, in her last interview with Edmund could see nothing in it but "folly". "No harsher name than folly given! So voluntarily, so freely, so coolly, to canvass it! No reluctance, no horror, no feminine, shall I say, no modest loathings? This is what the world does. For where, Fanny, shall we find a woman whom nature had so richly endowed? Spoiled, spoiled!" That is how Edmund described it to his cousin.

Then follows the "tidying-up" which concludes all Jane Austen's novels. Maria's *liaison* with Henry Crawford lasted only six months; they became "each other's punishment" and agreed to separate. Maria went to live with Mrs. Norris "in another country, remote and private" where "it may be reasonably

supposed that their tempers became their mutual punishment";
but at least "Mrs. Norris's removal from Mansfield was the great
supplementary comfort of Sir Thomas's life". We do not know
what became of Henry Crawford, nor does it matter. His sister,
Mary, on the other hand, does matter; for she had a culture and
wit, a capacity for kindness, and a candour, which sometimes
remind us of Elizabeth Bennet. But she had no principles. Her
outlook was secular, worldly, and frankly cynical about religion.
Despite her openly expressed contempt for the clergy, she
became genuinely in love with Edmund; and though he realized
that their outlook differed, Mary never did. She was also really
fond of her sister and brother-in-law, the Grants; and his
appointment to a Canonry at Westminster came in the nick of
time to make it possible for them to offer her a permanent home
in London. One may hope that she found a husband after all.

Meanwhile we are left with Edmund and Fanny—a much
chastened Edmund who had seen how near his blindness and
indecision had led him to a disastrous marriage, and Fanny whose
whole life had been so full of chastening that she now had little
except joy to look forward to. Lovers of *Mansfield Park* tend to
set their hearts on Fanny Price; and hers is indeed a beautiful
character. Shy, diffident, humble and infinitely unselfish, she has
firm Christian principles to which she adheres with rock-like
consistency; and she has also fire. In the soliloquy which Jane
Austen puts in her mouth after reading one of Edmund's letters
of indecision, Fanny's fire breaks into flame. "Finish it at once.
Let there be an end of this suspense. Fix, commit, condemn
yourself!" One can be sure that Fanny made not only an excellent
parson's wife, but also that she filled in the fatal deficiency in
Edmund's character, so that they could do together what he could
never have done by himself.

For Edmund, who was the hero in the novel, had principles
too; the same Church principles and ideals which Fanny had,
and he could stand up for them with conviction. It is sometimes
said that Edmund was a prig. But I do not see him in that light.
The revealing scene in the private chapel (now unused for a
generation) in the great house at Sotherton; the sarcastic remarks
of Mary Crawford's that "in those days—the parsons were very
inferior even to what they are now"—a remark for which she
apologises a little later on discovering that Edmund was to be
ordained—lead on to a conversation in the grounds outside when
Edmund's motive and vocation to ordination are set out with a
sustained warmth and conviction, sometimes rising to indignation,
which I feel sure are Jane Austen's own. His reasons for wishing
to be ordained are carefully given; his insistence that a clergyman
should expect a competence to live on; his admission that *some*
clergymen have unworthy motives and are indolent and his claim
that this was no ground for accusing *all*—all these shew the depth

and sincerity of his mind. And we gather later not only from the cynical comments and proposals of Mary Crawford and her brother but also from Sir Thomas Bertram's expectations that Edmund intended to reside in his parish. "A parish has wants and claims," says Sir Thomas, "which can be known only by a clergyman constantly resident"; and Edmund follows a moment later with, "Sir Thomas undoubtedly understands the duties of a parish priest." This is the only place in the novels, I think, where the endearing term "parish priest" is used; and it is significant of Jane Austen's view of Edmund. He may have been dull perhaps—though I am not so sure; but at least he was really good.

I have given this full space to *Mansfield Park* because it seems to me to go to the root of my subject. But there are, of course, others who must be briefly mentioned. The gouty Mr. Norris dies very early, leaving a dreadful wife behind him, of whom the less said the better. He was succeeded by Mr. Grant who is described as "indolent"; but Mrs. Grant, I think, must have been an attractive and kindly woman, able to make of the Mansfield parsonage a real social centre.

We come then to *Northanger Abbey* and the Morlands, father and son, and to Henry Tilney. The father was a "squarson", to use an old phrase—that is, both incumbent and patron of his living; blessed too with some private income of his own, and able to be handsome towards his daughters, but in no other way; not given to wit unless it were a pun, just as his wife preferred a proverb. One flaw alone he had to mar his perfect respectability, and that was given to him at his christening. His name was Richard. His son, James, who was an undergraduate at Oxford, was, I suspect, of his father's type; but as two and a half years must still elapse before he was ordained, it is hard to estimate how good a clergyman he would be. John Thorpe who knew James at Oxford swears that James was "one of the finest fellows in the world"; but as he was making his addresses to Catherine at the time, that was not surprising. Let us hope that there was something in it. According to Isabella, James's favourite colour was purple. But I cannot think that he ever reached it. James Morland and Henry Tilney are alike in this that our authoress's interest in them seems to be as potential husbands for her heroines. Otherwise they differ completely. Henry is a most attractive character; a man of the world in the best sense and fundamentally steady, but enjoying gaiety; a pleasant "tease"; and with sartorial interests which the fair sex often find agreeable. At that time there was little, if anything, to choose between a clergyman and a layman in dress, except in church; the day of Fielding's Parson Adams, who was wearing his cassock when tossed into a ditch, was gone, and that of the dog-collar had not yet come. Henry always bought his own cravats, and his taste was much admired; and unlike most clergymen, he could give quite a long dissertation on the best muslins for a lady's gown, and where to buy them at least cost. But what of his pastoral duties? One might think that he was so often at Bath or at Northanger that he cannot have been much in his parish at Woodston. Yet in fact he appears to have been normally there for Sundays, and sometimes for a meeting and other duties which kept him for three or four days longer. More decisive than anything, to my mind, is the fact that he kept his dogs there. That meant that Woodston was his home. And I surmise that when he brought his sweet Catherine there too, they were both of them so happy that they had no wish to go away from it for long. In that case Mrs. Hughes was right when she reported Henry Tilney as "a very fine young man, and likely to do very well".

We pass to *Emma* and Mr. Elton. Mr. Knightley's sketch of his character in the eighth chapter is borne out in the sequel. Fundamentally Mr. Elton is a man "in the make"; and having failed to marry money and position, he contented himself with marrying money and vulgarity. He was already self-satisfied and self-important when he married; and it is clear that, if ever these ambitious fires tended to die down, Mrs. Elton would bring her bellows and fan them into flame again. His refusal to dance with Harriet, who was without a partner, shews him to have been selfish too. Moreover, he was handsome and knew it, and was a great favourite wherever he went, not least in church; Miss Nash, indeed, even put down all the texts he had ever preached from since coming to the parish. Mr. Knightley was partly ironical when he described Mr. Elton as "a very good sort of man, and a very respectable Vicar of Highbury", and Emma was wholly so when she spoke of him as "the standard of perfection in Highbury both in person and mind". But he must have had his points. The occasion when Emma and Harriet met him visiting a poor and suffering family as they came out, and the discussion on how best to help them, is not the only indication in the book of his parish interests. And it was he who officiated at the wedding of the two who had read his character so well. That cataclysm of repentance which pervades the last eight chapters of *Emma*, in which Jane Austen makes the great words penitence, contrition and forgiveness ring out so plainly, had swept into its stream all that "small band of true friends who witnessed the ceremony"—Harriet and Frank Churchill and Jane Fairfax as well as the bride and bridegroom themselves; and I like to think that the Vicar's inability to tell his wife what everyone was wearing was due to the fact that he too had felt something of the spirit that was there.

Finally there is *Persuasion* and its two parsons. Mr Charles Hayter lived with his father, six miles away from his curacy; he was good-natured and cultivated; he had hopes "of getting something from the Bishop in the course of a year or two"; and he was certainly not of a practical turn of mind. However, he married his cousin, Henrietta Musgrove. Let us leave it at that. There lived close by a clergyman of very different mettle. Of all Jane Austen's clergymen, I think that Dr. Shirley, Rector of Uppercross "who for more than forty years had been zealously discharging all the duties of his office" is the one whom Jane Austen herself held in highest affection and esteem. "Dr. and Mrs. Shirley, who have been doing good all their lives"—could he not be persuaded to go and live seventeen miles away at Lyme Regis? Probably not, because "he is so strict and scrupulous in his notions." Many years ago I knew such a country parson, though he had been sixty years, not forty, in his parish. He was at Rugby under Dr. Arnold; and he was now over ninety. As I reached his Rectory, he was just back from a sick visit to a farmer, a mile and a half away in the downs. And he had christened and married the majority of his parishioners, and throughout had taught the children in day school as well as Sunday School. Eventually his family prevailed on him to retire. But let no-one underestimate the value of the continuous witness of such a country parson and his home. None knew it better than the father of English poetry, who has sometimes been called also the father of the English novel, Geoffrey Chaucer.

> Yet he neglected not in rain or thunder,
> In sickness or in grief to pay a call
> On the remotest whether great or small.
>
> He stayed at home and watched over his fold
> So that no wolf should make the sheep miscarry.
> He was a shepherd and no mercenary.
> Holy and virtuous he was, but then
> Never contemptuous of sinful men,
> Never disdainful, never proud or fine,
> But was discreet in teaching and benign.
>
> Christ and His Twelve Apostles and their lore
> He taught, but followed it himself before.

E. G. SELWYN

THE JANE AUSTEN SOCIETY

Report for the year 1960

THE JANE AUSTEN SOCIETY

(Founded in 1940 by Dorothy G. Darnell)

THE JANE AUSTEN SOCIETY

Report for the year 1960

Membership

Fifty-six new members joined the Society during the year, of whom eleven became Life Members. In addition, six existing members became Life Members.

Membership now stands at 825, of whom twenty-three live in the Commonwealth, one hundred and four in the U.S.A., and ten in other countries abroad.

Members are reminded that subscriptions are due on 1st January, and that this Report is the only reminder that they will receive. The Hon. Secretary would much appreciate prompt payment of the 5/- subscription, and will gladly provide a Bankers' Order form.

Annual General Meeting, 1960

The Annual General Meeting was held on Saturday, 16th July, at Chawton House, by kind permission of Major and Mrs. Edward Knight, when some 350 members and their friends were present.

The President of the Society, His Grace the Duke of Wellington, K.G., presided, and in his opening remarks spoke of the loss sustained by the Society in the death of Dr. R. W. Chapman, one of the Vice-Presidents. He asked that the minutes of the previous Annual Meeting be taken as read. There were no matters arising.

The Hon. Secretary presented the Report for 1959, and, in the absence of the Hon. Treasurer, the Accounts. The motion was seconded by Mr. Ralph Dutton, and carried.

The Election of Officers followed. The Hon. Secretary proposed the re-election of the Duke of Wellington as President, Mr. T. Edward Carpenter as Vice-President and Mr. John Gore as Chairman. This was seconded by Mr. Peter Knatchbull-Hugessen, and carried.

The President proposed the re-election, en bloc, of the Committee.

The meeting was addressed by Mr. John Gore, on "First Impressions . . . and Last", and by the Duke of Wellington on the "Houses in the Novels". Both of these addresses are printed in full at the end of this Report.

Mr. Carpenter was to have addressed the meeting, but unfortunately his train to London was held up, and in consequence he missed the train to Alton.

After the meeting members were able to see some photographs taken by Mr. Butler-Kearney in Jane Austen's House, of two descendants of Jane Austen's brothers ; Mrs. Shervington in a dress of the period, and Sarah Jenkyns in a dress which had belonged to Jane Austen.

The President closed the meeting with thanks to Major and Mrs. Knight for lending the house. Members had tea provided in aid of Chawton Church funds, for which nearly £50 was raised.

" Jane Austen in London "

Miss Winifred Watson's booklet " Jane Austen in London " was on sale after the meeting, when one hundred and twenty-eight copies were sold. Copies of Miss Winifred Watson's booklet can be obtained from the Hon. Secretary, price 3/6d. or 3/10d. by post.

Annual General Meeting, 1961

The Annual General Meeting will be held at Chawton House on Saturday, 15th July. The meeting will be addressed by Dr. Andrew H. Wright, Associate Professor of English at Ohio State University, who will speak on " Jane Austen from an American viewpoint."

Jane Austen Memorial Trust

Mr. T. Edward Carpenter, the Chairman, states that in spite of the bad weather, there were 3,903 visitors to Chawton Cottage during the year. He has redecorated one of the rooms on the first floor, and is arranging a running story of Jane Austen's homes, which will be engrossed by Miss Gertrude George. Above this will appear photographs and prints of the various places where she stayed. The Chief Librarians of Southampton, Bath and Winchester have helped Mr. Carpenter to find these.

Mr. Carpenter has also acquired two important relics. One is a silk shawl which belonged to Jane Austen. The other is the first edition of 1682 of Hooke's *"Ecclesiastical Polity"*, which has been presented to Mr. Carpenter by Croydon Corporation, through its Librarian, as a tribute to his work at Chawton Cottage. The interest in this large folio edition is that it came from the Fowle family, and is intimately associated with the Rev. John Fowle, the fiancé of Cassandra Austen, who died in the West Indies in 1797.

Correction

In an article published in the Report for 1959, I said that Jane Austen had two rings, each set with a December birth-stone : a turquoise and a garnet. The garnet ring, however, now in the possession of Mrs. Shervington, was not Jane Austen's, but belonged to a member of the family. The turquoise ring only was her personal property. I must apologize to the Austen family for this blunder and to readers of last year's Report.

ELIZABETH JENKINS

Dr. R. W. Chapman

Dr. Chapman's great reputation as a scholar and critic has been honoured in many publications since his death in April, 1960. Mr. John Gore in his obituary in *The Sphere* wrote that Dr. Chapman was for decades a well-known figure who was "an indivisible part of Oxford". Of Dr. Chapman's editions of Jane Austen's novels and letters, Mr. Gore says: "they will never be superseded as authorities. He put into them all his scholarship, years of research and a strictness in the sifting of evidence worthy of a Lord Chief Justice." He added: "I often wonder what Jane Austen would have felt if she could have foreseen that every word of almost every sentence she scribbled down at odd moments on her little desk at Chawton Cottage would one day be examined and tested, as through a microscope, by a great scholar." But he recalls one of Dr. Chapman's delightful aspects when he says: "he had a great sense of humour and proportion and was never pompous in his textual criticism."

My own memory of the Doctor is of a friend who, though awe-inspiring and severe, was kindness itself. When the Jane Austen Society was founded in 1940, it was Dr. Chapman's taking an interest in it, using his great influence on behalf of it, and giving us his invaluable suggestions and advice, that were largely responsible for the Society's having attained its present position. He was so critical and austere that it was an alarming experience to receive his opinions, though a wholesome one. This made it more charming that he should be so sympathetic with Jane Austen's heroines! Their youth and charm delighted him and he would take their part as if he had known them personally.

We can hardly say how much we owe to him or how great is our sense of loss.   E.J.

Photographs taken at Chawton Cottage

The Committee of the Jane Austen Society had photographs taken in Chawton Cottage in April, 1960. The idea had been a long-standing one. The strong family likeness in Mrs. Rupert Shervington to the sketch of Jane Austen, made by Cassandra

Austen and the possession by Mrs. Jenkyns, Jane Austen's great grand-niece, of a garment, with the claim of an unexceptionable pedigree to be Jane Austen's, made the Committee anxious to have a photographic record of the two.

The garment came to Mrs. Jenkyns, through one intermediary, from Jane Austen's niece Marianne Knight. It is made of bombazine, a shot brown and yellow with raised yellow spots. It has a high collar and long sleeves and opens all the way down the front like a coat, but the thinness of the material raised some doubts at first as to whether it could have been meant for outdoor wear. However, fashion books of the time say that, in 1806 for example, pelisses were worn of cambric and muslin, in comparison with which the bombazine is almost substantial. Although Jane Austen, writing to her sister on 25th January, 1801, described herself as "a tall woman", she was, it seems, not as tall as her great, great grand-niece Diana Shervington. To take the photographs, therefore, we put Mrs. Shervington into theatrical period costume, while the pelisse was worn by Jane Austen's great, great, great grand-niece, Miss Sarah Jenkyns.

It is interesting to see that, in the letter already mentioned, Jane Austen says she means to have for summer dresses, one brown cambric, and one white and yellow muslin, so the colours of the pelisse appear to have been among those she liked; while the letters contain several references to bombazine.

The photographs taken by Mr. Butler-Kearney, of which three are reproduced in this Report, were arranged to include something personally connected with Jane Austen. In that on the cover, Mrs. Shervington's pose has been copied from Cassandra Austen's sketch of her sister. In the one in silhouette, Mrs. Shervington is sitting at the work table said to have been Jane Austen's property. The third photograph shows Miss Sarah Jenkyns, wearing the pelisse, standing at the window which was cut in the wall of the living-room by Edward Knight, né Austen, when his mother and sisters took possession of the Cottage in 1809.

Sanditon and Bognor
by Lindsay Fleming

Sanditon, Jane Austen's last unfinished novel, describes the founding of a seaside resort.

Such a topic was no doubt in that era matter of common talk, but one may enquire whether any more direct inspiration might have suggested to Jane Austen the structure of her tale. The place that would appear most nearly akin to Sanditon in its history and appearance at the appropriate time was Bognor, or Hothampton as it was then sometimes named, and the prototype of the enthusiastic projector Mr. Parker could have been Sir Richard Hotham who founded Bognor as a seaside resort in the

latter years of the 18th century. The characteristics applied by the novelist to Mr. Parker (pp. 20-21, 23, 103) belonged in reality to Sir Richard Hotham. Hotham had just such aspirations as did Mr. Parker. William Hayley testified to Hotham's generous disposition, and George Romney "was pleased with the cheerful adventurous disposition of that commercial Knight." Miss Lascelles says she is sure the Parkers lost money by their venture.[1] Sir Richard Hotham did.

If Jane Austen never came to Bognor, it is possible she may have seen a copy of *The Origin and Description of Bognor*, by Dr. J. B. Davis (1807), or of *A New and Complete Guide to Bognor* (1814), as there are passages in "Sanditon" that would seem to echo paragraphs in these Guides. Mr. Parker's eulogy of Sanditon—"The finest, purest sea breeze on the coast—acknowledged to be so—excellent bathing—fine hard sand—deep water 10 yards from the shore—no mud—no weeds—-no sharp rocks— never was there a place more palpably designed by Nature for the invalid"—is almost a précis of this boost of Bognor in the 1807 *Origin of Bognor*.

"No spot on the coast of England is perhaps better calculated for the twofold purpose of sea-bathing and retirement than Bognor. Erected on the borders of a firm and sandy beach that extends for several miles from east to west, and commanding a wide expanse of sea, it is in every respect convenient, and desirable for those, who, in pursuit of pleasure, or of health, seek the renovating influence of maritime abodes.

"It must be obvious to every observer, that as there are no intervening objects to check the free passage of the air to this shore, it is here met with in a state of purity, a circumstance of the highest importance to those who are obliged rather to depend upon the sea breezes for restoration to health, than upon immersion in the briny fluid. Nor is this convenience, great as it may be, the only one. To the advantage of having a large tract of sand, very firm and compact, exposed at low water for pedestrian exercise, or recreation on horseback, or in a carriage, an agreeable descent of the coast may justly be added; inasmuch as it affords vast facility and comfort to those who bathe, and moreover inspires the timid with confidence and courage, when they commit themselves to the arms of Neptune."

These further passages may be compared:

In *Sanditon*: "In this row were the best Milliner's shop & the Library—a little detached from it, the Hotel & Billiard Room— Here began the Descent to the Beach, & to the Bathing Machines —& this was therefore the favourite spot for Beauty and Fashion".

---

[1] Mary Lascelles, *Jane Austen and her Art* (1948), p. 181.

View of Bognor

176

"Mr. P. could not be satisfied without an early visit to the Library, and the Library Subscription book . . . "

In *Origin of Bognor*: "This view of Bognor [see accompanying plate] is taken from one of the Bathing machines. It represents the Fox Hotel, and a smaller building, that comprises the Subscription room, the Milliner's shop, the Library and the Warm baths".

In *Sanditon*: "The Library of course, afforded every thing; all the useless things in the World that could not be done without, & among so many pretty Temptations . . . she took up a Book; it happened to be a vol: of Camilla. She had not Camilla's Youth, and had no intention of having her Distress,—so, she turned from the Drawers of rings and Broches, repressed farther solicitation and paid for what she bought."

In *Guide to Bognor*, 1814: "The Subscription-room is in a building erected still nearer to the sea than the Hotel . . . The Library is underneath the Subscription-room. The present proprietor, Mr. Binstead, has taken great pains to make it a desirable resort for intellectual amusement. A few years ago, it merely contained some indifferent novels: but now the visitor may find in this improved Library a very good collection of the most popular modern romances, novels, and tales, as well as a great variety of voyages, travels, memoirs, &c. Neither do books constitute the whole of its treasures. The proprietor has diversified his Library with an assortment of fancy articles, jewelry music, prints, colours, Tunbridge ware, &c. so that this may be justly said to be the only place of resort for those who seek to vary the tranquil pleasures of retirement by the recreations of a Library. He has added to the enjoyments of the place by providing a very excellent billiard table."

In *Sanditon*: "She . . . secured a proper House at 8 g pr week for Mrs. G.—"

In *Guide to Bognor*, 1814: "Houses may be hired at from three to twelve guineas per week in the height of the season."

If Jane Austen was casting about for a surname for one of her leading protagonists she might have thought not inappropriate to borrow a distinctive name belonging to one of the principal landowners of the Bognor district in 1817, that of William Brereton.

Editorial Note: Ingenious if unsupported by evidence. Contemporary guides to other rising watering-places offer similar parallels with *Sanditon*.

Jane Austen and Canals
Maurice Berrill

In the introduction to his edition of "Jane Austen's Letters" (Oxford University Press, second edition, 1952), Dr. R. W. Chapman wrote: "A familiar complaint is that they [the letters] have nothing to say about the great events that were shaking Europe— a kind of negative criticism seldom elsewhere applied to family correspondence." Be this as it may, there are many incidental references to matters of a more parochial nature and three of these references are to canals. This is not really surprising since Jane Austen, who was born in 1775 and died in 1817, witnessed the period of the "canal mania". Perhaps the surprising thing is that she should have mentioned them so little.

During a visit to Bath, Jane wrote on Tuesday, 5th May, 1801 to her sister Cassandra, then at Up Hurstbourne, Andover, and concluded her letter by the brief statement: "Last night we walked by the Canal"—presumably the Kennet and Avon where it runs through Sidney Gardens.

A week later, on Tuesday, 12th May, 1801, Jane again wrote to Cassandra and towards the end of her letter remarked: "My uncle . . . and I are soon to take the long-plann'd walk to the Cassoon." This is obviously the "Caisson" or lift with a vertical rise of 46 feet at Combe Hay on the Somersetshire Coal Canal. The Caisson Lock was built about 1798 by Robert Weldon and had already been abandoned by the time of Jane Austen's visit in favour of an inclined plane suggested by Benjamin Outram. The inclined plane then proved unsatisfactory and by 1805 a flight of twenty-two locks had been substituted, under the management of a joint committee of the Kennet and Avon, Wilts and Berks and Somersetshire Coal Canal Companies.

In April, 1811, Jane Austen was in London, staying in Sloane Street. She wrote to Cassandra on 30th April: "I congratulate Edward [her brother, of Godmersham Park, Kent] on the Weald of Kent Canal Bill being put off till another Session, as I have just had the pleasure of reading. There is always something to be hoped from Delay:

> Between Session and Session
> The first Prepossession
> May rouse up the Nation
> And the villainous Bill
> May be forced to lie still
> Against Wicked Men's will."

The precise reason for the family's objection to the proposed Weald of Kent Canal is not clear and indeed the Act was passed in 1812 for a line of canal from the river Medway at Brandbridges, near East Peckham to the Royal Military Canal near Appledore, projected by Rennie, though the work was never carried out. Was Godmersham Park, perhaps, on the intended line of construction?

THE ANNUAL ADDRESS

First Impressions . . . and Last

I have called my paper "First Impressions and Last". It is a reasonably descriptive caption. Certainly I am not an authority on Jane Austen, but, holding a dignified sinecure in your Society, I pay attention often enough to those who claim to be so.

I am sometimes puzzled by the extravagancies of some of Jane Austen's fans and admiring critics alike. Her fans allow no criticism of her as a woman. Her literary critics examine every other sentence she wrote down in her novels to estimate its *pre-meditated* art. I think both go too far. The little we know of her admirable character—derived chiefly from her family letters—does not justify us in treating her as a super-woman, while her private life and letters are irrelevant to higher criticism of her novels. She was certainly a super-novelist but she was a very human and humble-minded woman, and in her circumstances quite likely to be thought ordinary enough in some quarters. She was a witty woman and wit is never premeditated. Great novels are not built up with prefabricated phrases. They grow of themselves like great oaks nourished by some rare quality in the soil in which they are rooted; but no doubt the *Dolly Dialogues* or Saki's *Reginald* can owe their brilliance to prefabricated fireworks.

Except for conceding that personal experiences *must* be one source of all artistic creation, the woman and the novelist are surely two, not one. Both are rightly subjects for criticism, but *separately* and not too meticulously. We know very little of the inner life of authors or indeed of our nearest and dearest. Outward circumstances tell us very little. *John Inglesant* was written by a Birmingham dynamite manufacturer, who never saw Italy. With Jane Austen, the story's the thing and I sometimes think her critics lose sight of the wood for the trees. She, I am sure, never expected, never would have wished, that posterity (if she thought of posterity) should make her out either a saint or a wizard, or otherwise *mummify* her. What is more dreadful than the female novelist who never dismounts from her Pegasus?

Pride and Prejudice was the first novel to which I was introduced; it was read to me by my Mother a year before I went to a private school. Reading aloud was a drawing-room pastime, and novels read out-loud, if well read, have a strong claim on our life-long loyalty and love. *Pride and Prejudice* remains my first favourite among the world's novels. My Mother had no more desire or perhaps ability to judge *Pride and Prejudice* critically than I had in 1894, or indeed have now. To us it was a delightful and amusing story, and I do not doubt that its continued popularity with the general public is due less to its literary merits, as discovered to us by trained critics, than to the fact that its plot is the age-old Cinderella fairy story that takes so many forms. And, after all, it is we, the average readers, faithful to this or that novel generation after generation, who have selected the classic novels. Critics never established or denied a classic. I sometimes smile when they "seed" for us "the twelve best". They are only playing a game with the counters we supplied to them. And what a game it is which puts *War and Peace*, *Moby Dick*, *Pride and Prejudice* and *Wuthering Heights* into the same pack.

I still read *Pride and Prejudice*, then, with uncritical delight. But not without twinges of sharp pain. I still suffer agonies for Jane and Elizabeth when their Mother's vulgarity reaches its nightmare heights while Darcy and Bingley are guests at their dinner table; and I have felt that Somerset Maugham made no shrewder suggestion than that Miss Austen might with advantages have made Jane and Elizabeth the daughters of an earlier and wiser marriage. For my part, I positively *like* to think that Jane Austen lived and died "an amateur", and am never made unhappy by the charge of provincialism. Genius is clear-sighted and can recognize its own merits. She lived just long enough to learn of the high commendation accorded her by acknowledged literary lions of her day; but her desire for anonymity withheld from her, even in her own family circle, a successful author's confirmation by the public of her literary status. Time mercifully spared her a T/V interview by flatterers. I feel sure she never saw herself as a classic and I think her genius can best be appreciated by her admirers today by refusing to set her up in white marble in a niche. Rather we should acknowledge her handicaps and even weaknesses, the better to establish the full miracle of her genius, and see to it that "still the wonder grew how one small head could carry all she knew."

The library of *Austeniana* contains at least a dozen important books; I have derived particular confirmation for my own opinions about her and *Pride and Prejudice* from two: Margaret Kennedy's admirable short study in the *English Novelists* series and Somerset Maugham's *Ten novels and their authors*. Mr. Maugham, I believe, got many a sour look from the Jane Austen Society. He had laid impious hands on the marble statue in the shrine. He had gone so far as to call her "provincial." But both he and Margaret Kennedy (who raised no hackles on Janeites) appear to regard *Pride and Prejudice* as on the whole the best constructed of her novels and surely estimate her worth, if not next idolatry, yet as near idolatry as her votaries can ask. After all, Maugham ranks it high among the world's ten best.

"*Provincialism*" is perhaps as difficult to define today as "Gentleman." It was not so difficult in the early nineteenth century. If one defined it (for those days) as the inability to be one's natural self in any sort of company, high or humble, and the inability to discuss easily the latest trends and fashions of London and to speak the language of London, *that* would perhaps embrace the essentials, and I very much doubt if that definition would not (from the little we know of her) rope in Jane Austen. I think she was vulnerable to slights. Her own family was of the parsonage, and when (encouraged by Fanny Burney's triumphant proof that "lady scribblers" need not earn social ridicule) she sat down to write *First Impressions*, the vast gulf between the dignitaries of the Church and the parish priests and curates had only recently been narrowed. Social and religious changes had brought about this improvement in the status of the parson. Fielding and Richardson could give their parsons the happy ending of marrying the lady's maid and, as Margaret Kennedy observes, Richardson and Jane Austen died in the same reign. But before she died, the Oxford Movement was already stirring for its coming march in 1833.

Anyhow, the change in status of the parson was of recent growth; it brought it about that culture and education in the parsonage suddenly became and was recognized to be superior to the culture of the average Squire which, God knows, was not remarkable. It is reasonable to suppose that the cruel portraits of the Adams' and Trullibers, still kept in memory, might incite in the children of the parsonage a tendency to assert their own superior culture and to look down on the lack of it in many of their richer neighbours. I think it likely that Jane Austen decided that Mr. Bennett should be a Squire who preferred "an hour in his library" to an hour among his turnips or his cattle, in order to counteract the vulgarity of his wife and so comfort her darling Elizabeth. If, as Maugham impiously hints, Jane herself in girlhood perhaps spoke with a Hampshire accent, might not that fact, if it suggested provincialism, enhance the greatness of her achievements? An Oxford don called Dante provincial and presumably it described young Shakespeare.

One more incontestable social feature of her time is worth noting. Between the commonalty and the peerage there stood an artificial gulf—perhaps a ha-ha would be a better word—which convention accepted then. And under this convention the commonalty somehow tolerated, if it never excused, an insolence and patronage asserted by a few stupid members of the aristocracy which in modern eyes appears inexplicable, and was based on an article of faith in the superiority of their order. "Lady Catherines" were certainly larger than life-size, and it would be boring to belabour a dead donkey, if it were not that novels of high society—from Trollope to Emily Eden—*published as late as 1860*, photographically prove how very slowly this artificial ditch levelled up.

These facts of social history are relevant to judging the artistic rightness of the chief comedians of the novel, among whom Lady Catherine, Mr. Collins and Mrs. Bennet are clearly in the lead. You and I, the general readers, accept them gratefully and uncritically. We would not have them less foolish than they are shown us. Indeed, artistic balance and blind justice may have decided Jane Austen that Darcy must have as much cause to be ashamed of his Aunt, as Elizabeth of her Mother. When critics, going to another extreme of criticism, tell us that Jane Austen's men are too often cut out of cardboard, we can at least reply that they are substantial enough to fulfil the destinies she designed for her heroines—and that that suits us and her heroines. For you and me, the story's the thing.

But Mr. Maugham is a novelist of world renown and is entitled to apply his own skilled methods to his critical duty. He finds both Lady Catherine and Mr. Collins a trifle too grease-painted and farcical to be justified in pure comedy, but hedges with the opinion that pure comedy is not destroyed by the introduction of a modicum of farce. I cannot doubt that he is right in believing that a daughter of the Parsonage in 1800 would be vulnerable to slights from the aristocracy of her day (with whom she had but slight intimate acquaintance) and would be moved to uphold the higher culture of the "new" clergy over the slower advancing Squirearchy. I make no doubt that, when she and Cassandra paid their long visits to their kindest of brothers, the lucky Edward, in Kent, they experienced occasional slights in their treatment by his Kentish neighbours, and that they may have appeared as rather provincial ladies to that society of class-conscious landowners and M.P.s who enjoyed a closer acquaintance with London ways. And I *cannot* condemn, as many Janeites do, the "ingratitude" of Fanny Knatchbull in that famous letter hinting as much, written years afterwards in a sincere and reluctant effect to supply (what is so rare in our knowledge of Jane Austen) an authoritative light on her personality by an eye-witness.

Some critics, too (Harold Nicolson, or Professor Garrard, for instance) have stressed this provincialism in her surviving letters to Cassandra, and it is true that some of her criticisms of neighbours partake more of smartness than of wit. No one has been more generous than Mr. Maugham in defending them, for he says that the dying art of letter-writing is essentially to transcribe ordinary, intimate every-day conversation with pen and ink, and he compares Jane's letters very favourably with the stilted letters of men and women who wrote with an eye on future publication.

What's the odds if in her youth she accepted that the only happy destiny for portionless daughters lay in marriage, and if in consequence she considered marriage more coolly than passionately? The inward thoughts of men and women are not triable, and if the chief proofs that Jane could understand passion, are but an added sentence or two in her last novel or that enchanted scene of shy lovers meeting in Pemberley Park, we know still far too little about her to pontificate. What matter if Jane and Cassandra

182

appeared a little provincial to others more concerned with keeping up with the London Joneses? We know that her conversation with her intimates was a little nearer the frankness common in Fielding's day than was that of the society she met in Kent. In her novels, of course, she followed gracefully the then current convention of formalised speech in novel conversations. Achievement is best measured by the overcoming of handicaps, and genius which flowers on stony ground, is more wonderful than that generated in a hothouse. T. S. Eliot once said: "A great writer's disabilities often stand him in good stead."

Is the novelist's art, are manifestations of genius, *spontaneous* or are they achieved by infinite and deliberate adjustment with technical instruments? George Moore was not the pattern of all novelists in his massive exercise of meticulous revision. How often in novels, in plays, in political oratory, has a sentence emerged to hearten, delight or inspire generations in posterity which clearly slipped out *ex tempore*, sometimes even "regardless of grammar." *(Churchill's* "some *chicken*", *for instance.)* Apply that theory to one of Jane Austen's "immortal phrases." Mr. Collins, you recall, switched from Jane to Elizabeth very quickly. He did it "while Mrs. Bennet was stirring the fire." Critics have invited us, not without justification, to note what a bright and broad beam those seven words throw not only on Mrs. Bennet's posterior, but on her ulterior motives and character. But, I ask myself, were those seven words one of those premeditated gems which sent her scurrying and smiling to her little desk, or were they just a part of her daily stint composed between mixing Mrs. Austen's medicine or taking the jam off the boil? It *is* possible to elaborate too much, and in considering these seven words *I* do not stop to enquire, as Mr. Bennet of Collins: "May we ask if these pleasing attentions proceed from the impulse of the moment or are the result of previous study?"

I think Jane Austen thought and wrote wittily as a matter of routine and I am quite prepared to swallow not only her provincialism but to believe that she lived and died an amateur (as severe literary critics might define that word), a state which has never appeared shameful to a great man or woman who possessed the eternal humility of true greatness. At any rate, I am sure that the vital elements—the gaiety, the acute observation, the pure spirit of comedy, which makes *Pride and Prejudice* an everlasting delight, were contained in *First Impressions* before it was revised at Chawton and published under the title, borrowed *inter alia* from *Cecilia*, that labels its fame. And *First Impressions* quite certainly was the work of an amateur.

SOME amateur! *Some* chicken! Don't let us put her in the Deep Freeze.

JOHN GORE

Lacock Abbey from an engraving in Jones' Views 1829
It is suggested that Jane Austen had this house in mind when describing Northanger Abbey

Houses in Jane Austen's Novels
(Reprinted by permission of the Editor of the *Spectator*)

Jane Austen cared nothing for the visual arts. I am not sure she did not regard them as a snare likely to entrap those who should more properly be occupied exclusively with the study of the beauties of nature. It is true that she makes Elinor Dashwood draw and Henry Tilney and his sister talk about sketching, though it does not appear that they actually sketched much. But this sort of painting was intended to be merely a flattering imitation of Nature. To any other kind of painting, to sculpture and to architecture, she is, to put it as temperately as possible, indifferent. But, unfortunately, people have to live in houses, and the sort of houses they live in may enter pretty deeply into any presentation of their character and manner of life. Jane Austen cannot, therefore, quite get away from domestic architecture, and her powers of observation were so extraordinarily acute that the references she makes to houses are telling enough to enable us to construct them in our imagination.

Let us take some of the houses in the order of their age and try to visualize them. There are two Abbeys, Northanger and Donwell. Northanger, both inside and out, is described as fully as any house in the novels. It lay low and no distant view of it was possible, as might be expected of an Abbey. It had an "old" porch. This had doubtless been added by the son or grandson of the Tilney, who became possessed of the property at the time of the Dissolution. A porch in the sense of a projecting roof supported by pillars could not possibly have been called "old", but the term might well be applied to a projecting bay which might have been added to the original monastic buildings in the sixteenth century. The windows of the drawing-room retained their pointed arches, but mullions and tracery had been removed and the rooms had been completely modernized. Externally, however, two sides of the quadrangle, were "rich in Gothic ornaments." These are difficult to visualize, and I am doubtful whether the author had any genuine monastic buildings clearly in mind when she wrote it. I have an impression—though I can adduce no facts in its support—that Jane Austen when writing about Northanger, was thinking of Lacock Abbey in Wiltshire, which she may well have seen on her journeys from Hampshire to Bath. But such an impression would have been a general one and would not go so far as to differentiate between richness and plainness of ornamental detail. Inside the house there was a broad oak staircase, richly carved, which sounds as though it had been inserted in late Stuart days, and we might hazard that the reception rooms were coeval with it. The best bedrooms had been furnished during the five years previous to Catherine Morland's visit in the manner of Hepplewhite or Sheraton. A little filling in of the outlines gives us a very clear picture of what Northanger was like.

Godmersham Park from an engraving in Neales Seats 1826

It is suggested that Jane Austen had this house in mind when describing Mansfield Park

Donwell was smaller than Northanger and its surroundings more formal and old-fashioned. It had large gardens and many trees in rows and avenues. The house covered a good deal of ground and was rambling and irregular, with many comfortable and one or two handsome rooms. As might have been expected it contained a large number of cabinets, probably of lacquer, stored with collections of shells, medals, cameos and corals. There were books of engravings, and those representing St. Mark's Place, Venice, and views of Switzerland were examined with particular attention by Mr. Woodhouse.

Sotherton was an Elizabethan house, a large, regular, brick building standing low. Towards the end of the seventeenth century much had been done to the "lay-out" round the house. An avenue, which was of a respectable size, about 110 years later, was planted from the West side of the house to the top of the hill. This avenue, together with the walls, bowling green and terrace walk bordered with fine iron railings, which dated from the same epoch, stood a bad chance of survival at the time the story was written, but we do not actually hear of their destruction. As Mr. Crawford was in favour of their removal, there seems every reason to hope that they were eventually spared. I am inclined to think that it was also Mr. Rushworth's great-grand-father who fitted up the chapel in James II's time. Jane Austen tells us that this was done with a profusion of mahogany, and this is one of her rare slips, as mahogany was not imported except in very small quantities till thirty years later. It is not so serious a slip as the apple blossom which the party assembled at Donwell saw at mid-summer. William Kent was dead when the rooms at Sotherton were furnished and decorated by Mr. Rushworth's grandfather in the 1760's, but I am inclined to think that their solid mahogany, rich damask, marble, carving and gilding smacked much more of his manner than the more finnikin style of Robert Adam, who had just returned from Italy and was beginning his successful career at that time. Sotherton was filled with family portraits which interested no one except Mrs. Rushworth.

Uppercross was obviously a William and Mary or Queen Anne House. It had "an old-fashioned square parlour, with a small carpet and shining floor". The walls were panelled and hung with portraits of ancestors, the men in brown velvet and the ladies in blue satin. These pictures were evidently Knellers or something like Knellers. The ever-indulgent Mr. and Mrs. Musgrove had allowed their daughters to import their harp, grand piano, flower-stands and small tables into these staid surroundings, and now we can all see what the parlour at Uppercross looked like.

There is not much to go on in forming a mental picture of Mansfield Park. It was a large house with two main floors and an attic storey lit by dormer windows in the roof. Fanny Price's bedroom was in an attic. The erection of the stage for the theatricals damaged the plasterwork, which was therefore in high relief. Very likely it was the work of the Italian plasterers, Artari or Bagutti, who decorated the houses of Gibbs and his contemporaries. Mansfield Park was, I conclude, a Palladian house dating from the 1730's or 1740's, and was very likely inspired by Godmersham, which Jane Austen knew so well.

Rosings was built by Sir Lewis de Bourgh and was almost certainly from the designs of Robert Adam. One of the fireplaces cost £800, and was no doubt quite the best that Carter, the great chimney-piece maker, could do for his clients, the Adam brothers.

There is nothing to tell one what Barton Park or Kellynch Hall looked like. Pemberley may have been an Elizabethan or Jacobean house as it had a gallery, but the furniture was all Chippendale or later. Although it does not form the background of any scene in *Sense and Sensibility*, Colonel Brandon's house, Delaford, is described by Mrs. Jennings in some detail. It was an old-fashioned place quite shut in with great garden walls. It had a dovecote, delightful stewponds, a pretty canal and an old yew arbour. In short it was a typical South Country manor house of the Wren period. Longbourn is difficult to date, but we know from the testimony of Lady Catherine de Bourgh that it had some decent rooms in it. Probably it was very much like Hartfield, which was a medium sized compact house dating from about 1770.

The parsonages are all characterized and none of them had any architectural pretensions, though we may for once agree with General Tilney in thinking that a patched-on bow would have ruined Woodston. The "viranda" at Uppercross Cottage was in the very latest fashion. Before we leave the architecture of Jane Austen's novels it may be noted that additional point is added to the futility of John Thorpe's drive to Blaise Castle by the fact that it was a brand new "castle" on which the paint had hardly dried at the time that Catherine Morland was made to shudder deliciously at its mediaeval terrors.

WELLINGTON

THE JANE AUSTEN SOCIETY

Report for the Year 1961

Charles Thomas Haden

190

THE JANE AUSTEN SOCIETY

Report for the Year 1961

Membership

Forty-seven new members joined during the year and there were eleven new Life Members. Total membership now numbers 865.

Members are reminded that subscriptions are due on 1st January and this Report is the only reminder that they will receive.

The Hon. Secretary would much appreciate prompt payment of the 5/- subscription, and will gladly provide a Bankers' Order form.

Annual General Meeting, 1961

The Annual General Meeting was held on Saturday, 15th July, at Chawton House, by kind permission of Major and Mrs. Edward Knight, when some 300 members and their friends were present.

In the absence of the President, Mr. John Gore, Chairman of the Society, presided.

Opening the meeting, the Chairman welcomed Dr. Andrew H. Wright, the speaker, and asked for the minutes of the last Annual General Meeting, which had been published in the Annual Report, to be taken as read. There were no matters arising.

The Hon. Secretary presented the Report for 1960. The motion was seconded by Major R. A. S. Hartman, and carried.

The Hon. Treasurer presented the accounts. The resolution was moved by Mr. Harmshaw, seconded by Mrs. Sarsfield-Hall, and carried.

The Hon. Secretary proposed the re-election of the Duke of Wellington as President, Mr. T. Edward Carpenter as Vice-President and Mr. John Gore as Chairman. This was seconded by Mr. Henry Burke, and carried.

The Chairman proposed the re-election, en bloc, of the Committee.

Mr. T. Edward Carpenter, gave an account of the work of the Jane Austen Memorial Trust.

The meeting was addressed by Dr. Andrew H. Wright, Associate Professor of English at Ohio State University, who spoke on an American Point of View of the Novels. A vote of thanks was proposed by Mrs. Robbins, seconded by Sir John Hubback, and carried.

The Chairman closed the meeting with a vote of thanks to Major and Mrs. Knight. Tea was provided in aid of Chawton Church funds, raising a sum of £38.

Chawton Church

The Jane Austen-Dorothy Darnell Memorial Pew in Chawton Church was dedicated by the Archdeacon of Basingstoke on Sunday, 8th January. Miss Beatrix Darnell was present.

In this Report will be found photographs showing details of the pew, and an interior of Chawton Church, showing its position, the second square-ended pew from the right.

Annual General Meeting, 1962

The Annual General Meeting will be held at Chawton House, on Saturday, 21st July, when Miss Margaret Lane (Countess of Huntingdon) will be the speaker.

Chawton Church

Chawton Cottage

Mr. T. Edward Carpenter, Chairman of the Jane Austen Memorial Trust, has agreed to admit members of the Society free to Chawton Cottage, in return for an annual donation from the Society. Members are asked to sign the book provided for the purpose.

This arrangement also includes those friends brought by members to the Annual General Meeting.

"The Austens' London Doctor," by Winifred Watson

Extract by permission from a longer article in
"The Lady," 27th October, 1960

Almost a hundred and fifty years ago, in 1812, innovation came to Sloane Square in the form of the new Chelsea and Brompton Dispensary. Housed in a little building, low-roofed, and surrounded by iron railings, it stood for many years on the corner opposite the site of Sloane Square station.

Serving the poor and the insignificant, the Dispensary had its own staff, a physician and a surgeon. The surgeon, Charles Thomas Haden, if he had lived, would have become Whistler's sister's father-in-law.

He was the son of a surgeon in Derby, educated at Rugby, M.D. of Edinburgh. In his London practice, his life crossed that of Jane Austen; he was the "medical man" who brought her brother, Henry, safely through a "severe illness" in the autumn and winter of 1815.

Jane Austen and her niece, Fanny, were staying with Henry Austen at the time of his illness, and there are frequent references to Mr. Haden in her letters, from which it is evident that, for a short time, he played quite an enlivening part in the daily lives of Jane Austen and Fanny Knight. He sometimes dined at Henry Austen's house; we are told of his good manners and clever conversation. One evening, when he was expected and they suddenly heard that two ladies had invited themselves for the same occasion, Jane says, "It will be an evening spoilt to Fanny and me."

In one of the letters written during Henry's illness, Jane remarks sadly to her sister, Cassandra, that Mr. Haden "has never sung to us. He will not sing without a P. Forte accompaniment." Fanny had only her harp.

A man who liked to use his time and his talents to the very utmost, Haden started a women's paper, which must have been a godsend to mothers in Regency London. Dr. Alcock published a collected edition of all the issues, in one volume, in 1827, under the formidable title of "Practical Observations on the Management and Diseases of Children," and wrote a biographical

The Chelsea and Brompton Dispensary

introduction. These collected newspapers throw a very clear light on the chancy conditions under which even the Mrs. Darcys of that day had to bring up their children.

Mr. Haden's opinion of nurses was very low: a time might come, he said, when their opinions would deserve attention, but it would have to be under a very different order of things. He seems almost to have had prophetic powers sometimes, but, as he says himself,

"When a new view of things opens to anyone, the prospect is sufficiently boundless if the eyes only take the right direction."

Some of his advice sounds very modern. "Infants should be treated like rational beings, be spoken the truth to, and be never deceived . . . Perhaps the best exercise which an Infant can take is that which Nature dictates, when the child is allowed to lie on the ground or on a mattress with as few clothes on as possible." He even went so far as to design a sort of babies' battledress, having noticed how irritating to them was the elaborate dressing and undressing which the clothing of that day demanded.

The babies' mothers also came in for their share of advice. He was a great advocate of a morning shower bath, and much opposed to what he called "London habits of life . . . deficient exposure of the body to the open air, a deficiency of exercise, an indulgence in late hours both at night and in the morning . . . as London women are essentially sedentary, their digestive organs suffer . . . if young women were educated more with a reference to health, and less to personal accomplishments and delicacy of appearance, the number of inefficient mothers would be reduced."

In addition to his private practice, as we have already seen, Mr. Haden had accepted, in 1814, the post of surgeon to the Chelsea and Brompton Dispensary, probably, in those days before disinfectants were known, not a very healthy place. By 1823 he had developed definite signs of lung trouble. "More fully aware of his situation than was likely to be supposed by those who only witnessed his serene and cheerful hours," he went into the country, his native Derbyshire, "in the hope of experiencing relief by rest and a purer atmosphere."

A pathetic letter quoted by Dr. Alcock belongs to this period: "You must excuse the abruptness of my letters, because I cannot conveniently write. I am better somewhat, but in bed, and seldom even in the sitting position. From the complaint, however, that remains, and from my emaciation, pallor, and other symptoms I fear the worst; but never mind, I am prepared for that worst; and only regret leaving the many friends I possess, and the fine field for doing good."

However, after several months he had recovered enough to "take gentle exercise and enjoy the society of his friends," and, in the letter which follows, he evidently was feeling more optimistic.

"If I live to be a workman in London again, I hope to be able to place myself so as to be a nucleus for much being done by our younger friends. One of the best parts of the French system is the mode in which all the best of the Doctors, the working ones, are surrounded by eager young men."

Perhaps his own commonsense treatment might have cured him, but in 1823 he accepted an invitation to go with Sir William Curtis on a cruise to the Mediterranean in his yacht. It did him no good, and he was only able to get as far as Malta. Here he died, at the age of thirty-eight, having somehow managed to appear in his usual health and spirits up to within half an hour of his death. He is buried in the Protestant burying-ground, near the Quarantine Harbour, Malta, where a simple stone is erected.

Part of the advice contained in Mr. Haden's "Observations" was to the effect that a parent should decide, very early in a child's life, what trade or profession he wished him to enter, and should start training him with that in mind from his very first lessons. In the case of his own little son, Francis Seymour, who was only six when Mr. Haden died, this theory seems to have proved very successful.

Born the year after Jane Austen died — in 1818 — Francis Seymour Haden, or Seymour Haden, as he was usually called, was destined to be a surgeon, like his father and grandfather. He practised with great success at the address which he described as "the old house in Sloane Street"—number 62—where he had been born, and from which his father used to go "with a speed that you can imagine," as Jane Austen told Cassandra, to attend on Henry Austen. Its exterior is still, in 1960, one of the few unspoilt frontages left in Sloane Street; and still, one notices incidentally, bears the badge of the medical profession in plates at the front door.

The "Strange Business in America,"
By Bernard Ledwidge

"A strange business this in America, Dr. Grant. What is your opinion? I always come to you to know what I am to think of public matters."

Such are the words which Fanny Price overhears Tom Bertram address to the local vicar, while she is languishing as a wallflower during her first ball at Mansfield Park. This remark of Tom's has for two reasons a particular interest: it relates to public matters, which as a rule Jane Austen regards as outside her sphere; and it refers to America, of which she makes no other mention in her six novels.

2. Jane throws no direct light upon what the strange business in America was. She changes the subject without more ado in accord-

ance with her usual practice when her male characters venture to talk to each other instead of to her females.

With a less meticulous writer it might be reasonable to assume that she was not in fact thinking of a particular political event in America at all. But it would be wrong to believe this of Jane Austen. All that we know of the strict rules of her art suggests that she probably did know exactly what she was referring to when she put these words into Tom Bertram's mouth. As R. W. Chapman has observed:

"Her regard for accuracy in those parts of her work which belonged to the real and not to an ideal world were quite unlike that of authors in general." (1).

Perhaps it is worth seeing whether, by the exercise of a little of the ingenuity which Jane requires in her readers, it is possible to establish what event Tom was talking about.

3. The most promising first step is to try and fix the date of Fanny's first ball. Jane began writing "Mansfield Park" in about February, 1811, and finished it in the middle of 1813. She writes throughout as if the central events in the story took place shortly before she began to narrate them, that is to say, towards the end of the first decade of the nineteenth century. Nowhere in the book is the actual year mentioned, but indications are plentiful that Jane was writing with a fixed chronology in mind. All the indications, with one exception which can be explained, suggests the same calendar.

4. The clearest chronological pointer comes late in the story when Fanny is languishing in her parents' noisy, dirty, child-crowded house in Portsmouth, and pining to return to the quiet and comfort of Mansfield Park. Fanny's return is, however, delayed until after Easter, because no-one from Mansfield Park can find time to fetch her before then. At this point Jane observes:

"Easter came particularly late this year as Fanny had most sorrowfully considered on first learning that she had no chance of leaving Portsmouth until after it . . ." It happens that there was one year, and one only, in the general period which we know the novel must cover which had a really late Easter. This was 1810 in which Easter Sunday fell upon April 22nd, almost as late as Easter can be, and the latest Easter of Jane's adult life. There is supporting evidence earlier in the book which suggests the same time sequence. When Fanny's midshipman brother William visits Mansfield Park on leave in the autumn before Fanny's visit to Portsmouth, we are told that he

"in the course of seven years had known every variety of danger which sea and war together could afford." No date earlier than 1809 could have given William seven years of both sea and war, for the war with France was only resumed in 1802, after a year's peace. No feasible later date for William's visit will give Fanny a late Easter at Portsmouth. This sequence also provides us with the most plausible timing for Sir Thomas Bertram's visit to his estates in Antigua from which the revenues had been seriously diminishing. We know that he was away for just over two years and returned home in the same autumn as that of William's visit. If we date this in 1809, it follows that Sir Thomas set out for Antigua in the summer of 1807. This was precisely the moment when an absentee West Indian landowner might well have felt the need to visit his estates, for it was on May 1st of that year that the Act abolishing the slave trade in the British Empire came into force. Indeed there is evidence in "Mansfield Park" that Sir Thomas's visit was connected with the slave trade, for one evening soon after his return home, Fanny "asked him about the slave trade."

5. There is only one clue which does not fit in with our proposed calendar. The balance of evidence is decisive enough to permit the conclusion that "Mansfield Park" was written upon the calendar of 1809 and 1810.

6. If this is so, we can place Fanny's first ball with tolerable certainty in the latter half of September, 1809. We know that it was arranged soon after the return to Mansfield of Henry Crawford who had spent the first fortnight of September shooting on his Norfolk estates. The ball can hardly have been as late as October, for that would not allow time for the episode of the amateur theatricals, which takes place between it and the return, still in October, of Sir Thomas from Antigua. It seems then that it was in the second half of September that Tom Bertram and Dr. Grant discussed the strange business in America.

7. A study of "The Times" for that period reveals that all the news from America relates to the same topic, one of great importance to Anglo/American relations in general and of particular concern to a young man like Tom Bertram, who derived from the West Indies a large part of the income which he so consistently overspent and who had recently returned thence. This was President Madison's proclamation of August 9, 1809, to the effect that the British Orders in Council restricting American trade with other Powers had not been withdrawn, as he had previously been led to suppose, and that consequently Anglo/American trade, which had been resumed as recently as June 10 by a previous Presidential proclamation, was once more suspended.

"The Times" of September 12, 1809, announced the arrival of American papers bearing the first news of President Madison's proclamation. The renewed suspension of American exports to an England cut off from trade with Europe by Napoleon's blockade, was naturally of capital importance. There was immediately a great rise in the prices of American produce. "The Times" of

Captain Charles Austen R.N.

Captain Francis Austen, R.N.

Septembetr 13 and September 19 carried the story further as fresh news arrived from America.

8. Any of these copies of "The Times" might have been lying before Tom Bertram when "he took a newspaper from the table and looking over it said in a languid way: 'If you want to dance, Fanny, I will stand up to you.'" Fanny denies wanting to dance and Tom, relieved, drops his newspaper and makes unflattering remarks about dancers and about Dr. Grant. Then, finding the doctor sitting closer to him than he had thought, Tom is obliged to cover his tracks by hurriedly opening a conversation with him. The first thing that enters his head is obviously what struck him most in the paper he has just been reading. This is absolutely true to life, a perfect piece of Austenian observation. But it is not unreasonable to suggest that Jane would not have been quite satisfied with it unless she could visualise the actual newspaper Tom Bertram had been reading and the actual item of news which made an impression on a young man obviously disinclined as a rule to read anything serious. This requirement is admirably met by President Madison's proclamation. It foreshadowed a threat to the income from the family estates in Antigua, because the whole British position in the West Indies was endangered when trouble with America loomed.

9. It may be objected that Jane Austen did not begin to write "Mansfield Park" until 1811 and could hardly at that date have remembered President Madison's proclamation of 1809. But there was a reason why events in America were of such interest to Jane in the summer of 1809 that she might well have remembered them even in 1811. Charles, the younger of her two beloved sailor brothers, was due home that summer from duty with the Royal Navy off the West Indies and North America. Jane mentions his impending return in a letter written in July, 1809. But in fact Charles's return was postponed until 1811. Perhaps it was the deterioration in Anglo/American relations following the President's proclamation that changed fleet plans and delayed him. If so, Jane would have had a particularly family reason, of the kind which weighed with her most, for remembering President Madison's proclamation.

10. Another piece of evidence shows that Jane and her brothers did devote thought to the question of British policy towards the United States and had decided ideas upon the subject. This is in a letter which Jane wrote to her niece Martha Lloyd from the London house of her banker brother Henry in September, 1814. Martha was herself the granddaughter of one of the last colonial Governors of South Carolina, the Honourable C. Craven, and may have retained a hereditary interest in the rebellious colonists which prompted Jane to write to her of their affairs. What Jane says, speaking of Henry, is: "His view, and the view of those he mixes with, of Politics is not cheerful—with regard to an American war

I mean—they consider it as certain and as what is to ruin us. The Americans cannot be conquered and we shall only be teaching them the skill in war which they may now want. We are to make them good sailors and soldiers and gain nothing ourselves." (2).

Jane Austen lived through all the perils of the Napoleonic wars without being moved to record the fear that they might result in the ruin of Britain. But it seems the Austens had already absorbed the fact that America was a different proposition from any European country. The Americans lived in a land so vast that even the Royal Navy could not defeat them. War with them was therefore likely to be fruitless and might even be disastrous. When the news of the battle of New Orleans reached England, Jane would have been entitled to say to Martha Lloyd: "I told you so."

11. On the whole, there is enough evidence not only of Jane's general care) for accuracy when she writes of the real world, but also of her interest in America to warrant the suggestion that she knew exactly what she was talking about when she made Tom Bertram speak to Dr. Grant in September, 1809, of a strange business in America. Jane knew that the business was the Presidential proclamation of August 9, 1809, reimposing the embargo on American trade with the British Empire; that it would be in the newspapers at the time of Fanny's first ball; and might well catch Tom Bertram's eye.

References

1. R. W. Chapman. "Jane Austen. Facts and Problems." Clarendon Press, Oxford. 1948

1 or 2. Letter to Martha Lloyd of September, 1814. (No. 99.1. in "Jane Austen's Letters." Collected and edited by R. W. Chapman. Oxford University Press. 1952).

Jane Austen from an American Viewpoint

When, a dozen years ago, I first came to Chawton, the idea that I should ever address the Jane Austen Society was one which I was very far from entertaining. It was an honour that I dreamt not of, and the dream is no less an honour for having come true. I am an enthusiastic reader of Jane Austen, but I am by no means omniscient, as are your Committee and your noble President and Mrs. Stallybrass and Mr. Gore—and no doubt scores of others. The only distinction I can claim, and I must claim it for all it is worth, is that of perhaps being the only person here this afternoon who is both a reader of Jane Austen and a native of central Ohio. Hence the title of my remarks, which I trust gives me licence to be autobiographical; and you, the distinguished members of the Jane Austen Society, if you learn nothing new about Jane Austen herself, can have the anthropological—or is it merely sociological ?

—pleasure of observing how Jane Austen survives a transplantation to the plains west of the Allegheny Mountains.

For me, the summer of 1949, to which I have alluded, marks a beignning so far as Jane Austen is concerned: the beginning not of my admiration for her, but of my decision to articulate that admiration. And I owe much of the impulse to a meeting which took place in that year on the platform of Paddington Station. My distinguished correspondent wrote: "I am over six feet tall, and what hair I have is white." This was, as I hardly need tell you, Dr. Chapman. We drank coffee at the Great Western Hotel, and talked; and I shall never forget that talk, or our subsequent exchange of letters. When, therefore, I went to the Annual General Meeting of the Jane Austen Society in that memorable year I felt already, thanks to Dr. Chapman, at home among Austenians. And I should very much like to record here this afternoon within the Society to which he was devoted and to which he contributed so much, the sense of gratitude that this American feels to him.

Dr. Chapman was what a scholar ought to be: both learned and wise; not merely pertinacious, but discriminating; high-principled and sympathetic; generous—as I know at first hand—to the young; intelligent, judicious and—in all the best senses of the word—witty. It is good to know that his great work will keep his memory green not only among ourselves, but among readers of Jane Austen who will not have had the pleasure, the privilege, and the delight of knowing him.

Let me begin with the easy and agreeable task of recording a well-known fact: that of Jane Austen's popularity in my country. There are many ways of documenting this point, but instead of giving an historical survey of Jane Austen's invasion and occupation of America, I shall read you a few sentences from a letter written more than a century ago from one Miss Eliza Susan Quincy of Boston, Massachusetts, to Admiral Sir Francis Austen. Miss Quincy identifies her father as successively "Member of Congress from Boston, Mayor of that City, and President of Harvard University, the oldest literary institution in America": (Austen Papers, p.301). Miss Quincy wrote as follows to Jane Austen's brother: "Since high critical authority has pronounced the delineations of character, in the works of Jane Austen, second only to those of Shakespeare, transatlantic admiration appears superfluous.—Yet it may not be uninteresting to her family to receive an assurance that the influence of her genius is extensively recognised in the America Republic—even by the highest judicial authorities.

"The late Mr. Chief Justice Marshall, of the Supreme Court of the United States, and his associate, Mr. Justice Story, highly estimated and admired Miss Austen, and to them we owe our introduction to her society.—For many years, her talents have brightened our daily paths, and her name and those of her characters, are familiar to us as 'household words.' " (6 January, 1852. Printed in R. A. Austen Leigh, ed., Austen Papers 1704-1856, London, privately printed, 1942, pp.296, 297). Thus Miss Quincy.

And it is true that Jane Austen was admired by many of my fellow countrymen, even beyond the boundaries of Boston, which used to like to think—and not without some pardonable pride—that it was the whole world. Among the most intelligent and sensitive remarks about Jane Austen are those by William Dean Howells, a native of my own state. To multiply examples would be easy for me, but dull for you.

And yet, there is another side of the picture. In my part of the world, in the year before Jane Austen was born, Lord Dunmore—in a successful battle, by the Ohio rivei, against the Shawnee who was governor of Virginia—led eleven hundred backwoodsmen Indians. During Jane Austen's infancy the American Revolution began. And it was not until she was twenty-eight years old, in 1803, that Ohio became a state of the union. Those of you who have read Mrs. Trollope's highly-coloured account of her sojourn in America, of her wild and romantic effort to found a department store in Cincinnati, will know that there was not in Ohio anything very closely resembling the country society which Jane Austen knew and about which she wrote. Nowadays, of course, you can buy Coca-Cola in Chawton and Cadbury's chocolate in Cleveland; but these commercial miracles only obscure the differences which remain. Jane Austen makes it possible to see these differences in high relief.

At my university, over the campus of which swarm twenty-five thousand students, the great majority of them residents of Ohio, there are numbers of young men and women who every year read Jane Austen for the first time. You will perhaps hardly be surprised to be told that among new American readers of Jane Austen — young, ingenuous and keen readers, often extremely intelligent readers — the first impression is frequently that of bewilderment. Hampshire is a long way from Ohio—not simply geographically, but also spiritually. There never has been in American letters any writer who bears the faintest resemblance to Jane Austen; Jane Austen shows us that the English and the American civilizations are, for all their ties of affection, interest and sympathy, nonetheless distinct and distinguishable. And Jane Austen with fine modesty supposed her readers to be rather like herself, from much the same background, and well acquainted with the "3 or 4 Families in a Country Village," as she put it, that she worked on.

The great theme of American literature, which of course reflects the history of America herself, is of apostasy, rebellion, renunciation. Or, to put the matter less negatively, it is the theme of individual fulfillment despite established church, despite society, despite community—despite history itself.

The greatest of all American novels—"Moby Dick"—chiefly celebrates a flight from the homeland. Walt Whitman is the self-styled hero of his own defiantly idiosyncratic, and at the same time, characteristic "Leaves of Grass." Huckleberry Finn is most nearly fulfilled when, floating down the Mississippi on a raft, he is farthest from the town in which he was at best an outcast anyway—and Mark Twain found Jane Austen unendurable. Not that Americans have ever felt that man can subsist entirely by himself—except for Henry David Thoreau. Indeed, the epitome of a typically American dilemma is contained in a remark of Emerson's. "Solitude," Emerson said, "is impractical and society fatal."

To speak, therefore, about Jane Austen from an American viewpoint is to consider the foreignness of her novels, as they strike an American reader. For there exists the temptation, to which I and perhaps some of my fellow countrymen have occasionally or in the first place succumbed, to read Jane Austen as though she were in her novels celebrating the achievement, or lamenting the frustration of loneliness: that is to say, to make Jane Austen reflect our own image, rather than hers. This is, of course, a very natural and no doubt inevitable predisposition, and I record its existence here to underscore the fact that Jane Austen is surely among the most English of writers. To see in her novels a theme of isolation—and there exists an article in a scholarly journal which purports to find just that—is to see what is not there.

You remember that in Kipling's stort "The Janeites," a character called Macklin says that Jane Austen did leave lawful issue, that issue being Henry James. ("The Janeites," Debits and Credits, London, 1926, pp.153, 154). Kipling is no doubt right in suggesting that Henry James is the American writer who more nearly than any other resembles Jane Austen. And yet to compare these two novelists is to see that the differences are far more numerous and far more significant than the resemblances.

James knew England well. He lived here for forty years and at the end of his life he became a British subject. His novels exhibit because they dramatize society in a way that few other American novels do. Like Jane Austen, James makes fine discriminations, and he repeatedly shows the disadvantages—for him the tragic and sometimes fatal disadvantages—of being unable to distinguish minutely. Christopher Newman, in "The American," is by virtue of his nationality and what it signifies, unable to detect the difference between facade and essence in the French noble family whose daughter he wishes to marry. Isabel Archer, that delightful heroine of "The Portrait of a Lady," marries a man not nearly good enough for her because she cannot distinguish between pretence and actuality. In Henry James, as in Jane Austen, one gets a sense of the shape of certain sections of society, of the way individual members of society are incorporated into the fabric under examination. Neither Jane Austen nor James runs the gamut: intensity within a small area, rather than Balzackian comprehensiveness, is their strength.

And yet, after all, it is the contrasts rather than the resemblances which finally strike one as establishing the connection, or marking the disconnection, between Jane Austen and Henry James. To put the matter very briefly indeed: the characteristic Henry James heroine burns her bridges; the Jane Austen heroine puts her bridges in good order. It is impossible to imagine Daisy Miller, that "inscrutable combination of audacity and innocence" (as James describes her), in Jane Austen; Emma Woodhouse is audacious and innocent, but she is not, I think, inscrutable. The ultimate destiny of the Henry James heroine is renunciation. Caroline Spencer in "Four Meetings" renounces Europe; Isabel Archer in "The Portrait of a Lady" renounces happiness; Daisy Miller renounces life itself. But the ultimate destiny of a Jane Austen heroine is marriage and happiness: acceptance, that is to say, and fulfillment. Henry James thought that his native ground was for an artist stifling; Jane Austen, her letters make the fact abundantly clear, did not feel herself to be artistically disadvantaged by residence in Chawton. No wonder there is a temperamental failure of sympathy between James and Jane Austen.

James admired Jane Austen, but he could not conceal in his praise of her a note of exasperation. In a lecture which he delivered in 1905, called "The Lesson of Balzac," he adverts to a number of novelists as they seem to belong to certain times of the day or states of the weather. "Why is it," James asks, "that the life that overflows in Dickens seem to me always to go on in the morning, or in the very earliest hours of the afternoon at most, and in a vast apartment that appears to have windows, large, uncurtained, and rather unwashed windows; on all sides at once? Why is it that in George Eliot the sun sinks forever to the west, and the shadows are long, and the afternoon wanes, and the trees vaguely rustle, and the colour of the day is much inclined to yellow? Why is that in Charlotte Bronte we move through an endless autumn?" And then, to get to our subject, James turns (I think) slightly subacid when he asks: "Why is it that in Jane Austen we sit quite resigned in an arrested spring?" ("The Question of Our Speech and The Lesson of Balzac," London, 1905, pp.81, 82). Surely we are justified in detecting here that arrested sympathy which, in James, is not altogether usual. And if James had difficulty in appreciating Jane Austen, what about other less intelligent readers?

Last year Mr. Gore spoke of Jane Austen as provincial. Of course he is right. And all writers are provincial in that they cannot—even when they are trying very hard indeed—escape the facts of their birth, their nationality, their education, their special circumstances — including geographical circumstance. Henry James, though he was educated in Europe, and though he spent more than half his life in England, remained to the end thoroughly American: even in London and in Rye he was, and he knew it, an outsider. Thomas Mann, for all his cosmopolitan fervour, never—and we are all grateful for it—escaped his inheritance as the son of a grain merchant in Lübeck. And who among us would ever mistake Mr. Auden for an American or Mr. Eliot, despite his knowledge of the taste of Wensleydale, for a native of these isles ?

The task of the reader, of course, is to accommodate himself to the frame of reference, to the predispositions, of the writer whose work he is encountering. For some Americans Jane Austen is more difficult than others because she is so specially English; and the central quality of her Englishness lies not—I hasten to say— in being provincial in a pejorative sense of that word; but in being, in a wholly ameliorative sense, insular: possessed, that is to say, of a sense of proportion; taking for granted a certain harmony in political, social and individual organization; assuming not only the desirability but the possibility of consonance — within the village, the neighbourhood, the county. Beyond the county what happens cannot be apprehended, and is therefore hardly a subject of contemplation.

There is in Jane Austen a sense of social settledness, and— where necessary—an argument in favour of accommodation to the world. It is fair to say that the Jane Ausen heroines begin as imperfect members of society and then learn how to be social and thus fully human beings. When Catherine Morland has shed her Gothic illusions and recovered the good sense which is her happy native endowment, she is at last marriageable. When Marianne Dashwood learns sobriety of temper she can regard with intelligent favour an alliance with a middle-aged (as she thinks) considerably waistcoated soldier. When Elizabeth Bennett's eyes are no longer beclouded with prejudice she can marry a squire whose pride has fallen before the imperatives of affection. As for Fanny Price, she alone among the Jane Austen heroines must be adjusted to, rather than herself be accommodating: when Fanny comes to be understood and appreciated for the person she really is (rather than the irremediably ignorant and inferior girl that is the figment of Aunt Norris's patronising imagination), then Edmund Bertram deserves the good luck of making her his wife. When Emma Woodhouse, the most brilliant of all Jane Austen's creations, learns to know herself, she can form accurate ideas about the heirs of Donwell. And when Anne Elliot, chastened by nearly a decade of unhappiness, meets a suitor who at least is worthy of her—not Commander, but Captain, Wentworth—all is going to be well.

Jane Austen's novels end with marriage, that most fundamental of institutions: and the Jane Austen marriages signify not simply or merely happiness ever after, but the achieved enlightenment that justifies and makes promising the relationships established by that sacrament. This enlightenment is always by way of a social awareness that makes definition of the self possible.

In all of Jane Austen there is, I think, no more completely un-American passage than the one I am going to read to you from chapter 11 of Book I of "Sense and Sensibility." Elinor Dashwood is talking to Colonel Brandon about her sister. "A few years," Elinor says hopefully, "will settle her opinions on the reasonable basis of common sense and observation; and then they may be more easy to define and to justify than they now are, by any body but herself."

"This will probably be the case," Colonel Brandon replies; "and yet there is something so amiable in the prejudices of a young mind, that one is sorry to see them give way to the reception of more general opinions."

"I cannot agree with you there," says Elinor. "There are inconveniences attending such feelings as Marianne's, which all the charms of enthusiasm and ignorance of the world cannot atone for. Her systems have all the unfortunate tendency of setting propriety at nought; and a better acquaintance with the world is what I look forward to as her greatest possible advantage." (Chapman ed., p.56).

I do not want to leave the impression that Americans are un worldly; but we are anti-worldly; and like some other citizens of the world we pretend contempt for it when we are embracing its values, such as they may be. But to *preach* worldliness: that does not happen in America.

Jane Austen, despite her willingness to accept the world, is too intelligent to wax unqualifiedly enthusiastic. There are surely few more accurate and at the same time more u n s p a r i n g portraits in all of English literature than that of Aunt Norris. No: Jane Austen does not romanticise, rhapsodise, idealise. And it seems to me that a very agreeable passage in "Persuasion" illustrates her fine detachment. Sir Walter Elliot may, I suppose, be described as a disappointed idealist. It is he, the epitome of personal vanity—it is Sir Walter rather than Jane Austen—who is discomfited by the appearance of the women in Bath. "The worst of Bath was, the number of its plain women. He did not mean to say that there were no pretty women, but the number of the plain was out of all proportion. He had frequently observed, as he walked, that one handsome face would be followed by thirty, or five and thirty frights; and once, as he had stood in a shop in Bond Street, he had counted eighty-seven women go by, one after another, without their being a tolerable face among them. It had been a frosty morning to be sure, a sharp frost, which hardly one woman in a thousand could stand the test of. But still, there certainly were a dreadful multitude of ugly women in Bath; and as for the men! they were infinitely worse." (Chapman ed., pp.141, 142).

What we all of us, English and American, finally learn to look for in Jane Austen is not facile acceptance of the world that is given her, not what nowadays is all too often called conformity: but something rarer, finer, and extra—or super-national. I mean: comic balance. All of us here today are bound to Jane Austen by ties of affection, not merely because she is the most cheering novelist ever born, but because she knows how to put gravity in its place. There is a kind of bravery in Jane Austen, and I should like to conclude by illustrating this facet of her art. In "Sense and Sensibility" Jane Austen is so wonderfully skilled that we can be deeply concerned about Marianne's distress — we can share her distress at Willoughby's barbarous treatment of her, and yet never quite lose the comic edge. Thus Mrs. Jenning's efforts to be helpful to Marianne are irresistibly attractive because they are so well meant, and irresistibly amusing because of the way Jane Austen describes them. "Marianne was to have the best place by the fire, was to be tempted to eat by every delicacy in the house, and to be amused by the relation of all the news of the day. Had not Elinor, in the sad countenance of her sister, seen a check to all mirth, she could have been entertained by Mrs. Jenning's endeavours to cure a disappointment in love, by a variety of sweetmeats and olives, and a good fire." (Chapman ed., p.193). Elinor herself is too close to her sister's misery to be amused, but we are far enough away to be both touched and delighted by Mrs. Jenning's warm-hearted ineptitude. From one viewpoint, Jane Austen illuminates the contrasts between the English and the American civilisations. From another, she brings us closer together, in the bonds of admiration and love transatlantically forged because we can all of us, through the medium of a common language, share in Jane Austen what is in the firmament of literature nothing short of a glory.

ANDREW WRIGHT

Detail from Patchwork Quilt, made by Mrs. Austen, Cassandra and Jane, and now at Jane Austen's house at Chawton

THE JANE AUSTEN SOCIETY

(Founded in 1940 by Dorothy G. Darnell)

THE JANE AUSTEN SOCIETY

Report for the Year 1962

———o———

Sixty-nine new members joined during the year and there were seventeen new Life Members. Total membership now numbers 929

Annual General Meeting, 1962

The Annual General Meeting was held on Saturday, 21st July, at Chawton House, by kind permission of Major and Mrs. Edward Knight, when some 350 members and their friends were present.

The Duke of Wellington presided and, in opening the meeting, asked for the Minutes of the last Annual General Meeting, which had been published in the Annual Report, to be taken as read. There were no matters arising.

The Hon. Secretary presented the Annual Report and, in the absence of the Hon. Treasurer, the accounts for 1961. This was seconded by Mr. J. Butler-Kearney and carried.

The Hon. Secretary proposed the re-election of the Duke of Wellington as President; Mr. T. Edward Carpenter as Vice-President; and Mr. John Gore as Chairman. This was seconded by The Hon. Mrs. Eggar, and carried.

The President proposed the re-election, en bloc, of the Committee.

The meeting was addressed by Miss Margaret Lane (Countess of Huntingdon), who took as her theme Jane Austen's use of the Domestic Interior.

A vote of thanks was proposed by Sir Charles Stirling, K.C.M.G., K.C.V.O., seconded by Mr. M. Hemphrey, and carried.

The meeting was closed by the President thanking Major and Mrs. Knight for lending Chawton House for the meeting, after which tea was provided in aid of Chawton Church Funds, for which some £45 was raised.

Annual General Meeting, 1963

The Annual General Meeting will be held at Chawton House on Saturday, 20th July. The meeting will be addressed by Miss Elizabeth Jenkins.

Early Success of Mr. Darcy

"Pride and Prejudice" was published in January, 1813. On May 1st of that year, Miss Annabella Milbanke (who married Lord Byron in 1815) wrote to her mother:

"I have finished the novel called 'Pride and Prejudice,' which I think a very superior work. It depends not on any of the common resources of Novel writers, no drownings, no conflagrations, nor runaway horses, nor lap-dogs and parrots, nor chambermaids and milliners, not rencontres and disguises. I really think it is the **most probable** fiction I have ever read. It is not a crying book, but the interest is very strong, especially for Mr. Darcy. The characters which are not amiable are diverting, and all of them are consistently supported. I wish much to know who is the author or **ess** as I am told."

Printed in "Lord Byron's Wife," p.159, Malcolm Elwin (Macdonald; 1962); reproduced by kind permission of the Earl of Lytton.

Jane Austen's Memorial Tablet

Following last year's annual meeting, a correspondent raised the question of the provenance of the brass tablet in Winchester Cathdral beneath the Jane Austen Memorial Window. This information was supplied by Mr. W. J. Carpenter Turner and is here recorded for information and for record:

"This memorial was placed in the Cathedral in 1872, and it appears that it was erected out of the proceeds of the **"Memoir of Jane Austen"** by the Rev. J. E. Austen. The design was entrusted by the family to Mr. Wyatt, the architect who restored Bray Church."

Mr. Carpenter Turner supplies the source of his information—Vaughan's **"Winchester Cathedral — its Monuments and Memorials."** This book contains other references to Jane Austen, among which one may be set on record. Her funeral was conducted by the Rev. T. Watkins, one of the Petty-Canons.

From a School in Eastern Nigeria

"I found that the third year were reading 'Pride and Prejudice,' and was amazed to find how much the story and the characters appealed to them. I should have thought Jane Austen's England too far removed from life in West Africa, but the story of a mother with five daughters to marry and of love triumphing over difficulties was one of which they grasped the essentials at once, and they became enthuiastic partisans of Elizabeth and Jane, and sworn enemies of Lady Catherine de Bourgh, whose discomfiture, when read in class, they applauded.

Memorial Tablet in Winchester Cathedral

Who was John Lyford ?

Readers of Jane Austen's letters will remember that she several times refers to a family called Lyford. On one occasion, in the late October of 1798, she and her parents were returning from a visit to the Edward Austens in Kent to the Rectory at Steventon in Hampshire. Towards the end of the third day's journey the party reached Basingstoke, where Mrs. Austen, who was unwell ". . . received much comfort from a mess of broth and the sight of Mr. Lyford, who recommended her to take twelve drops of laudanum when she went to bed as a composer, which she accordingly did." This Mr. Lyford promised to call at Steventon in the course of the next few days. He is thus gradually revealed to be the Austen's family doctor, John Lyford, **Surgeon and Man-midwife,** as he had been called under the **Basingstoke** entries in a **Directory of Hampshire,** published some years earlier in 1784. Mrs. Austen continued unwell; and it is presumed that Mr. Lyford did in fact call from time to time at Steventon. He was certainly there on November 30th and joined the Austens for dinner. He expressed himself well satisfied with his entertainment, but was puzzled by his patient. "He wants my mother to look yellow and to throw out a rash, but she will do neither."

We also hear of a Mr. Lyford—perhaps the same John Lyford—prescribing for the Austens later at Southampton, where they lived from October, 1806, until February, 1809. It will be remembered also that it was in order to be under the care of a Mr. Lyford that Jane Austen was taken from Chawton to Winchester a little before her death in 1817. "Our nearest **very good** is at Winchester, where there is a Hospital and capital Surgeons." This last Mr. Lyford must have been Giles King Lyford, surgeon in ordinary at the county hospital there, and was probably a nephew of the earlier John Lyford of Basingstoke.

Going back now to the year 1796, while the Austens were living at Steventon, we find Jane Austen, then aged twenty, attending balls at various places in the neighbourhood. She was at this time interested, to say the least of it, in the attentions of Tom Lefroy, a nephew of the Rector of Ashe and later Chief Justice of Ireland. Of another young man, however, who was present at a ball on January 8th of that year, she writes: ". . . to my inexpressible astonishment, I entirely escaped John Lyford. I was forced to fight hard for it, however." Who was this unacceptable John Lyford ? About a week later a letter reveals that he was a friend of Edward Austen, who had gone to spend a day with him, and also that "John Lyford and his sister bring Edward home today, dine with us, and we shall all go together to Ashe." This was to another ball, but there is no letter to tell us whether or not on this occasion Jane Austen again escaped John Lyford. We do not, in fact, hear of him again until December 18th, 1798, when it is reported: "Miss Lyford is gone into Suffolk with her

Brother and Miss Lodge." Clearly a marriage was in the wind. "Everybody is now very busy making up an income for the two latter. Miss Lodge has only 800£ of her own and it is not supposed that her Father can give her much, therefore the good offices of the Neighbourhood will be highly acceptable. John Lyford means to take pupils." On Thursday, January 17th, 1799, Jane Austen attended another ball, which was probably one of the Basingstoke assemblies, at which John Lyford was once again present. On this occasion he was, in fact, one of Jane Austen's partners. Perhaps he was more acceptable now, seeing that his marriage was less than three months away. There is no letter to mention this marriage, which took place at Great Blakenham, near Ipswich, on April 19th, and unfortunately the next mention of John Lyford is a comment on his death, which followed shortly afterwards in June, 1799. It is a characteristically shrewd one: "John Lyford's history is a melancholy one.—I feel for his family, and when I know that his wife was really fond of him, I will feel for her, too . . ." And that is all that the letters of Jane Austen can tell us about John Lyford.

He was the eldest surviving son of John Lyford, Surgeon and Man-midwife—an elder son, also called John, having died before the birth of the second—and was born in 1769. He was baptised at Basingstoke on August 31st; he was at Eton as a King's Scholar from 1782 until 1786; and he was an Exhibitioner at Queen's College, Oxford, where he became a Bachelor of Arts in 1790. Some time before this he must have decided on the law as a career, for, in the November of the previous year he had been admitted a member of Lincoln's Inn. Two more years passed, but no more was heard of the legal career; and on February 21st, 1793, he was made a Deacon and ". . . licensed to serve the Chapels of Basing and Nately in the parish of Basingstoke in the County of Southampton with a stipend of £50 per annum." Just over a year later "John Lyford A.M., of Queen's College, Oxford," was ordained Priest. Two years later — and a welcome augmentation of his stipend it must have been—he was elected a Michel Fellow of his College.

It was such a John Lyford that Jane Austen worked hard to escape at the ball in the January of 1796, with whom Edward Austen spent the day and who came, along with his sister, to dinner at Steventon and on to the ball at Ashe. Jane Austen knew that in the event of his marriage he must resign his fellowship and be reduced again to £50 per annum. Now it is clear why, when his eventual marriage with Miss Lodge was in the offing, friends speculated about their joint resources and also why John Lyford proposed to take pupils — a practice common enough among the country clergy and one carried on by Jane Austen's father himself. In this state of mind John Lyford returned from Suffolk into Hampshire, danced with Jane Austen on January 17th, performed a marriage at Basing on March 26th and two more an March 27th, and then went back to Suffolk for his own marriage on April 9th. He died on June 12th and was buried in the Holy Ghost Litten at Basingstoke on June 16th. A grave there bears an almost indecipherable incription which, as we know from a copy made many years ago by a local antiquary, reads: ". . . in memory of the Rev. John Lyford, M.A., late of Queen's College, Oxon, who died June 12th, 1799, aged 29 years." This inscription is followed by another commemorating his mother, who died in the following November, and also his father—the original ". . . John Lyford, surgeon . . ." who lived on to die in his eighty-ninth year in 1829.

It is amusing to note that Mrs. John Lyford, the erstwhile Miss Lodge, for whom Jane Austen had reserved her sympathy in 1799, married again in 1801. She then wrote: "Mrs. John Lyford is so much pleased with the state of widowhood as to be going to put in for being a widow again; she is to marry a Mr. Fendall, a banker in Gloucester."

WILLIAM JARVIS

The Sources of Jane Austen's Kentish Ties
by the Rev. Canon S. Graham Brade-Birks, D.Sc., F.S.A.,
Vicar of Godmersham

Horsmonden lies some seven miles to the east of Tunbridge Wells and in the pleasant rolling countryside of the High Weald of Kent not far from the Sussex border. Here in the sixteenth and seventeenth centuries several generations of the Astyn or Austen family were prosperous "clothiers," * manufacturers of woollen cloth, and here, today, you will still find their memorials in the parish church and see two of their attractive gabled homes, Broad Ford, often written "Broadford," where John Austen, Jane's great grandfather, lived until his early death in 1704; and Grovehurst, where his parents and grandparents had their home and built up their considerable fortunes.

The busy looms had brought prosperity to a family which had its roots deep in Kentish soil, for there is good reason to believe that these Austens were descended from William Astyn of Yalding (seven miles or so north of Horsmonden, ‡) who died in 1522.

The John Austen we have mentioned left his widow with many debts and seven children ; and his very rich father dealt most ungenerously with all but the eldest son. The struggle of Mrs. John Austen to bring up her other children was successfully accomplished and makes a heroic tale into which we must not enter here. †   One son, Francis, eventually became a very wealthy

*Hasted **History of Kent** ii (1782), pp 387-8; iii (1790) p. 48; W. & R. A. Austen-Leigh, **Life and Letters,** 1 *et seq.* ‡Not the next parish as has been stated, Wagner **Historic Heraldry of Britain,** p. 119. †**Life and Letters** pp. 2-3; her own account is given in full in **Austen Papers,** pp. 3 *et seq.*

Broad Ford
Photo: Douglas Weaver, Ashford, Kent

Grovehurst
Photo: Douglas Weaver, Ashford, Kent

Sevenoaks solicitor ; another, William, Jane's grandfather, was a medical practitioner, but he died young, leaving four children of whom a promising only son George, six at the time, was befriended by his wealthy Uncle Francis and was educated at Tonbridge School and St. John's College, Oxford. He took holy orders in 1760 and as related below, became Rector of Steventon the following year. He married Cassandra the daughter of the Rev. Thomas Leigh, Vicar of Harpsden and they had six sons and two daughters. Our main interest is in the third son, Edward, and the younger daughter, Jane, the novelist.

Godmersham, the Kentish spot dearest no doubt to Jane's heart, is twenty-five miles as the crow flies from Horsmonden and much further by road, but the two were linked with one another and with Hampshire in a rather complicated manner, as we shall see.

We have already noticed that the Austens of Horsmonden descended to the novelist Jane's great-grandfather, John. He had a sister, an earlier Jane Austen, who married Stephen Stringer and their daughter Hannah Stringer (her father's co-heiress) married William Monke. This couple in their turn had a daughter who was her father's co-heiress, Jane Monke ; she, in 1729, married Thomas May (formerly Brodnax) of Godmersham. This gentleman, the son of William Brodnax, had taken, in 1727, the arms and surname of May, by Act of Parliament, on succeeding to the estates at Rawmere, Sussex, of his mother's cousin, Sir Thomas May who died childless in 1718 ; his widow died in 1726. His new found wealth now enabled Thomas May to build, on the site of his former modest residence, the present mansion at Godmersham, now Godmersham Park, which he began in 1732. He called his new home Ford Place, from its proximity to the ancient crossing of the Kentish Stour a hundred yards away. He commemorated his good fortune by incorporating three shields of arms in the very fine frieze on the south wall of the entrance hall of his mansion, those of Monke to the east, his own new arms (May quartered with Brodnax) in the centre and those of Brodnax towards the west.

A few years later he succeeded to the estates of the family of Knight of Chawton, Hampshire and so in 1738 he had to go to Parliament again for an Act to change his name for the second time. The well-known antiquary, Samuel Pegge, was Vicar of Godmersham from 1731 to 1751 and it is he who recalls the observation of a Member of Parliament on this second occasion: "This gentleman gives us so much trouble, that the best way would be to pass an act for him to use whatever name he pleases." *

With his new estates in Hampshire, Thomas (Brodnax, May) Knight inherited the advowson of Steventon and so in 1761 he was able to present his second-cousin the Rev. George Austen, Jane's father, to the living. Thus was established a new link between Godmersham and the Austens in Hampshire which was to be strengthened in the next generation when the only, and childless, son of this Godmersham benefactor, himself another Thomas Knight, adopted Edward Austen, George's third son (not his second, as frequently stated‡). On the death of the widow of Thomas Knight the younger in 1812, Edward Austen, already resident in the great house at Godmersham, inherited all the Knight estates and took the arms and surname of Knight.

Thus Jane Austen's association with Kent arose from two distinct circumstances, the former was her Horsmonden ancestry and the other, more compelling, the position of her brother Edward as the squire of that delightful estate at Godmersham, in the North Downs, eight miles from Canterbury, where he made his home. Edward was seven years older than Jane and her respect for his position and his wealth is clearly evident in some of her letters and must have been further emphasized by his seniority and his hospitality. There was no doubt that she was impressed and delighted by the ease and comfort she enjoyed when she was able to visit the mansion at Godmersham.

Godmersham, two miles long, lies in an attractive, well-wooded, rather steeply-sided part of a fertile valley which is here about two miles wide. Its river, the Kentish Stour, runs roughly from south to north with the church of St. Lawrence the Martyr on its left bank in the middle of the parish, eight miles from Canterbury and six from Ashford. The main road, made about eighteen forty, and the railway, built in the seventies, run nearly parallel to the river. A mile to the west along the ridge and above Godmersham Park, in the same direction, runs the so called Pilgrims' Way, a prehistoric track probably of Neolithic age. Near the bottom of the valley, one on either side, are two Roman roads which also run parallel to the river. The one on the west of the valley can easily be traced but it is now disused ; the other Roman road leads directly to Godmersham from Wye about three miles away. The church, vicarage and mansion lie in that order south to north on the west bank of the river, while the short village "street" and adjacent houses grouped near the post-office form a hamlet to the east of the river. Except for the railway, the main road and its houses and those of the "street," Godmersham today, in its main features, is the Godmersham of Jane Austen's day. The southern part of the parish is called Bilting and the north-eastern part of it Eggarton, both mentioned by Jane in her letters.

*__Anonymiana__, p. 331. ‡See even J. E. Austen Leigh, __Memoir__, p. 12 and Lord Brabourne's edition of the __Letters__, i, p. 10.

221

The Rev. George Austen presenting his son, Edward, to Mr. and Mrs. Thomas Knight. It is suggested that the left-hand female figure is Mrs. Austen's mother, Mrs. Harriet Knatchbull. (Original about 22 x 18 inches)

Jane's first recorded visit to Kent was when she was a little girl of twelve. With her sister Cassandra, she was taken by her parents to visit her father's uncle and benefactor, Mr. Francis Austen, then a widower ninety years of age, living at the Red House, Sevenoaks.* Her half-cousin, Philadelphia Walter, wrote at this time that she was "not at all pretty & very prim, unlike a girl of twelve : but it is hasty judgement. . ." ‡

As the years passed, Jane's familiarity with Kent and Kentish families grew from her visits to her brother Edward's homes in East Kent, first at Rowling in the parish of Goodnestone, from which she wrote to her sister in September, 1796† and later at Godmersham where Jane with her parents and her sister was a visitor in the autumn of 1798 § soon after Edward and his family, upon the insistence of the widowed Mrs. Knight, had made the mansion at Godmersham their home.

Mrs. Catherine Knight had just gone to live at the White Friars, Canterbury and there Jane was not only able to meet many of her brother's friends in the city and neighbourhood but she also greatly enjoyed the diversions provided by the Assembly Rooms and The Concert Hall.

Ashford too had its attractions for, as at Meryton, troops were stationed there and the Assembly Rooms provided many an evening's enjoyment for the young people. There is plenty of other local colour in the letters and not a few of the families Jane met have their present day decendants filling important places in the public life of Kent.

---

*Not (as in **Austen Papers,** p. 2) "The Old House," which belonged to relatives. ‡**Austen Papers,** p. 131. †**Letters** 4-7 (in Chapman's edition). §**Letter 9.**

223

Address Given at A.G.M., 1962

I am usually bored by speakers who apologise too much, hoping to disarm criticism by explaining beforehand how ill-equipped they are for the task they have undertaken to perform. Dearly as I love him on the printed page, I should find Mr. Collins insufferable in life. But in my own case I do want to disarm you just a little, for I am addressing an audience of experts on Jane Austen, and am very far from being one myself. I regard her simply as the most consistently entertaining novelist in the language, whom I have read and re-read at long intervals during my life with increasing pleasure; but I could never hope, like beloved Cynthia Asquith, to win any prize in a memory test on her work; nor could I, like her perceptive biographer, Miss Elizabeth Jenkins, pin-point any place or event in her life at a moment's notice; nor dream of embarking, in the steps of the incomparable Dr. Chapman, on even the smallest atom of textual criticism. My reason for being with you today is a sentimental one. I like to pay my debts, and to keep myself, as far as possible, reasonably solvent; and my debts, in this connection, are considerable. Of my debt to Jane Austen herself I need hardly speak: it is a debt of such lasting and continuous pleasure that I find it difficult to be wholly at ease with anyone who frankly admits they cannot share it. Then, like most of us, I am grateful for a compliment, and when your Chairman astonished me in April by suggesting that I should talk to you today, my heart warmed at once to the whole committee, and I felt that to be among you in July was a pleasure not to be missed. But there is more in it than that. I have long owed a personal debt to Dr. Chapman, whom I first met at one of the meetings of this Society, and whose work, and wit, and scholarship and company have contributed so much to the interest and gaiety of my existence that I responded at once to the idea that I might at last, and in public, be able to pay him a small and grateful tribute.

There are two more names which my heart insists shall be mentioned in the same breath. One is Lady Cynthia Asquith, whom I heard speak on the heroines of Jane Austen on that same day when I first met Dr. Chapman, and who became a loved and admired friend, contributing to the richness of life with her vitality and talent to within a few days of her death. And the other is Miss Elizabeth Jenkins, who has performed the same rare service as the other two—enthralling me with her work as a writer, and contributing very materially to my happiness by the friendship and hospitality which flow from that elegant Regency house of hers in Hampstead, and by that talent for precise and intimate conversation on all topics which I prize above most things, and which in these days of hurry and no-time-for-anything is lamentably rare.

But as well as the temptation of being able to say in public these things which I have long felt in private, there was another temptation about your Chairman's suggestion which I was too self-indulgent to resist. When the suggestion was made, I was about to set off for East Africa to do something very different. I was going out to live in the wilds for a good many weeks, cut off from the normal distractions and annoyances of normal life, and the thought of going out there with my old shabby pocket editions of Jane Austen, and re-reading them at leisure in the bush, was so attractive that I was quite unable to resist it. It did'nt turn out like that, of course. I found myself plunged into fresh difficulties, with no leisure or solitude by day and no light but a feeble hurricane lamp by night; but even so, I re-read four of them: and the experience of taking that highly civilized world with me into the long grass, and the strange preoccupations, and the heat, was one that I would on no account have missed. This re-reading, I must confess, completely upset the theory I set out with, but that kind of upset is stimulating in itself, and is the very thing that I want to talk to you about today. I am not, I am afraid, going to be very helpful to **you.** In fact, I am going to ask you some questions: and since I am among experts I have a very good hope that by tea-time I shall have the answers.

To give you the history of these questions—which are really one big question with one or two little trivial ones in the margin —I shall have to go back some way. I have in my possession a charming book of engravings, published in 1779, called **The Seats of the Nobility and Gentry** in a Collection of the most interesting and Picturesque VIEWS, Engraved by W. Watts, from Drawings by the most eminent Artists, with descriptions of each VIEW; and it is one of my favourite books for a winter evening because, as I have long recognised, it enables me to identify, to admire, and study the details of many of the houses known to me from Jane Austen. It doesn't, of course, contain the Prices' house at Portsmouth, or anything low; it doesn't even contain a decent and commodious parsonage, or anything of that sort; but it does afford a fine choice of Pemberleys, a nice range of Abbeys for either Donwell or Northanger, some convenient great houses, parks and halls which will do for Kellynch, Norland, Mansfield or Uppercross, and a few charming cottages and lodges, which if a little on the ambitious side, with weeping willows and deer, and ladies in hats and veils walking beside the ornamental water, will do well enough for some of the less grandiose establishments. After all, we know well enough from Mr. Robert Ferrars what a cottage can be made to contain—'My dear Lady Elliott,' said he. 'do not be uneasy. The dining-parlour will admit eighteen couples with ease; card-tables may be placed in the drawing-room; the library may be open for tea and other refreshments; and let the supper be set out in the saloon.'

My book, of course, shows me only the exteriors of these houses, but I know well enough, as we all do, what the interiors are like. We all have a lively vision of the grandeurs of Pemberley —the long gallery with its portraits, the windows opening down to the ground with yellow satin curtains, in the saloon ; we could sketch a plan of the drawing-room at Hartfield, marking the exact site of Mr. Woodhouse's armchair and the table where Emma and Harriet do needlework or draw ; we know exactly how the supper-table (presumably in the dining-room) is moved forward to the fire, with dishes of minced chicken and scalloped oysters on it, and of course some soft-boiled eggs and gruel for the cautious, and a fruit tart, and a dish of custard which the host does **not** advise.   We know that at Donwell, where the drawing-room contains plenty to amuse one—'books of engravings, drawers of medals, cameos, corals, shells,'—the service in the dining-room leaves something to be desired, since Mrs. Elton tells us that anything is 'very likely to happen with the Donwell servants, who are all, I have often observed, extremely awkward and remiss. We know, to come to humbler and more intimate apartments, exactly what the east room at Mansfield Park is like, the 'little white attic', 'this nest of comforts' in spite of its wanting a fire, where Fanny shivered in privacy in the winter, and we have an excellent idea of the compact comforts of Captain Harville's lodgings at Lyme, and that other and very different naval officer's home, the Prices' at Portsmouth, where the rooms were too small and everybody slammed the doors and shouted.

So vivid, indeed, has my private vision always been of every domestic interior in Jane Austen's novels that I always turn with a particular eagerness, and some distrust, to any illustrated edition that comes my way, to see whether the artist has got it right or not. Usually, of course, he hasn't. Only in Miss Joan Hassall's engravings in the Folio Society's edition do I find what I am looking for—a perfect response, in period, elegance and feeling, to Jane Austen's magical evocations of proportion and space, of comfort and refinement or the want of them, of furniture, sofas, tables, work-baskets, albums, harps and pianofortes.

So with this lively impression in my mind of the domestic interiors in Jane Austen's novels, and the moving and comical scenes that they enclosed, I thought what a pleasure it would be to re-read the novels with the specific purpose of paying them special attention, of trying to analyse her method of setting her interior scenes, with that feeling for good furniture and elegance, for dress and muslins and finery, which she reveals so unself-consciously in her letters. I set off with my pocket editions, as I thought, with this prospect before me, and you will perhaps imagine my surprise, my increasing dismay, and eventually bewilderment when I found that all those interiors of great house and cottage and parsonage which we know so well are conjured up, so to speak, out of thin air, and very nearly without the aid of description.

Now this is a very curious thing, and surprised me more than I can say, for though I am a person who derives an extreme pleasure from the visual world I am not particularly imaginative about it ; and I don't believe I have a clearer impression of these familiar interiors than anyone else who enjoys and has made a habit of reading the novels. I began with **Mansfield Park,** of which I believed I had a particularly clear impression, and was amazed to discover that there is hardly a word of interior description in it from beginning to end. She tells us so little about the well-ordered house, in fact, that it is hard to guess how we form so sharp an idea of it. It is almost as though she feels it unnecessary to describe a large, quiet, orderly and dignified house because every one must know what it should be like, and any word of description would be superfluous. The servants, for instance, are anything but obtrusive ; the house runs on oiled wheels and apparently by magic. We know there are footmen, because Mrs. Norris 'insults them with injunctions to despatch'; we know that Lady Bertram's maid is called Chapman, and that there must be several housemaids, since one of them interrupts Fanny's conversation with Edmund on the stairs, and on the night of the ball the head housemaid is sent, rather late, to help her to dress; but beyond these passing references they remain invisible. The only object mentioned in the drawing-room is the sofa, which is almost a physical extension of Lady Bertram, like the fringe she is always knotting and which gives her so much trouble; and indeed the only room described at all is that little attic room of Fanny's, which we know so well because—and this is a very rare exception in Jane Austen—she lovingly mentions some of the objects in it. 'The comfort of it'. she tells us, 'in her hours of leisure was extreme . . . Her plants, her books—of which she had been a collector from her first hour of commanding a shilling— her writing desk, and her works of charity and ingenuity, were all within her reach. . . .The room was most dear to her, and she would not have changed its furniture for the handsomest in the house, though what had been originally plain, had suffered all the ill-usage of children ; and its greatest elegancies and ornaments were a faded footstool of Julia's work, too ill-done for the drawing-room, three transparencies, done in a rage for transparencies, for the three lower panes of one window, where Tintern Abbey held its station between a cave in Italy and a moon-lit lake in Cumberland, a collection of family profiles, though unworthy of being anywhere else, over the mantlepiece, and by their side, and pinned against the wall, a small sketch of a ship sent four years ago from the Mediterranean by William, with *H.M.S. Antwerp* at the bottom, in letters as tall as the main-mast.

I have ventured to give this description almost in full because it is so rare in Jane Austen as to be almost unique ; and if you are going to tell me that the Prices' squalid house in Portsmouth is surely described in equal if not greater detail I must confess

Chawton House from the East

that I thought so too at first, and turned to it eagerly, for a second set-piece at least in **Mansfield Park.** But I was quite wrong.

Except that we are told that the parlour into which Fanny is shown was so small that her first conviction was of its being only a passage-room to something better, the whole appearance and atmosphere of the house are built up **not** by visual impressions, but in terms of discomfort and noise. Doors bang; grubby little boys crash about and wrestle on the stairs; the bell doesn't ring, and everybody shouts for what they want; Mr. Price kicks things out of his way in the passage and calls loudly for a candle, which takes a long time in coming; the parlour door is slammed until Fanny's head aches; there are quarrels on the landing; there is a wrangle about a pocket-knife; somebody's shirt-sleeves are mislaid and finally run to earth in the kitchen drawer. It is all noise and movement, sound and discomfort, which produce the striking visual impression.. Only the cramped quarters are insisted on, and that only subjectively : 'The smallness of the rooms above and below, indeed, and the narrowness of the passage and staircase, struck her beyond her imagination. She soon learned to think with respect of her own little attic at Mansfield Park, in that house reckoned too small for anybody's comfort.

By the time I had turned to **Pride and Prejudice** I was aware that interior description is a thing that Jane Austen disciplined herself to do without. In the whole of that great and almost perfect novel, whether we are at the Bennet's or at Netherfield, or Pemberley, or Rosings, or Mr. Collins's parsonage, we are made to see them without the aid of description. I am inclined to think it the most extraordinary sleight-of-hand in the whole of fiction. Turn your mind for a moment to the work of a great contemporary and admirer of Jane Austen, and consider the descriptive force—altogether too overpowering for my taste—being deployed at this very time by Sir Walter Scott. Take a look at another great woman writer, born in the year before Jane Austen died, and see how totally opposite, how inconceivably different, is her method of setting out an important interior. You can **see** how Charlotte Brontë does it; she does it like a painter, working in colours, masses and light; using everything, in fact, from which Jane Austen deliberately abstains. I would like to remind you of a short passage in **Jane Eyre,** the description of the red room, in which Jane as a child is locked in disgrace by her aunt: "The red room was a spare chamber, very seldom slept in; I might say never; yet it was one of the largest and stateliest chambers in the mansion. A bed supporter on massive pillars of mahogany, hung with curtains of deep red damask, stood out like a tabernacle in the centre; the two large windows, with their blinds always drawn down, were half shrouded in festoons and falls of similar drapery; the carpet was red; the table at the foot of the bed was covered with a crimson cloth; the walls were a soft fawn colour, with a blush of pink in it; the wardrobe, the toilet-table, the chairs were of darkly polished old mahogany. Out of these deep surrounding shades rose high, and glared white, the piled-up mattresses and pillows of the bed, spread with a snow-white Marseilles counter-pane. Scarcely less prominent was an ample, cushioned easychair near the head of the bed, also white, with a footstool before it; and looking, as I thought, like a pale throne."

And to that fine set piece, so skilfully prepared for the onset of childish terror, I would like to add one remarkable sentence from **The Professor,** in which Charlotte Brontë, working again like a painter, like Goya, in black and white, conjures up the breakfast room of the little Brussels hotel in which the narrator receives his first foreign impressions of Belgium: "I repaired to the public room; that, too, was very large and very lofty, and warmed by a stove; the floor was black, and the stove was black, and most of the furniture was black; yet I never experienced a freer sense of exhilaration than when I sat down at a very long, black table (covered, however, in part by a white cloth), and, having ordered breakfast, began to pour out my coffee from a little black coffee-pot."

These are both very telling passages of interior description, based wholly on masses of light and shade, with exclamations of colour; could anything be more different from the oblique and abstemious methods of Jane Austen, who, though she will go so far with the outside of a house as to tell us it was a "spacious, modern-built house, situated on a sloping lawn," that it had, or hadn't, a park, a plantation or a shrubbery—though, as I say, she is prepared to tell us this much, to admire a private demesne or recommend a landscape, we are no sooner inside the front door than she falls mysteriously silent; and we are left, solely from our knowledge of the people she is concerned with, and from a few apparently trivial hints that she lets fall by the way, to construct the interiors out of our own fancy. And this is exactly what we do, with peculiar success, making remarkably serviceable bricks without straw, and wondering afterwards, if we ever (as I naively did) take the bricks to pieces, how on earth we ever managed to do it.

The puzzle has been partly solved, I think, by Virginia Woolf, who once wrote in a memorable essay on Jane Austen: "She stimulates us to supply what is not there." That is certainly part of her famous sleight-of-hand: she takes such an immediate grasp of our attention, so firmly directs our imagination on to her characters, and the exact social milieu in which they have their being, that our inner eye obediently supplies everything that she had economically left out, which her classic feeling for shapely simplicity tells her is unnecessary, and which she knows the reader will invent for himself if she gives him the merest suggestion here and there.

These hints, which our imagination picks up and uses visually, are always conveyed through the behaviour of her characters, for her first concern is with the human heart, and her second with the manners of society; and she never allows us a word of description unless it is certain to enlarge our understanding of the one or the other.

A case in point is Lady Bertram's sofa; that sofa is more often mentioned, I believe, than any other piece of furniture, with the possible exception of Marianne Dashwood's instrument; and they are mentioned only as they contribute to our understanding of indolence, or of romanticism. Description for description sake, however fine, is something that I suspect Jane Austen would have found vulgar. In **Northanger Abbey,** the only novel in which she slightly indulges in it, it is done purely for purposes of mockery— for laughing at precisely the kind of atmosphere that Charlotte Brontë, and many other novelists, would have found stirring. The drawing-room at Northanger, you remember, when Catherine Morland first stepped into it, was very far indeed from her fearful imaginings, and to give us a glimpse into Catherine's mind a description of the room and furniture is unavoidable.

"An Abbey! Yes, it was delightful to be really in an Abbey! But she doubted, as she looked round the room, whether anything within her observation would have given her the consciousness. The furniture was in all the profusion and elegance of modern taste. The fire-place where she had expected the ample and ponderous carving of former times, was contracted to a Rumford, with slabs of plain, though handsome, marble, and ornaments over it of the prettiest English china. The windows, to which she looked with peculiar dependence, from having heard the General talk of his preserving them in their Gothic form with reverential care, were yet less than what her fancy had portrayed. To be sure the pointed arch was preserved, the form of them was Gothic, they might be even casements, but every pane was so large, so clear, so light! To an imagination which had hoped for the smallest divisions and the heaviest stonework, for painted glass, dirt and cobwebs, the difference was very distressing." And when she cautiously entered her bedroom, you remember, she was at first reassured to find that "it was by no means unreasonably large, and contained neither tapestry nor velvet" — details which give us an opportunity of laughing both at our eager heroine and at Mrs. Radclyffe.

In the other novels there is, I think, nothing to compare with these deliberate description-pieces, which are done strictly for a purpose, to display the novel-fed romanticism which caused Catherine to care for "no furniture of more modern date than the fifteenth century." Where other interior descriptive passages occur, much more briefly and obliquely introduced, they serve to contribute to a character, and it is by knowledge of the character that we in turn are able to conjure up the room. We are given some clues to the interior of Captain Harville's lodgings at Lyme, because the effect he has had on the lodgings will give us the man. We need to know "all the ingenious contrivances and nice arrangements of Captain Harville to turn the actual space to the best possible account, to supply the deficiencies of lodging-house furniture, and defend the windows and doors against the winter storms to be expected . . . "His lameness prevented him from taking much exercise; but a mind of usefulness and ingenuity seemed to furnish him with constant employment within. He drew, he varnished, he carpentered, he glued; he made toys for the children; he fashioned new netting-needles and pins with improvements; and if everything else was done, sat down to his large fishing-net at one corner of the room."

Jane Austen loved the practical abilities of sailors, and even spared us a glimpse of domestic comfort aboard a man-of-war, in the interest of showing us that Admiral Croft's wife was every bit as alert and practical as her husband. "Women," said Mrs. Croft, "may be as comfortable on board as in the best house in England. I believe I have lived as much on board as most women, and I know nothing superior to the accommodations of a man-of-war . . . I speak, you know, of the higher rates. When you come to a frigate, of course, you are more confined; though any reasonable woman may be perfectly happy in one of them; and I can safely say, that the happiest part of my life has been spent on board a ship. While we were together, you know, there was nothing to be feared."

Once one has become aware of this remarkable conjuring trick in Jane Austen's work, the discrepancy between the extreme spareness of her descriptions and the lively picture we have of the scenes which she has **not** described, it becomes a habit to pause over the few concrete objects which she does mention, to consider them as the odd wisps of straw which imagination picks up like a nesting sparrow, or—since I'd better not change my metaphor so recklessly—as the few odd straws to be found inside those bricks which a responsive imagination makes so well out of non-existent materials. Being so few, they are striking. They are always put there deliberately, and never wasted; they tell us a lot, and are sometimes also puzzling. Consider, for instance, the court-plaster which both Emma and Harriet apparently keep in their pockets. It serves its purpose, of course, since nothing could be more ludicrous than a bit of old sticking-plaster when preserved as a romantic memento of Mr. Elton, and it displays the idiot innocence of poor Harriet to perfection. But it also sets me wondering, and makes one of those trivial marginal queries to which I would like answers. For what purpose did young ladies carry sticking plaster in their apron pockets? Can it be to do with needlework? Did they prick their fingers with needles, cut them with scissors, to such an extent that plaster was part of their equipment, like bobbins or thimbles? It seems unlikely; in the course of a lifelong addiction to my needle, I've never yet required a surgical dressing. Did

232

they constantly cut their fingers with pen-knives, as Mr. Elton once did, to require the immediate provision of court-plaster ? Was this a normal hazard involved in the mending of pens ? It is evidently one of the things which Jane Austen takes for granted, this carrying of sticking plaster in young ladies' pockets, as being too universal to require comment; and I should like to have someone explain it to me.

And then again, how do you revive a young lady with lavender water ? When I read of Elinor doing this for Marianne, after her shattering encounter with Willoughby at a London party, I imagine her dabbing her forehead and temples with a moistened handkerchief; but a few pages further on, when Marianne has become hysterical with grief, we find that "some lavender drops, which she was at length persuaded to take, were of use"—and I am all at sea again, since clearly one **swallows** the stuff, a medication which I find it hard to believe in.

But these minutiae are of no importance ! They are marginal scribblings which amuse me in the same domestic spirit which prompts me to notice the cut of a flounce or the pattern on a footstool in a nineteenth century painting The alphabet letters which the little Knightleys play with, cut out of stiff paper and lettered by their aunt's hand ; Lady Bertram's fringe and Mrs. Jenning's carpet work; the 'rage for transparencies' and the painting of fire-screens—these are some of the very few details which do not contribute to any knowledge of character, but which touch in the detailed background of intimate life. Jane Austen is economical to the point of parsimony with her descriptions, and it still remains one of the mysteries of her genius, which I can do singularly little to explain, that we have so fine and firm an impression of her domestic scenes. It is true indeed that she magically stimulates us to supply what is not there. She is prodigal in telling us what her principal characters think, more prodigal still in telling us what they feel—and here I must digress for a moment to state my conviction that she is generally underrated as a novelist of **feeling.** I am more moved by the secret history of Anne Elliott's heart, and by the undisciplined woe of Marianne Dashwood's—and how could Sir Harold Nicolson ever have called Marianne 'insufferable' ?—than I am by the far more romantic treatment of more emotional novelists. It seems to me that for all her classical perfection, her wit, her irony, and that cheerful heartlessness of which some critics complain, she knew as much as can possibly be known about certain types of female heart in the vicissitudes of love. And she knew very well too, without ever glancing at the sort of indelicacy so fashionable today, the whole range of sexual attractions as displayed by handsome young men. This is particularly clear in her artful presentation of those young men of whom her moral sense insists that we shall disapprove Ah, those young men ! Willoughby, Wickham, and of course the entrancing, and surely less heartless and dangerous,

Henry Crawford! There is no spinterish primness in her approach to these; she knew what she was writing about; there is ardour under the surface of her well-behaved approach; and I am surprised that she is still not always given credit for it.

But this a digression, and a self-indulgent one at that. All I intended to do was to set out a puzzle, and to invite you to solve it. What people think, what they say, how they feel and what they do, Jane Austen is scrupulous to tell us; the background of all this activity she leaves generally to us. Her descriptive set pieces are remembered because they are so rare; when they occur they are brief, only a few lines; and because I have a feeling that some of you are waiting to remind me of that cheerful half-paragraph which tells us all we need to know about Christmas at Uppercross, I will remind you myself:

'Immediately surrounding Mrs. Musgrove were the little Harvilles, whom she was sedulously guarding from the tyranny of the two children from the Cottage, expressly arrived to amuse them. On one side was a table occupied by some chattering girls, cutting up silk and gold paper; and on the other were tressels and trays, bending under the weight of brawn and cold pies, where riotous boys were holding high revel; the whole completed by a roaring Christmas fire, which seemed determined to be heard in spite of all the noise of the others. Charles and Mary also came in, of course, during their visit, and Mr. Musgrove made a point of paying his respects to Lady Russell, and sat down close to her for ten minutes, talking with a very raised voice, but from the clamour of the children on his knees, generally in vain. It was a fine family piece.'

And so it is, almost in the manner of Dickens, and we have a very clear picture of it. But where we get the others from, which we carry about with us as part of our enjoyment of Jane Austen, but which she has never, when we come to look for them, given us, I leave it to yourselves to determine.

Margaret Lane

21. 7.62.

Essay Competition

The Committee considered that the essays submitted to them were of a high standard.

The three prizewinners, in order of merit, were:

1st, Sophia Marshall, Winchester County High School;
2nd, Celia Howard, Gosport County Grammar School;
3rd, Sheila Beal, Gosport County Grammar School.

The prizes will be presented at the Annual General Meeting.

THE JANE AUSTEN SOCIETY

Report for the Year 1963

Table, believed to have belonged to Jane Austen, bequeathed to the
Jane Austen Memorial Trust by the late Mr. Arthur Jeffress

235

THE JANE AUSTEN SOCIETY

Report for the Year 1963

――――o――――

Sixty-one new members joined during the year and there were 11 new Life Members. Total membership now numbers 948. Of these, 109 live in the U.S.A., 22 in the Commonwealth outside the United Kingdom, and nine in other countries.

Members are reminded that subscriptions are due on 1st January, and that this Report is the only reminder that they will receive. The Hon. Secretary would much appreciate prompt payment of the 5/- Annual Subscription, and will gladly provide a Bankers' Order form.

Annual General Meeting, 1963

The Annual General Meeting was held at Chawton House, by kind permission of Major and Mrs. Edward Knight, on Saturday, 20th July. The Duke of Wellington presided. Almost 400 members and friends attended.

Opening the meeting, the President referred to the retirement from the office of Chairman of Mr. John Gore, who had agreed to continue as literary adviser. He also referred to the Essay Competition, and to the co-operation of the County Education Officers and of the Headmasters.

He asked that the minutes of the last Annual General Meeting, which had been published in the Annual Report, be taken as read. There were no matters arising.

The Hon. Secretary presented the Annual Report for 1962, and, in the absence of the Hon. Treasurer, the Balance Sheet. It was proposed by Commander Holmes, seconded by Miss Harris, and carried, that these be adopted.

It was proposed by the Hon. Secretary, seconded by Miss Diana Morgan, and carried, that the Duke of Wellington be re-elected as President.

It was proposed by Sir John Russell, seconded by Miss Hay, and carried, that Mr. T. Edward Carpenter and Mr. John Gore be elected Vice-Presidents.

It was proposed by Mr. John Gore, seconded by Sir Hugh Smiley, and carried, that Lt.-Col. Sir William Makins be elected Chairman.

The President proposed the re-election, en bloc, of the Committee.

Mr. T. Edward Carpenter gave a short account of the activities of the Jane Austen Memorial Trust.

The prizewinners in the Essay Competition received their prizes from the President.

The meeting was addressed by Miss Elizabeth Jenkins, who discussed the taste of Jane Austen's day.

A vote of thanks was proposed by the Rev. J. P. Bushell, seconded by Mrs. Field, and carried.

The meeting was closed by the President thanking Major and Mrs. Knight for lending Chawton House for the meeting, after which tea was provided in aid of Chawton Church Funds, when a sum of over £50 was raised.

Annual General Meeting, 1964

The Annual General Meeting will be held on Saturday, 18th July. The speaker will be Lord David Cecil, C.H.

A Link with America

The painting reproduced here, of "Christ's Rejection by the Elders," and its companion picture, "Christ Healing the Sick," should be of particular interest to the members of the Jane Austen Society.

Both pictures, and their American painter, Benjamin West, were a "talking point," in September, 1814, and they were the subject of sincere comment from Jane Austen.

It has been said that "Jane Austen cared nothing for the visual arts," but her opportunities were incredibly limited by modern standards. Such as they were, I think, she made the most of them. One of her brothers—Henry—was a faithful follower of the arts, and when she stayed with him in London, he always took her to the current picture exhibitions. Though Jane Austen, as she said herself, usually inclined to attend "more to the company than the sight."

This occasion seems to have been an exception, however. She wrote to her friend Martha Lloyd in 1814:

Friday, September 2nd.   23, Hans Place.

—I have seen West's famous Painting, and prefer it to anything of the kind I ever saw before. I do not know that it **is** reckoned superior to his "Healing in the Temple," but it has gratified **me** much more, and indeed is the first representation of

238

Christ Rejected by the Elders
(Courtesy of the Pennsylvania Academy of Fine Arts)

our Saviour which ever at all contented me. "His Rejection by the Elders" is the subject—I want to have you and Cassandra see it—

"Christ Rejected by the Elders"—a painting 22 feet long, is in the Pennsylvania Academy of Fine Arts. "Christ Healing the Sick" was once, I believe, in the Tate Gallery. But my efforts to trace it, in 1961, were unsuccessful.

Winifred Watson

23, Hans Place

Captain and Mrs. S. J. Thomson, the owners of 23, Hans Place, have, with help from the Jane Austen Society, put up a commemorating plaque, which we reproduce.

Lydia Languish, Lydia Bennet, and Dr. Fordyce's Sermons

The youngest Miss Bennet in **Pride and Prejudice** and Miss Languish, the comic heroine of Sheridan's play **The Rivals,** are both called Lydia; they are both of the kind to be attracted by a young man's military uniform, what Sir Lucius O'Trigger calls "a bit of red cloth." They both think favourably of the romantic possibilities of an elopement: Miss Languish sets her heart on eloping and Lydia Bennet elopes indeed. Though viewed by their creators with very different degrees of indulgence they are both very silly girls. One might be content to leave it at that if it were not for a further revealing detail: they are both made to show a marked lack of response to the celebrated **Sermons for Young Women** (1765) by an eminent Presbyterian, the Rev. Dr. James Fordyce. Lydia Languish has allowed some pages of her copy of Fordyce's **Sermons** to be torn up to make curl-papers **(The Rivals** Act I Sc. II). When Mr. Collins is invited to read aloud to the ladies of Longbourn on his first evening there he chooses, "after some deliberation," Fordyce's **Sermons.** "Lydia gaped as he opened the volume and before he had with very monotonous solemnity read three pages she interrupted him" **(Pride and Prejudice,** Ch. XIV).

One would have expected anyhow that Jane Austen would have read or seen Sheridan's famous play. It is known that she liked sometimes to make use of names which had already acquired suitable associations for her. "Lydia" she uses only this once; no doubt it was her knowledge of Miss Languish that had surrounded that name for her with a suitable aura of youthful silliness.

A word may be added about Dr. Fordyce's **Sermons for Young Women.** They are by no means contemptible and might well deserve a place in Mr. Bennet's library or in the drawing-room at Longbourn; it is not quite clear from whence they are "produced." Everything considered, Dr. Fordyce's views are not illiberal. His manner of writing must however have appeared stiff and old-fashioned to the company at Longbourn and his phrases are often such as would be all too congenial to Mr. Collins. Dr. Fordyce's habit of referring to "my fair auditory" or "my fair hearers" would come naturally to the lips of Mr. Collins who addresses Elizabeth as "my fair cousin." Dr. Fordyce's disapproval of novels would also recommend him more to Mr. Collins than, one imagines, to the Bennets; and the pronouncement which the Presbyterian divine makes on dancing, "I can see no reason for declamation against the moderate and discreet use of dancing," has the same air of conscious liberality about it as Mr. Collins' comment on Mr. Bingley's ball, "I am by no means of opinion, I assure you . . . that a ball of this kind given by a young man of character to respectable people can have any evil tendency." In

The Rev. Dr. James Fordyce—1720-1796

From the original portrait by Tassie, reproduced as a Medallion by Josiah Wedgwood in the 1780's, now in the Wedgwood Museum, by whose courtesy it is reproduced.

242

fairness to Dr. Fordyce one must remember that he was speaking in the pulpit and thirty or forty years earlier. Jane Austen chooses not to tell us what pages of Fordyce's **Sermons** Mr. Collins lit upon that evening at Longbourn. There is a passage of the first sermon "On the Importance of the Female Sex, especially the younger Part" that has particular relevance to the adventures of Lydia Bennet. "The world, I know not how," says Dr. Fordyce, "overlooks in our sex a thousand irregularities which it never forgives in yours; so that the honour and peace of a family are in this view much more dependant on the conduct of daughters than of sons; and one young lady going astray shall subject her relations to such discredit and distress as the united good conduct of all her brothers and sisters, supposing them numerous, shall scarce ever be able to repair." Mr. Collins echoes this sentiment when writing to Mr. Bennet on the subject of Lydia's elopement. "Be assured, my dear Sir, that Mrs. Collins and myself sincerely sympathise with you, and all your respectable family, in your present distress, which must be of the bitterest kind because proceeding from a cause which no time can remove . . . you are grievously to be pitied, in which opinion I am not only joined by Mrs. Collins, but likewise by Lady Catherine and her daughter, to whom I have related the affair. They agree with me in apprehending that this false step in one daughter will be injurious to all the others, for who, as Lady Catherine herself condescendingly says, will connect themselves with such a family ?" **(Pride and Prejudice**, Vol. III, Ch. VI).

It seems not unlikely that Dr. Fordyce's **Sermons to Young Women** have contributed a little to the making of Mr. Collins. Nothing that Dr. Fordyce himself says is absurd. but Mr. Collins by using his pulpit phraseology in the wrong place and at the wrong time produces an impression of stiff-necked self-importance that is all his own.

E. E. Duncan-Jones

Chawton in 1753

In 1606, William Symonds of Winchester, by will, bequeathed to the Mayor and Corporation of Winchester all his property in Chawton, with the stipulation that the rents obtained therefrom should be used for the relief of the poor in the city of Winchester.

In 1753 the Corporation employed the well-known surveyor William Godson to map out their estates; the survey, part of which is produced here, shows the Chawton property (hatched). By the

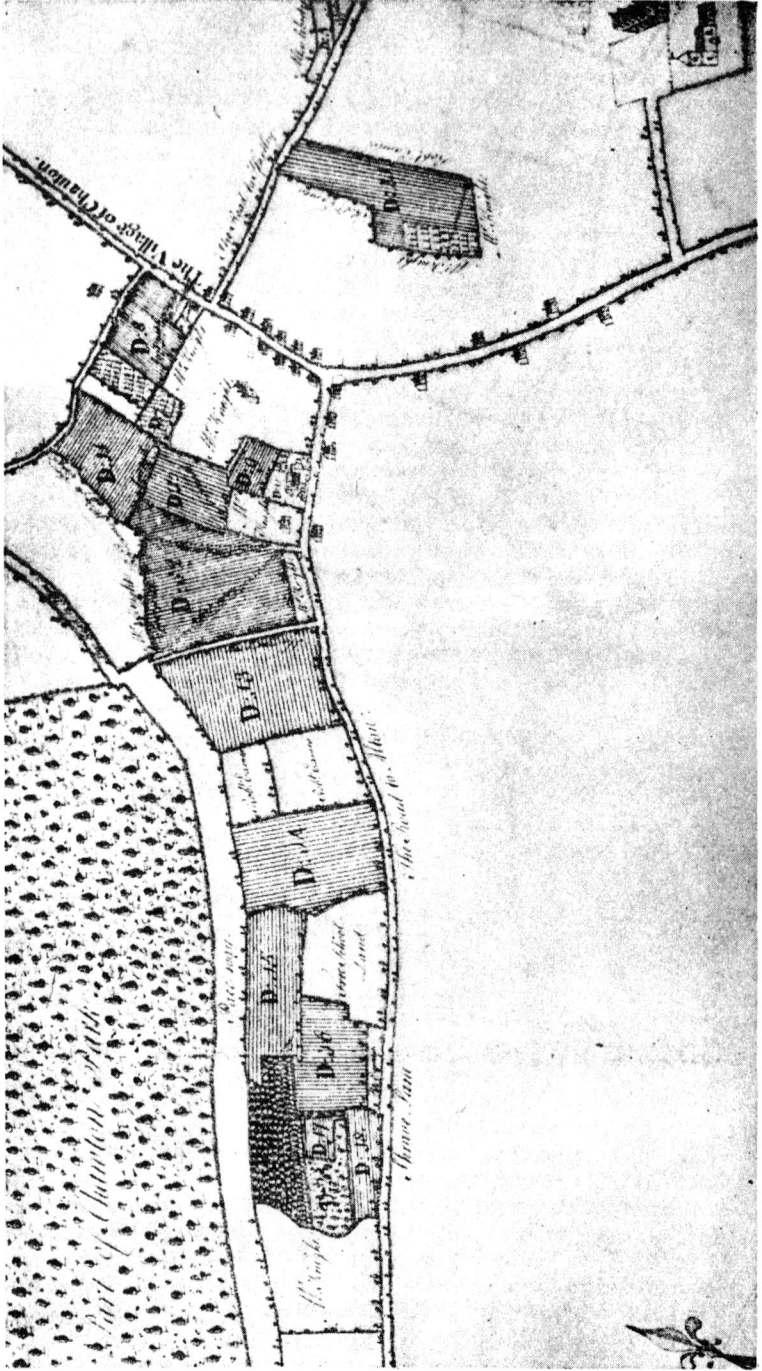

Chawton in 1753

beginning of the 19th century it consisted of about 160 acres of land, an old farm house and some outbuldings, leased to William Baigen in 1812 for 40 years at £20 a year. The land was scattered, in four different parts of the parish, and part of it was taken by the Mid-Hants Railway Company in 1864 for the construction of the railway. By this time, the administration of the Chawton estate was vested in the Charity Commissioners, and they sold off the rest of the land in 1869.

Apart from the Winchester interest, this survey of 1753 also shows some of the property of the Knight family who had been lessors of the manor house since 1524, and owned the site since 1571. Presumably the Mr. Knight referred to on this map was Thomas Knight, senior; after the death of his son in 1794, the property passed to Edward Austen.

Barbara Carpenter Turner

Miss E. Jenkins' Address 1963

On Thursday, February 4th, 1813, Jane Austen wrote from Chawton to Cassandra Austen at Steventon, to say that Mrs. Austen had been reading Pride and Prejudice aloud to a small circle consisting of Martha Lloyd, Miss Benn and Jane herself, and this had given the writer her first opportunity of hearing what the book sounded like now it was in print. Her impression on the whole had been favourable, but she said:

"The work is rather too light and bright and sparkling—it wants shade; it wants to be stretched out here and there with a long chapter of sense, if it could be had; if not, of solemn, specious nonsense, about something unconnected with the story—an essay on writing, a critique on Walter Scott or the history of Bonaparte." The remedies she proposed make one believe that she did not view the draw-back very seriously, and the epithets she used: light, bright and sparkling, it seems to me, characterize not only this, her most striking if not her greatest work, and evoke one of the immediately recognizable characteristics of all her work, but they call up the image of the era in which the works were written: that period of achievement in writing, music, painting, architecture and design, which included the years from 1788 to 1820, the period covering those three separate periods when the Prince of Wales acted as Prince Regent for his deranged father: an era almost exactly that of Jane Austen's own, since she was born in 1775 and died in 1817.

The very word Regency calls up the vision of something bright and elegant, of vigorous, formal simplicity and natural grace. It is the more striking by contrast with the period from which it emerged, the early eighteenth century with its wigs and hoops and full skirted coats and beautiful but solid furniture, and with that which succeeded it, the scene created by the congestion and garishness and mechanical power produced by the rapid and enormous development of the Industrial Revolution. Distinctive and brief, it is invested, in our longing eyes, with the light that never was on sea or land; but of course, common sense and common humanity, remind us of its dark hues and sombre elements. Then, too, since it was England, the weather must often have been bad; indeed we know it was; Jane Austen had a walker's interest in the weather, and her letters are often full of rain. In November, 1808, it came into the store closet at Southampton. Jane began by moving the contents away from the damp area, but at last she had to say: "The contest between us and the store closet has now ended in defeat. I have been obliged to move almost everything out of it and leave it to splash itself as it likes." In 1813 she said: "July begins unpleasantly with us, cold and showery, but it is often a baddish month." In the March of 1816 she exclaims:

"Our Pond is brimful and our roads are dirty and our walks are damp and we sit, wishing every bad day may be the last."

These are disadvantages we experience ourselves, but then, ordinary life had a harshness that has been mercifully removed from our own. One need only read Cassandra's brief account of Jane's last hours, dying of a malignant disease without sedatives and pain-killing drugs:

"She said she could not tell us what she suffered. When I asked her if there was anything she wanted, her answer was: she wanted nothing but death."

But this is not the emphasis that suggests itself in the beautiful remains of the period. We know the elements were there, but in some mysterious way, they subside and give place to others—as we sometimes say of a face: Yes, now you mention it, he **has** a short nose or a long upper lip, but it doesn't strike you when you look at him.

What is this aspect of the age, so peculiarly its own, that we seize upon wherever we find it ? It is easier to recognize than to describe. If we are looking over a collection of articles in a junk shop, how startlingly any relic of the Regency proclaims itself, if we are lucky enough to come upon it ! Among plastic beakers, battered electric torches, necklaces that look like strings of sucked sweets, aluminium photograph frames, a plate whose "contemporary" decoration consists of a row of shapeless coloured patches arranged round the rim, how we dart and pounce upon a pepper pot, made of valueless metal, but shaped like a little urn, or a glass picture of the death of Nelson, in which a crudely coloured print has been pasted underneath a sheet of green glass, the whole framed in shiny maple wood. Made to be sold for public houses, sold cheaply, then. We shan't buy it cheaply now.

How was it that the same spirit inspired the productions made for rich and poor: the painted china of Derbyshire, Bristol, Swansea, and Wedgwood's factory at Stoke, for the dining rooms and tea tables of the great, and for the humble family, the Sunderland ware of black transfers on a white ground and a rim of rosy-lilac lustre: that the sense of form showed itself not only in the classically inspired chairs and sofas from the workshops of Chippendale and Sheraton, but in the rough, beautiful chairs and tables and corner cupboards made for cottages? I think one answer is: the smallness of the population. In 1800, the combined populations of England and Wales barely reached ten million. In so small a society, one idiom of taste can dominate all walks of life, and the taste in this instance was, I suggest, moulded by two factors:

One was the innate sense of the beautiful, fostered by the fact that people were never entirely cut off from the unspoiled beauties of English scenery. The towns, including even London, were full of gardens and lanes, and as soon as you left the town, you were in the country. The sight of beautiful buildings in beautiful landscape was a perpetual experience for them. For us: to drive from London to Leatherhead, say, or down to Rochester, through the endless, traffic-congested streets with their coagulated, toppling erections of multiple stores and shops and municipal flats and towering offices of glass and concrete: is one continuous mental agony, sharpened by the sight here and there of a little neglected terrace of exquisite proportions, each house with its symmetrical facade of sash windows and pillared, fan-lighted front door: the only object worth preserving within a radius of miles, but a slum tenement now, because no one who could afford to live elsewhere would live in the ceaseless uproar of a main road. Is it any wonder that we have no music, no painting, no poetry, no novels, which can compare with the best of what had been produced by 1863? But honesty compels one to admit that we have something else. Jane Austen and her family settled in Chawton in 1809, and in that year the journal devoted to fashion, La Belle Assemblée, carried this story on the page it reserved for interesting events. A man had been apprehended by the local authorities of a country town and put into the lock-up, and before he could be brought before the magistrates he was dead. An autopsy revealed that there was nothing in his stomach but grass. During the twenty-four hours he was in official hands, he had collapsed and died of starvation. The authorities did not feel that they had been to blame. If the man had had money for food, they would have bought food for him. As he had no money, naturally he could have no food. This event shocked people; if it had not been thought shocking, it would not have rated any space among the topicalities of La Belle Assemblée. It had happened because the system had been logically and ruthlessly carried out when there was no one at hand with the sense to act in the interests of human decency. Bad things happen today for the same reason but not things as bad as that. You can still die of starvation in England, but you can't do it according to the book of rules.

But for the producers and the consumers, the era of the Napoleonic Wars was one of great prosperity; and the other factor I would suggest as giving its characteristics to the taste of the period was merely one of date. This was the last era during which man controlled the machine. The machine-made objects of the early nineteenth century are as beautiful as if they had been made by hand; the machine was then an extension of the powers of the hand: a length of wall-paper or of printed cotton from a press or a mill of 1800, or a chest of drawers from a Regency cabinet maker, for which the nails and screws and the handles and the brass inlay had come from a factory, were some of the most beautiful objects of their kind ever produced. The taste that created them was man's. The same can hardly be said of the gross of plastic ash-trays produced by one punch of the handle.

If we choose the year 1810, midway between Trafalgar and Waterloo, we can see the conscious image of the time in an aquatint depicting a London square. The houses are pale and exquisitely formal; no buildings overtop them; the blue sky with its white clouds is empty above the chimney pots. The garden, set out with young shrubs, is enclosed in an iron paling; the roadway about it is blissfully empty. One carriage, canary yellow with scarlet wheels, bowls away in the distance. In the foreground, two couples are walking, arm in arm. The clothes of both men and women are based on a classical design—in other words, they follow the lines of the human figure. The men's long, tight trousers show the form of their legs, their coats too are close-fitting except that they have tails. The stock and the small-brimmed hat complete the human outlines without distorting it. The women's clothes show the same principle. Their dresses are high waisted with long straight skirts, their shoes are flat. One wears a small hat, the other wears a handkerchief tied over her head as a girl would now; one of them is dressed in pale pink, the other in white.

One may exclaim that this print, though contemporary, is a disingenuous idealization of the actual scene. There is no mud or horse dung on the road. To complete the picture there should be a starving man holding out an imploring hand, while his weak, desperate moanings are ignored by the ladies and gentlemen as

248

part of the perpetual nuisance of beggars. But one ventures to believe that it is the self-conscious image of the age, the picture it likes to draw of itself, what it picks up and what it leaves out, that corresponds to a great extent, with the vision of its artists, except the most eccentric of them, and even these, if subjected to Marxist analysis, would I daresay be found to evince some signs of the prevailing idiom. And so, though Jane Austen writes faithfully in her letters of rain and ruined crops and dirty roads and leaking houses, she seems to us to epitomize the atmosphere of the time when she speaks of a day in October as "a very bright, crystal afternoon." Her favourite poet Crabbe does it too when he describes girls and young men wading on the shore:

> Now arm in arm, now parted they behold
> The glittering waters on the shingle rolled.
> The timid girls, half dreading their design,
> Dip the small foot in the retarded brine—
> And search for crimson weeds which spreading flow
> Or lie like pictures on the sand below—
> With all those bright red pebbles that the sun
> Through the small waves so softly shines upon.
> And those live, lucid jellies which the eye
> Delights to trace as they swim glittering by.

To leave for a moment the painters in words for the painters with a brush, I must speak cautiously for it is a subject on which I know very little, but I would suggest that the painters of the late eighteenth and early nineteenth centuries seem to have very often in their pictures the luminous, glowing look that water imparts to a landscape. Their fondness for painting water seems to have been most marked: one thinks of Wilson's "Boys Bathing" and his "The Thames at Twickenham," Crome's "Scene on the River at Norwich," his "Poringland Oak" and his "Moonrise over the Marshes of the Yare"; of the transparency of the water colourists, Cotman, Girtin, Bonington, and above all of Constable and his treatment of water and light, and of Turner and his vision of luminous space. Sir John Rothenstein in his "Introduction to English Painting" quotes a statement made by the French Impressionists themselves, that they had been preceded by Turner in their aim of "applying themselves with passion to the rendering of the fugitive phenomena of light."

Moving once again from the sphere of paint to that of language, what a contrast meets us when we look thirty years ahead, to 1851, and the stupendous description of fog that opens Bleak House ! Where though it is daytime, the sickly gas burns ineffectively in the choking fumes, "the smoke, lowering down from the chimney pots, contains flakes of soot as large as snowflakes" and there is "as much mud in the streets as if the waters had but newly retired from the face of the earth, and it would not be wonderful to meet a Megalosaurus forty feet long, waddling like an elephantine lizard up Holborn Hill." There had been London fogs under the Regency, the French traveller Simond noticed them, but this was how they came after thirty years of increasingly rapid industrial expansion, that had filled the air with smuts and choked the streets with traffic and mud.

Jane Austen said of picture exhibitions in general: "My preference for men and women always inclines me to attend more to the company than the sight," and her own practice was to give visual description a minor place in her work; but when she describes anything, how masterly she does it. One cannot claim as an example of description characteristic of the age, the passage in Mansfield Park where she says that "everything that was solemn and soothing and lovely appeared in the brilliancy of an unclouded night and the contrast of the deep shade of the woods," such a description is timeless. But her description of the walk on the ramparts at Portsmouth does seem to me characteristic of the age that produced Constable. "It was really March, but it was April in its mild air, brisk, soft wind and bright sun occasionally clouded for a minute, and everything looked so beautiful under the influence of such a sky, the effect of the shadows pursuing each other on the ships at Spithead and the Island beyond with the ever-varying hues of the sea, now at high water, dancing in its glee and dashing against the ramparts with so fine a sound." While one of the very last descriptions she can ever have written might be an illustration, though in strongly realist idiom, to a guide to the Watering Places on the coast. It is the scene of Charlotte Heywood's arrival at the Parker's new house at Sanditon:

"Trafalgar House on the most elevated spot in the town was a light, elegant building, standing on a small lawn with a very young plantation round it, about a hundred yards from a steep but not very lofty cliff . . . Charlotte having received possession of her apartment, found amusement enough in standing at her ample Venetian window, and looking over the miscellaneous foreground of unfinished buildings, waving linen and tops of houses, to the sea, dancing and sparkling in sunshine and freshness."

Jane Austen says very little about dress in the novels but the little she does say is in accordance with the fashion that was a part of the universal preference for what was pale, airy and bright. The overwhelming popularity of muslin made it the most fashionable of all materials for women's dress: the plain sorts, white or coloured, woven on English looms, or the most beautiful and expensive kinds worked with gold or silver, imported from the East. The Regent's daughter, the ill-fated Princess Charlotte, whose extensive trousseau is described in the contemporary memoir by Mr. Huish, had a great collection of white muslin dresses; also "an India muslin worked in small gold spots, very thick," and "a

dress of transparent net worked in bright silver and dead silver."
On May 16, 1816, she and the Prince Leopold attended Queen
Charlotte's Drawing-Room on the occasion of their marriage,
and the Princess wore the dress that can be seen in the London
Museum. It looks like a dress and train entirely turned to silver
by an enchanter's wand; it is made of silver tissue, trimmed with
silver lace, and in the words of Mr. Huish: "the draperies are
elegantly supported with a most brilliant cord of real silver bullion,
and very superb silver tassels." The Princess wore on her head a
wreath of roses, buds and leaves, all set with diamonds and
mounted in silver. Though pale pink, pale blue, yellow and lilac
were all fashionable colours, the acme of elegance was white. A
glance at the catalogue of Princess Charlotte's trousseau confirms
this, so do Jane Austen's references to it. A sort of sumptuary
law seems to have been attached to its use; Mrs. Norris was
delighted to hear that the housekeeper at Sotherton had turned
away two housemaids for wearing white gowns, and in the same
novel occurs the conversation between Fanny and Edmund in the
carriage on their way to dine at the Parsonage. Fanny is wearing
the frock Sir Thomas Bertram gave her for the wedding of Maria
and Mr. Rushworth.

"I hope it is not too fine, but I thought I ought to wear it as
soon as I could, and that I might not have such another opportunity
all the winter. I hope you do not think me too fine."

"A woman can never be too fine while she is all in white.
Your gown seems very pretty. I like these glossy spots. Has not
Miss Crawford a gown something the same?" The glossy spots,
I think, on Fanny's gown would not be silver, but "satin-spot."
Mrs. Elton, the mistress of as many thousand pounds as would
always be called ten, had a white and silver poplin.

The mania for whiteness extended to buildings as well as
dress. The large tract of open land originally known as Mary-le-
bone Fields had fallen in to the Crown: and in honour of the
Prince Regent had been renamed The Regent's Park. The
Government invited tenders for laying it out and the result was the
half-circle of splendid terraces, chiefly the work of John Nash,
which begins west of the Park, with Hanover Terrace, and
continues eastwards with Sussex Place, Clarence Terrace, Cornwall
Terrace, York Terrace, Park Square, Cambridge Terrace, Chester
Terrace and ends with Cumberland Terrace, six of them named
for the family of George III. Pale as alabaster, they stand,
beautifully thrown up by the greenery of grass, shrubs and the
green-tufted islands in the ornamental water. Nash's use of milk-
white stucco earned him the quip:

Is not our Nash a very great master?

He finds us all brick and he leaves us all plaster.

251

Snuff Box, bearing a Cameo of the Prince Regent, in the possession of the Duke of Wellington

While these beautiful ranges of buildings were still being erected, Mr. Elmes took a walk around them which he describes in his work: "Metropolitan Improvements." The day is one in May, and in what he calls "this sparkling season of the year," he says the swans are floating on the silvery surface of the lake, spangled with ever-moving gems. He pauses outside a house in York Terrace, where, he says, lofty, well proportioned windows give light to the elegant drawing rooms; he breaks off to exclaim:

"But hark at that delightful harp! It comes from the open window with the tamboured muslin curtains. The lovely musician is revelling in all the brilliancy of Arpeggio variations." The Terraces past which he takes his sauntering stroll are the finest examples of building to be seen but building is going on apace in many areas. He is a little disturbed at the rapidity with which houses are going up. "It would be curious," he says, "to ask those gentlemen in what part of the neighbouring counties they intended that London should end? The rustic and primeval meadows of Kilburn are filling with new buildings and incipient roads, to say nothing of the charming neighbourhood of St. John's Wood Farm." Meanwhile, Mr. Elmes says, it is the height of the London Season and the town is "resplendently full." Carriages are thundering towards Regent Street, on their way to Buckingham Palace. One of them contains the Austrian Ambassador, Prince Esterhazy, who is wearing enough diamonds to buy an English manor. Prince Esterhazy was noted for the enormous quantity of diamonds he wore on his person. It was a fashion to which he kept throughout a long diplomatic career. At the coronation of Queen Victoria, crossing a bar of sunlight in the Abbey he shone like a rainbow; "as he dangled his hat, it cast a dancing radiance around."

The diamond, so much in keeping with the age's effects of clarity and brilliance, was imitated in that characteristic decoration of the period, the cut-glass chandelier. Simond, who visited Birmingham in 1809, saw flint glass being cut into pendants for chandeliers. He was astonished at the process:

"So hard a substance ground by the simple friction of a wheel, turning at high speed!"

He was also amazed at the factory's being lighted by hydrogen gas: "absolutely as bright as day!" "A leaden tube," he says, "runs round the apartment with a number of cocks, which, opened more or less, let off a little stream of gas which is set on fire, presenting a bright flame of several inches in length."

This product, cut flint glass, was used profusely in rich houses, nowhere to greater effect than in Carlton House, rebuilt and decorated for the Prince Regent by Henry Holland. Here, brilliant chandeliers depended from ceilings painted to imitate a blue sky mottled with white clouds. The shape of the chandelier was that of a great circle of cut glass pendants, supporting a ring of wax lights; the circle hung from a sheaf of strings of cut glass drops, the sheaf bound closer and closer together as it ascended to the ceiling, so that the effect was that of the basin of a fountain sparkling with prismatic lustres from which shot up into the painted sky, a lofty jet: motionless, but with light trembling all over the curves of its water-gleaming chains. In the Throne Room and the Circular Drawing Room of Carlton House the immense torrents of lustrous drops supported, not one, but three circles of lights, diminishing in size one above the other. Does one not feel that this spectacle was an expression in visual form of the music characteristic of the time: of the rapid, brilliant, exhilarating passages of Mozart played on a harpsicord, or of Rossini, whose opera "William Tell" was first performed in 1816?

When one thinks of the other art of public entertaining: acting, the name of Mrs. Siddons at first blots out that of everybody else; but though her popularity was enormous, Mrs. Siddons' acting can hardly be cited as an example of the spirit of the time: she was a tragic actress and her overpowering genius put her beyond fashion, but there was an actress, second only to Mrs. Siddons in her magical power over audiences, descriptions of whose art seem altogether in harmony with that of the painter and musician of the era. Mrs. Jordan reached the highwater mark of her career in 1814 with her dazzling appearance as Lady Teazle. Sir Joshua Reynolds who saw her in her early days, said: "She ran on to the stage as if it were a playground, and laughed from sincere wildness of delight." Hazlitt, who in 1814, was the dramatic critic on the Morning Chronicle, said "she talked far above singing; her singing was like the twang of Cupid's bow." Her contemporary biographer, Boaden, said she had: "An expression of face so brilliant, that seemed never to tire in giving pleasure. The sight of her was a general signal for the most unrestrained delight."

This ravishing creature became the mistress of the Regent's brother, the Duke of Clarence. The Duke make a settlement on her of £1,000 a year, but he made it on paper only. It was she who kept him, out of the large earnings she made when she was not obliged to leave the stage to lie in of his children. However, when the £1,000 was under discussion, the Duke sent her word that the old King thought it too much, and had recommended him to reduce it to £500. Mrs. Jordan replied by tearing off and sending to him a strip from the bottom of a play-bill, which said, "No money can be refunded after the raising of the curtain."

Of the man whose title gave the period its name, it is difficult to find much that is agreeable to say, except that his aesthetic bent amounted to genius and that his manners earned him the name of the First Gentleman in Europe. Nevertheless, stout, dandified, disreputable as he was, I, at least, have been a little surprised at the vicious hatred he aroused in the populace, so that even in the triumphant year 1814, when London was en fête for the visit of the Allied Sovereigns, the Prince Regent could hardly show himself in the streets for fear of missiles being thrown through the glass windows of his coach. Unpleasant as he must have been, in his selfishness and his self pity, his corpulence and his folly, still one had thought of him more as a figure of fun than an object of passionate resentment. But I was made to think again by the sight of his portrait as a very young man, painted by Gainsborough, and shown at Kenwood House. I was astonished to see how very beautiful he had once been, and as one had thought of him as a laughable, self-indulgent trifler, I was disagreeably impressed by the expression of the beautiful young face: it is stony-eyed, with an air of callousness that must be seen to be credited. The remembrance of this picture interested me very much when I read the letter from Jane Austen to Martha Lloyd, first published by Dr. Chapman in 1952, on the affairs of the Regent's wife, Caroline of Brunswick, who, stout, dirty, improper and an unmitigated nuisance, had nevertheless aroused Jane Austen's compassion. The latter had, one believes, without a trace of that hostility to men as such, which is implied by feminism, a warm sympathy for members of her own sex. She said in *Sanditon :* "With due exceptions; woman feels for woman very promptly and compassionately." In her letter of February 1813, she says: "Poor woman, I shall support her as long as I can, because she *is* a woman and because I hate her husband. I am resolved at least always to think she would have been respectable, if the Prince had behaved only tolerably to her at first."

This letter, written as it was, two years before Jane Austen visited Carlton House at the Prince Regent's invitation, sent through his librarian Mr. Stanier Clarke, puts that episode, and Jane Austen's attitude to it, into clearer focus. No letter of hers remains giving her own account of the visit, and one remembers that her family never produced, as they might naturally have done, any tradition of her having been greately elated, or even of her laughing at herself for being so. That she accepted the invitation was a matter of course, but what does emerge in her letter to Mr. Stanier Clarke, is her anxiety to have confirmed, beyond a possibility of mistake, what he had said to her as to the Regent's permission to dedicate to him any work she had on hand. Uncertainty on such a point was unbearable As she said: "I should be equally concerned to appear presumptuous or ungrateful." What a charming light is for the moment thrown on the Prince Regent. He had heard through the doctor attending Henry Austen that the authoress of *Sense and Sensibility, Pride and Prejudice* and *Mansfield Park.* was now in London, staying with her sick brother, and he told Mr. Stanier Clarke to offer to show her over Carlton House and to pay her any attention in his power. Mr. Stanier Clarke was, one fears, a foolish man in his private capacity. He wanted Jane Austen to write a novel about him, but his letter as the Prince Regent's librarian is a model of gentle courtesy and sense:

"It is certainly not incumbent on you to dedicate your work now in the Press to his Royal Highness, but if you wish to do the Regent that honour, I am happy to send you the permission. The Regent has read and admired all your publications."

That the work: "by his Royal Highness' permission, most respectfully dedicated," should have been "Emma," not, one supposes the most generally beloved of her novels, but perhaps the consummate achievement of her art, and that while this book was actually in Murray's hands, Jane Austen was shown that chef d'oeuvre of Henry Holland, the Circular Drawing Room at Carlton House, brings together two of the highest examples of the period's art. The Circular Drawing Room was on the first floor, and Holland had decorated it in tones of lavender, silver and sky-blue. There were porphyry columns at intervals around the walls, and between them four chimney-pieces of violet marble, above which four looking-glasses reflected and redoubled the images of five crystal chandeliers.

The really very complicated nature of Jane Austen's art makes one, the older one grows, the more hesitant to say anything about it, but I suppose it cannot be wrong to say that it gives an appearance, altogether misleading though this is, of simplicity, and in the two most light-hearted, though not the least serious of the four great novels, *Pride and Prejudice* and *Emma*, the over-all impression is one of radiance. Her quality of vision is of course the reason for this, but I would suggest that though a shimmering brightness lies over the whole work except when the emphasis is necessarily sombre, the concentration of brilliance occurs in those conversations between men and women which take place before th crisis of a declaration is reached. The actual proposals, with the single exception of Captain Wentworth's which is made by a letter written almost at Anne Elliott's elbow, are all chiefly conveyed by reported speech, or by sentences of the briefest kind. Though they are infinitely satisfying and convincing, they are so because we read them in the perspective of what has gone before. When Eleanor Dashwood, hearing that it is not Edward whom Lucy Steele has married, but his brother Robert, runs out of the room and begins to cry as if she would never stop, what do we need to hear about Edward's proposal except what we do hear: "His errand at Barton was a simple one, it was only to ask Eleanor to marry him."

The first proposal of Mr. Darcy is indeed given to some extent verbatim, but this is not the true love-scene, it is not the proposal proper. This is one of those conversations showing how fully Jane Austen understood that even when people are scolding and quarrelling, they do not speak with that full orchestration of feeling unless they are, for some reason, very much interested in each other. When Darcy, leaning against the chimney-piece, white with anger, his eyes fixed on her face, says to Elizabeth:

"Am I expected to rejoice in the inferiority of your connections?" one admits he wouldn't have said it if he had not been, for the time being, a brute and a bear, but he would not have said it, either, if he had not had a passion for the woman he was insulting.

The corresponding conversation in *Emma* is the one in which Emma and Mr. Knightley discuss Harriet Smith's refusal of Robert Martin:

"Then she is a greater simpleton than I ever believed her! What is the foolish girl about?"

"O to be sure! it is always incomprehensible to a man that a woman should ever refuse an offer of marriage. A man always imagines a woman to be ready for anybody who asks her!"

"Nonsense! A man does not imagine any such thing. But what is the meaning of this? Harriet Smith refuse Robert Martin!"

"Mr. Martin is a very respectable young man, but I cannot admit him to be Harriet's equal."

"Not Harriet's equal! No, he is not her equal, for he is as much her superior in sense as in situation . . . Emma, your infatuation about that girl blinds you . . . She is pretty, and she is good tempered, and that is all. The advantage of the match I felt to be all on her side."

"You are a very warm friend to Mr. Martin, but, as I said before, are unjust to Harriet . . . Supposing her to be, as you describe her, only pretty and good natured, let me tell you, those are not trivial recommendations . . . I am very much mistaken if your sex in general would not think such beauty and such temper the highest claims a woman could possess."

"Upon my word, Emma, to hear you abusing the reason you have, is enough to make me think so too. Better be without sense, than misapply it as you do."

That argument will never be finished. I have tried to collect fragments of evidence to support an idea of the prevailing aesthetic climate in which Jane Austen lived; but I must now admit of what secondary importance these considerations are. Some novelists we enjoy now, quite consciously for their period charm; but the author of that conversation is not one of them. Though we may amuse ourselves in trying to assess how far great artists reflected or influenced their time, their value to us is that they inhabit the sphere outside time.

Elizabeth Jenkins

THE JANE AUSTEN SOCIETY

Report for the Year 1964

Title page of Elizabeth Austen's Music Book
(See article on Page 264)

THE JANE AUSTEN SOCIETY
(Founded in 1940 by Dorothy G. Darnell)

THE JANE AUSTEN SOCIETY

Report for the year 1964

———o———

Ninety-four new members joined during the year, of whom 24 became Life Members. In addition, 12 old members became Life Members. One hundred and twelve members live in the U.S.A. Total membership is now 995.

Members are reminded that subscriptions are due on 1st January, and that this Report is the only reminder that they will receive. The Hon. Secretary would much appreciate prompt payment of the 5/- Annual Subscription, and will gladly provide a Bankers' Order Form.

Annual General Meeting, 1964

The Annual General Meeting was held at Chawton House, by kind permission of Major and Mrs. Edward Knight, on Saturday, 18th July. The Duke of Wellington presided and over 500 members and their friends were present.

In opening the meeting, the President stated that following the 1963 Essay competition, the Committee had decided to look for a wider field. The Winchester College authorities had accepted the idea in principle.

The President said that Lady Scott and Mrs. R. L. McAndrew had resigned from the Committee, and expressed the thanks of the Society for all the work they had done.

He asked that the minutes of the last Annual Meeting, which had been published in the Annual Report, be taken as read. There were no matters arising.

The Hon. Secretary presented the Report for 1963. This was seconded by the Hon. Mrs. Clive Pearson, and carried.

The Hon. Treasurer presented the accounts for 1963. It was proposed by Mrs. Pyke, seconded by Mrs. Banyard, that these be adopted, and carried.

It was proposed by the Hon. Secretary, seconded by the Rev. A. L. B. Hay, and carried, that the Duke of Wellington be re-elected President, that Mr. T. Edward Carpenter and Mr. John Gore be re-elected Vice-Presidents, and that Lt.-Col. Sir William Makins, Bt., be re-elected Chairman of the Society.

The President proposed the re-election, en bloc, of the remaining members of the Committee.

It was proposed by Lady Scott, seconded by Mrs. McAndrew, and carried, that Lady Stirling and Mr. Hugh B. Powell be elected to the Committee.

The meeting was addressed by Lord David Cecil, C.H., who discussed Jane Austen's Juvenilia and unpublished works.

A vote of thanks was proposed by Sir Steuart Wilson, seconded by Mrs. Wade, and carried.

The meeting was closed by the President thanking Major and Mrs. Knight for lending Chawton House for the meeting, after which tea was provided in aid of Chawton Church funds, when over £80 was raised.

Annual General Meeting, 1965

The Annual Meeting will be held at Chawton House on Saturday, 17th July. The speaker will be Mr. L. P. Hartley.

————o————

Extracts from the Morning Chronicle

INTERESTING NOVEL.—In 3 vols. price 15s.
SENSE and SENSIBILITY; a Novel. By
LADY A——.
Printed for Thos. Egerton, Whitehall, and may be had of
every Bookseller in the Kingdom.

In 3 vols. 12mo. price 18s. in boards,
PRIDE and PREJUDICE: a Novel. By a
LADY, Author of Sense and Sensibility.
Printed for T. Egerton, Whitehall, and may be had of all
Booksellers.

The Jane Austen Society possesses three copies of The Morning Chronicle for Nov. 28, 1811; Feb. 9, 1813; and April 1, 1813; each containing something interesting about Jane Austen.

Mr. R. A. Austen Leigh in "Life and Letters of Jane Austen," says that **"Sense and Sensibility"** was advertised in The Morning Chronicle three times; first, on October 31, 1811, as "A Novel, called Sense and Sensibility, by Lady—," secondly, on Nov. 7, as "an extraordinary novel, by Lady—;" the third advertisement occurs in the edition Nov. 28. The Morning Chronicle, consisting of four pages only, devotes two or more columns to "Books published this day," and among the items listed here on Nov. 28, occurs the following:—

Interesting novel in 3 vols., price 15/-.

Sense and Sensibility, a novel. By Lady A—.

Printed for Thomas Egerton, Whitehall, and may be had of every book-seller in the kingdom.

"Lady—" and "Lady A" are printers' errors for Jane Austen's nom-de-plume, "A Lady."

In the issue dated Feb. 9, 1813, "Books published this day," include:

In 3 vols., 12 mo., price 18/-, in boards.

Pride and Prejudice : a Novel. By a Lady, author of Sense and Sensibility.

Printed for T. Egerton, Whitehall, and may be had of all booksellers.

The notices in the Books published this Day column are publishers' advertisements. Egerton published **Sense and Sensibility, Pride and Prejudice** and **Mansfield Park;** with **Emma,** Jane Austen changed to Murray.

A roving glance at The Morning Chronicle is very interesting: "*To Parents and Guardians,*" "*A Valuable Free-hold Estate,*" and "*To be sold, a handsome Bay Gelding, a capital gig-horse,*" recall the advertisements Edmund was so pertinaciously reading in chapter xxxiv of **Mansfield Park.**

The most interesting of the entries is that in the issue of April 1, 1813.

The unfortunate Princess Charlotte, daughter of the Prince Regent and his estranged wife, Caroline of Brunswick, was used as a shuttle-cock in the game of mutual aggravation played by her parents with each other, while as heir to the throne of England, she was of the highest news value to journalists. The Princess visited her mother on the death of the latter's mother, the old Duchess of Brunswick. The Morning Post printed an emotional and magnanimous speech in which, according to them, the Prince Regent had given his daughter permission to do this, adding: "This, it must be allowed, was manly, generous. The young Princess felt and acknowledged it so; she threw her arms round the neck of her Royal Father, thanked him with all that fine sensibility that forms so distinguishing a characteristic of her nature, and departed, with a pious ejaculation to Heaven."

The Morning Chronicle quotes this passage, then says, that in fact, the Prince Regent answered the Princess's first letter of entreaty by saying she'd better not go till after the Duchess's funeral; to a second letter he returned no answer at all. Whereupon the Princess said: "Silence gives consent," and went off to her mother.

This article, serving the double purpose of conveying hot news and pouring scorn on a rival paper's coverage, the Morning Chronicle headed: **Sense and Sensibility.**

The title gives rise to some speculation. Was this phrase in use as a title or quotation or common saying, before Jane Austen used it as the title of her first novel in 1811 ? The title of **Pride and Prejudice** she of course took from a speech in Fanny Burney's **"Cecilia."** As this was published in 1782, it was assumed that Jane Austen, a devoted reader of Fanny Burney, had formed her first title on a suggestion from this phrase (though the latter is not an antithesis), and took the phrase itself for her second one, and up till now, nothing we have been able to discover contradicts this view. It would seem, therefore, that Jane Austen's first novel introduced its title into contemporary speech. An instance very similar is provided by the title of Lord Snow's latest novel, though here the author first set the phrase going, then took it as a title for his own book, as he explains in the preface to "Corridors of Power."

Elizabeth Jenkins

—————O—————

Elizabeth Austen's Music Book

This book has been given to the Society by Miss N. Cassandra Hardy, great-grand-daughter of the owner, Elizabeth Bridges, who, in 1791, married Edward Austen, the second of Jane Austen's five brothers.

Edward Austen had been adopted by the wealthy Thomas Knights and made heir to their properties of Godmersham Park, in Kent, and Chawton Great House, in Hampshire. He and his wife lived at first at Rowling, in Kent, but in 1799, five years after Mr. Knight's death, his widow wanted to leave Godmersham and let the Edward Austens, who already had five children, occupy it at once instead of waiting for her death. The reason they gave for at first refusing this suggestion is most interestingly illustrated in the "Knight Letters and Journal, 1784-5," privately printed by the Hon. Mrs. Clive Pearson in 1963. The letters to her sister-in-

Elizabeth Bridges, wife of Edward Austen

265

law were written by Mrs. Knight, then aged 31, during a tour of France on which her husband took her for her health. In all the interest of foreign travel, some of which she enjoyed very much, Mrs. Knight constantly speaks of her longing to be back at Godmersham Park. "I should really have been just as well at dear Godmersham, what a pity it was to leave it." "We talk of it without ceasing, and whenever I lay *(sic)* awake in my bed, I think of nothing else."

Since her passion for the house was so well known, the young people at first would not consent to the arrangement, even though it was her own; but Mrs. Knight had made up her mind. She wrote to Edward: "You may assure yourself and my dear Lizzie, that the pain I shall feel in quitting this dear place will be no longer remembered when I see you in possession of it." The Edward Austens accordingly took possession of Godmersham in 1799, when Jane Austen was 24.

Jane's relations with this brother and sister-in-law appear to have been uncloudedly happy. Her letters to Cassandra show that she was somewhat critical of her brother James, who was melancholy and difficult, and of his wife, Mary, who required some forbearance, but they contain no word of criticism of Edward, sensible, cheerful and kind; or of Elizabeth, the beautiful, affectionate, gracious mistress of his large household.

In 1796, while the Edward Austens were still at Rowling, Jane was staying with them, and they went to dine at the house of Elizabeth's parents, where they danced after dinner. Elizabeth played one set of country dances and Lady Bridges another. Jane, untasked, danced all the time.

In 1798 Elizabeth's fifth child was born, and Jane said how charmingly pretty she looked in her convalescence, in all her white draperies, making a comparison unfavourable to poor Mary in a similar situation.

In 1799 Jane pretended to take umbrage at some remark of Elizabeth's on her method of copying music. "Elizabeth is very cruel about my writing music, and as a punishment for her I should insist on writing out all her's for her in future, if I were not punishing myself at the same time."

In the same year Jane was at Bath with the Edward Austens, and during the important examination of the season's millinery, Elizabeth gave her a straw hat trimmed with purple ribbon.

Elizabeth's last appearance in Jane's letters is given during the latter's visit to Godmersham in June, 1808, where as usual she enjoyed the luxury and elegance of the great house, "ate ice and drank French wine and was above vulgar economy," little knowing how soon this light-heartedness was to be eclipsed. In this month Elizabeth was five months' pregnant with her eleventh child. On

Jane's arrival, the eldest niece, Fanny, took her to her room, the Yellow Room; and presently the beautiful mother, attended by a troop of her small children: Marianne, seven, Charles, five, and Louisa, four, came into the room "for a moment," to give the guest an affectionate welcome. To her sister-in-law's attentive eyes she did not look at all well.

Jane left Godmersham early in July and Elizabeth died in childbirth on October 10th. She never bore the name of Knight, as Edward did not assume it till Mrs. Knight's death in 1812.

The music book with her name inside it contains sonatas for the harpsichord or piano forte by Maria Hester Reynolds, by whom it is signed on the title page, and is dated 1786.

Edward frequently brought his family to Chawton Great House. In 1812 they stayed there for five months. On one of these occasions the music book must have been brought with them, as in living memory it always lay on the piano there. Jane Austen must almost certainly have been familiar with the sight of it, at Godmersham or Chawton, or in both houses.

Elizabeth Jenkins

————o————

Jane Austen's Last Illness

Reprinted by permission from the BRITISH MEDICAL JOURNAL, *18th July, 1964, vol. ii, pp. 182-183*

Jane Austen died at 4.30 a.m., on 18th July, 1817, at the age of 41 from an ailment the nature of which has never been ascertained, or, so far as I am aware, seriously discussed. No information was furnished by the doctors who attended her, and her relatives were reticent about her illness, so that we are compelled to rely chiefly on the few comments made by the patient herself in the letters that have survived. Fortunately Jane Austen was an accurate observer, and though she made light of her troubles until near the end, one can rely on her definite statements.

The onset of her illness was insidious, but we know that she began to have a feeling of weakness or tiredness round about July, 1816, and within a few weeks she experienced severe pain in the back, for in a letter dated 8th September she wrote to her sister saying:

"Thank you, my back has given me scarcely any pain for many days. I have an idea that agitation does it as much harm as fatigue, and that I was ill at the time of your going away from the very circumstances of your going."

That comment is noteworthy. Three months later (16th December) she refused an invitation to dinner, giving as a reason:

"I was forced to decline it, the walk is beyond my strength (though I am otherwise very well)."

A month later, though she told her neice Caroline that she felt stronger, in a letter to her friend Alethea Bigg, she for the first time confesses that her illness is serious:

"I have certainly gained strength through the winter and am not far from being well; and I think I understand my own case now so much better than I did, as to be able by care to keep off any serious return of illness. I am more and more convinced that *bile* is at the bottom of all I have suffered which makes it easy to know how to treat myself."

"Serious return" and "all I have suffered" are significant words. The self-diagnosis of "bile" must indicate some gastro-intestinal irritation, probably nausea or vomiting or both. Up to that time she appears to have been treating herself.

Little information is available for the month of February, 1817, though we learn that there was pain in one knee, which was there-fore wrapped in flannel, but in a letter dated 23rd March, and written to her favourite niece, Fanny, we find important evidence:

"I certainly have not been well for many weeks, and about a week ago I was very poorly; I have a good deal of fever at times and indifferent nights, but am considerably better now and recover-ing my looks a little, which have been bad enough, black and white and every wrong colour. I must not depend upon ever being blooming again. Sickness is a dangerous indulgence at my time of life."

She was evidently distressed by her changing facial appearance.

Two weeks later, on 6th April, a letter written to her brother, Charles, tells of severer attacks:

"I have been really too unwell the last fortnight to write anything that was not absolutely necessary; I have been suffering from a billious attack attended with a good deal of fever . . . I was so ill on Friday and thought myself so likely to be worse that I could not but press for Cassandra's return with Frank."

Obviously the attacks or crises were becoming more serious and she was now apprehensive. The last two available letters were written in May and show deterioration. On 22nd May she wrote to her dear friend Anne Sharpe a despairing letter which, however, contains several important clues:

The room at 8, College, Street, Winchester, in which Jane Austen died—
"We have a neat little Drawing room, with a Bow-window overlooking
Dr. Gabell's garden."

(From a letter to J. Edward Austen, dated Tuesday, 27th May, 1817)

Photographed by courtesy of Mr & Mrs. J. R. Darling

"In spite of my hopes and promises when I wrote to you I have since been very ill indeed. An attack of my sad complaint seized me within a few days afterwards—the most severe I ever had and coming upon me after weeks of indisposition, it reduced me very low . . . My head was always clear, and I had scarcely any pain; my chief sufferings were from feverish nights, weakness and languor."

In the same letter she tells her friend that she had arranged to go to Winchester so as to be under the care of a well-known surgeon there, Mr. Lyford. The other letter was to her nephew, Edward, and mentions that the appearance of her face was still distressing:

"I will not boast of my handwriting; neither that nor my face have yet recovered their proper beauty, but in other respects I am gaining strength very fast."

In this letter she also mentions that she was eating her meals in a rational way and was employing herself, though lying on the sofa most of the day.

Two other witnesses must now be called. First, just before the move to Winchester her niece Caroline paid her a visit and later she was able to remember that her Aunt Jane was sitting down, dressed in a dressing-gown, looking very pale, and speaking in a weak and low voice. This testifies to her anaemia, for when in health, Jane Austen had a rich colour. The last and very important piece of evidence is to be obtained from the letter in which Cassandra Austen describes the last few hours of her sister's life in such moving words. The letter was written to Fanny Knight on 20th July, 1817. The important passage is the following:

"On Thursday I went into the town to do an errand your dear Aunt was anxious about. I returned about a quarter before six and found her recovering from faintness and oppression; she got so well as to be able to give a minute account of her seizure and when the clock struck six she was talking quietly to me. I cannot say how soon afterwards she was seized again with the same faintness, which was followed by sufferings she could not describe, but Mr. Lyford had been sent for, had applied something to give her ease and she was in a state of quiet insensibility by seven at the latest. From that time till half past four, when she ceased to breathe, she scarcely moved a limb."

One further fact must be mentioned. Henry Austen, Jane's favourite brother, whom she had nursed through a serious illness in 1815, who greatly encouraged her writing and helped to get her novels published, and who seemed to be very prosperous, went bankrupt in March, 1816. This was a terrible mental shock to Jane, and might well have precipitated any disease susceptible of being influenced by mental shock.

Here then we have the story of an illness coming on soon after a severe mental shock, beginning with an insidious languor and a pain in the back, progressing steadily yet with definite periods of intermission, and attended by critical attacks of faintness and gastro-intestinal disturbance, yet unaccompanied by any noticeable pain anywhere, whether in abdomen, chest, or head. During the intermissions, the intelligence was acute and the appetite good. The end came in one of the crises in which faintness was a very noticeable feature.

No doubt many of the above symptoms might be accounted for by a number of conditions, but there are very few diseases which could account for them all.

There are indeed some abdominal diseases that give no signs and yet may progress and cause no other symptoms than great weakess and anaemia. Tabes mesenterica and some other forms of tuberculosis should also be considered, but such conditions are not attended by acute painless crises. Latent cancer of the stomach might cause severe anaemia and weakness before it became obvious, but should not give rise to prolonged fainting attacks, and with cancer the course is progressively downhill. Yet after reading all the evidence many times I had almost come to the conclusion that cancer of the stomach would most readily account for most of the symptoms when I bethought myself of two pathological conditions, either of which would account for most of them— Addison's or pernicious anaemia, and Addison's disease of the suprarenal capsules. Neither of these diseases had at that time been recognised, and when Thomas Addison made his investigations he at first found difficulty in discriminating the one from the other. Both give rise to an insidiously developing weakness and languor, to anaemia, and to severe gastro-intestinal disturbances. Both are liable to intermission during which the patient feels much better and is hopeful of recovery. Yet, in the absence of all laboratory assistance, Addison found one symptom that, in the majority of cases, enabled him to distinguish between the two conditions, and that was the appearance of the skin. In the disease which he found constantly associated with a pathological condition (usually tuberculosis) of the suprarenal bodies he noted that the skin in certain parts changed to a darker colour, usually brown but sometimes almost black, and the face was nearly always affected. He summarized the main distinguishing features as follows:

"The leading and characteristic features of the morbid state to which I would draw attention are: anaemia, general languor and debility, remarkable feebleness of the heart's action, irritability of the stomach and a peculiar change of colour of the skin."

In some cases the dark patches of the skin are mingled with

271

areas showing a lack of pigment—a true black and white appearance.

Though I had read the letter of 23rd March, 1817 many times, it was long before I realised the true significance of that symptom which is almost pathognomonic(1) of Addison's disease in Jane Austen's pathetic lament:

"Recovering my looks a little, which have been bad enough, black and white and every wrong colour."

Again, when she wrote to her nephew two months later she was distressed that her face had not recovered its beauty. There is no disease other than Addison's disease that could present a face that was "black and white" and at the same time give rise to the other symptoms described in her letters.

Addison's disease is usually—Wilks said always—due to tuber-culosis of the **suprarenal capsules**(2), and it is likely that it was so in Jane Austen's case. The disease ran its course rapidly, indicating an active pathological process that might well account for any fever. Pain in the back has been noted in Addison's disease by several observers.

If our surmise be correct, Jane Austen did something more than write excellent novels—she also described the first recorded case of Addison's disease of the adrenal bodies.

Addendum : In the letter to Anne Sharp dated 22nd May, 1817, Jane Austen wrote—"This Discharge was on me for above a week, and as our Alton Apothy did not pretend to be able to cope with it, better advice was called in. Our nearest, **very good,** is at Winchester, where there is a Hospital and capital Surgeons, and one of them attended me, and **his** applications gradually removed the Evil."

This "Discharge" has been variously interpreted. The most probably view is that the word Discharge was Jane Austen's way of describind diarrhoea. Addison's disease is often accompanied by vomiting and diarrhoea. The word vomiting is not mentioned in the letters, though it must be indicated by the word "bile," and by a similar delicacy Jane Austen preferred to use the word "discharge" for the more common term, diarrhoea.

ZACHARY COPE

NOTE. The extracts quoted above are taken from *Jane Austen's Letters*, collected and edited by R. W. Chapman. 2nd ed.

(1) Conclusive sign or proof.

(2) Two small glands, each weighing about two drachms, situated one on each side of the body close to the corresponding kidney.

Jane Austen's Lesser Works

When I was asked to speak here today, my first feeling was one of pleasure. It is an honour to be invited to address the Jane Austen Society a second time. When, however, I began to consider my task, I felt less happy; for the occasion clearly demanded something new; and what had I new to say about Jane Austen? I had talked and written of her many times and my few fresh thoughts about her six glorious masterpieces were exhausted.

Then it occurred to me: what about those works of hers which are not masterpieces? Jane Austen has left a few fragments and by-products; squibs and skits written in her youth, juvenilia of various kinds, one unpublished novel and two unfinished novels. All these have their interest; all the more because they are imperfect. They show what was innate in their author and what was acquired later; and they tell us something about the author's creative process, by showing a piece of his or her work in an experimental or an unfinished state. We understand Jane Austen's perfection better by examining what she does when she is failing to achieve perfection. What light then do these minor pieces of hers throw on her achievement? In order to make this clear may I say a few words upon the especial nature of her art? Why is it so outstanding? For two reasons, surely. One is aesthetic. No one has kept the rules of novel-writing more rigorously than she. First of all she stays within the range of her imaginative inspiration. This was limited on one side by her experience. She was careful only to write about the kind of life she had lived herself; the life of a female member of the small gentry of the late eighteenth and early nineteenth centuries, feminine, domestic, social. On the other side, her range was limited by the nature of her genius, which was that of a high comedian. Like Elizabeth Bennett, she was quick to note "follies and nonsense, whims and inconsistencies," and to laugh at them whenever she could. What made her laugh, made her write. Her creative range then was confined to social and domestic life observed in a spirit of comedy. She sticks to it vigilantly. Her art is also notable for the way it combines truth and delight. No plots give a greater effect of reality. Yet they are not, like reality, often dull and incoherent. She contrives to make their incidents fall unobtrusively into a shapely pattern and also to make her picture of life consistently amusing. This is partly because she is careful to write about themes and characters that are genuinely comical, and partly because she tells her tale in so entertaining a tone of voice. Her ruthless good-tempered irony sparkles through her every paragraph.

If the first reason for Jane Austen's eminence is artistic, the second is moral and intellectual. She indues these quiet tales of limited life with a universal significance. She makes her characters universal; her eye is so sharp that she penetrates below surface qualities to discern the universal human characteristics which they illustrate. These eighteenth-century gentlemen and ladies are revealed as archetypes, moral archetypes. Jane Austen is a serious comedian, like Molière, who satirises her figures in the light of a wise and firm moral standard. She believes that human beings should be honourable, unselfish, faithful. She also believes that they must be sensible. She does not sympathise with a morality that cannot be carried out in real life in such a way as effectively to promote the good and happiness of others. This realistic moral standard gives substance and weight to her books and contributes to give them their universal application.

Such is her achievement. Her minor and unfinished works throw light on it. Let us examine them in detail. The first group consists of a collection of skits all written before she was eighteen, and some when she was hardly fifteen years old. Among them is a comic History of England, some imaginary letters and a few parodies of the sentimental novels of the day. The best of these are very entertaining, particularly the tales entitled **Love and Freindship** and **Jack and Alice.** Two things strike one about them. In the first place, they are at once surprisingly clever and surprisingly normal. Jane Austen was never an eccentric or rebellious young person, but rather a typical young woman of her time and class, characteristically interested in dress and parties and flirtations and laughing at what most sensible girls of her acquaintance would have laughted at—silly sentiment and romantic highflown stuff. She also had a high-spirited taste for nonsense. What is abnormal about her is the accomplishment with which her nonsense and her mockery are expressed. At fifteen her writing is already marked by her characteristic neat stylishness, her crisp irony. This shows in brief sentences:

> She was a Widow and had only one Daughter, who was then just seventeen—One of the best of ages; but alas! she was very plain and her name was Bridget . . . Nothing therefore could be expected from her—she could not be supposed to possess either exalted Ideas, Delicate Feelings or refined Sensibilities—. She was nothing more than a mere goodtempered, civil and obliging Young Woman; as such we could scarcely dislike her—she was only an Object of Contempt.

Here is a more extended passage from a similar skit. Two young women, Sophia and Laura, are wandering in wild Wales lamenting the absence of their two lovers, Edward and Augustus:

> "What a beautiful sky! (said I) How charmingly is the azure varied by those delicate streaks of white!"
>
> "Oh! my Laura (replied she hastily withdrawing her Eyes

from a momentary glance at the sky) do not thus distress me by calling my Attention to an object which so cruelly reminds me of my Augustus's blue satin Waistcoat striped with white! In pity to your unhappy friend avoid a subject so distressing." What could I do? The feelings of Sophia were at that time so exquisite, and the tenderness she felt for Augustus so poignant that I had not power to start any other topic, justly fearing that it might in some unforseen manner again awaken all her sensibility by directing her thoughts to her Husband. Yet to be silent would be cruel; she had intreated me to talk.

From this Dilemma I was most fortunately relieved by an accident truly apropos; it was the lucky overturning of a Gentleman's Phaeton, on the road which ran murmuring behind us. It was a most fortunate accident as it diverted the attention of Sophia from the melancholy reflections which she had been before indulging. We instantly quitted our seats and ran to the rescue of those who but a few moments before had been in so elevated a situation as a fashionably high Phaeton, but who were now laid low and sprawling in the Dust. "What an ample subject for reflection on the uncertain Enjoyments of this World, would not that Phaeton and the Life of Cardinal Wolsey afford a thinking Mind!" said I to Sophia as we were hastening to the field of Action.

She had not time to answer me, for every thought was now engaged by the horrid Spectacle before us. Two Gentlemen most elegantly attired but weltering in their blood was what first struck our Eyes—we approached—they were Edward and Augustus—, Yes dearest Marianne they were our Husbands, Sophia shrieked and fainted on the Ground—I screamed and instantly ran mad—. We remained thus mutually deprived of our Senses, some minutes, and on regaining them were deprived of them again. For an Hour and a Quarter did we continue in this unfortunate Situation—Sophia fainting every moment and I running Mad as often.

This is the tone of the Jane Austen that we know: and it illustrates the same preoccupations. We can see that the girl who created Laura is going to create Marianne Dashwood, that the satirist of **Love and Freindship** was to grow into the satirist of **Northanger Abbey**. From the start Jane Austen was to be a debunker. Her comic History of England also discloses it. Listen to her on Mary Queen of Scots:

Oh! what must this bewitching Princess whose only friend was then the Duke of Norfolk, and whose only ones now Mr. Whitaker, Mrs. Lefroy, Mrs. Knight and myself . . . have suffered when informed that Elizabeth had given orders for her Death!

275

The youthful Jane Austen could feel romantic; but never so much so as to lose her humorous sense of reality.

All this goes to show that her primary basic inspiration was comic. Her gift for form, her moral insight, were to disclose themselves later: but her cool mocking sense of fun was with her from the first. So too was the crisp sense of phrase which aptly expressed it. Did any other of her gifts show themselves in these early pieces ? There are a few glimpses of her sense of character in the short story called **Catharine.** You will recollect in **Northanger Abbey** the flirtatious Isabella Thorpe and the vacuous platitudinous Mrs. Allen. Both are foreshadowed in this piece. Mrs. Allen is foreshadowed in Mrs. Stanley:

> "Queen Elizabeth," said Mrs. Stanley who never hazarded a remark on History that was not well founded, "lived to a good old age, and was a very Clever Woman."

Camilla is a sketch for Isabella Thorpe:

> All her stock of knowledge was exhausted in a very few Days, and when Kitty had learnt from her, how large their house in Town was, when the fashionable Amusements began, who were the celebrated Beauties and who the best Millener, Camilla had nothing further to teach, except the Characters of any of her Acquaintance as they occurred in Conversation, which was done with equal Ease and Brevity, by saying that the person was either the sweetest Creature in the world, and one of whom she was doatingly fond, or horrid, shocking and not fit to be seen.

Jane Austen's sense of character appears in a more extended form in her first full-scale work, the unpublished short novel entitled **Lady Susan.** In some ways it is unlike anything else she wrote. For one thing, it is set in a grander milieu, and for another, it deals with a more obviously wicked character. The central figure, Lady Susan Vernon, is a sort of aristocratic Becky Sharp, an unscrupulous adventuress, far more sensational in her evil-doing than any character in Jane Austen's later books. Further, the story is formally different from her other works; it is told in letters like **Clarissa Harlowe.** It starts with Lady Susan already saddled with a bad reputation; the action describes how she tries to get herself well married and received back into respectability. She also plots to achieve a worldly marriage for her reluctant and virtuous daughter. This daughter in the end is saved for a happier fate, while Lady Susan herself is united to a foolish baronet much younger than herself. The novel has its merits. It is lively and readable all through, and Lady Susan's own letters are un-usually entertaining. The end too is characteristically intelligent. The fact that Lady Susan is not punished for her evil-doing reveals Jane Austen's mature sense of reality. Already

she is aware that in real life the wicked are often successful. She also realised that a catastrophic end would be artistically
inappropriate. Anything darker would be out of harmony with
the light and mischievous tone of the book. All the same **Lady
Susan** is not a success. Jane Austen is working out of her imaginative range. She had no acquaintance with smart fast society and
has to describe it from hearsay; with the result that her picture
lacks the intimate reality with which she portrays the country
gentry. Further, Lady Susan is too sinister a figure to be effectively
treated in Jane Austen's particular comedy vein. If she is to be
satirised effectively it should have been flippantly or savagely. Jane
Austen's satiric vein was neither. She evades her problem by
burlesquing it: Lady Susan is represented as owning up to her own
evil-doing with a sort of joyous impudence, which is more entertaining than convincing:

> Upon the whole I commend my own conduct in this affair
> extremely, and regard it as a very happy mixture of circum-
> spection and tenderness. Some Mothers would have insisted
> on their daughter's accepting so great an offer on the first
> overture, but I could not answer it to myself to force
> Frederica into a marriage from which her heart revolted; and
> instead of adopting so harsh a measure, merely propose to
> make it her own choice by rendering her thoroughly uncom-
> fortable till she does accept him.

This is amusing but unreal. We get the impression that we
are listening to Jane Austen commenting on Lady Susan—not to
Lady Susan commenting on herself. She would never have risked
being so frank. It is clear from such a passage that if Jane Austen
does venture outside her moral and social range she fails to achieve
her characteristic equal blend of comedy and truth. Truth is
sacrificed to comedy.

More interesting than Jane Austen's juvenilia are the two
unfinished works of her maturity. **The Watsons** was written about
1803, fairly early in her mature career. She did not get further
than the beginning. In this we are told how Emma Watson, the
heroine, has just returned to her poor home in the country. The
first two chapters describe her going to the local ball where she
attracts the attention of the aristocratic Lord Osborne; and also
of a flashy young beau, Tom Musgrave. In the next chapters we
see her at home, visited by her brother and his vulgar wife.
Meanwhile, the hero, a quiet cleric called Howard, makes his first
appearance. The general impression made by **The Watsons** is
unequal. Howard is a wooden figure and Emma herself not fully
individualised. Nor is the texture of the story so continuously
sparkling as in Jane Austen's finished works; the beginning, in
particular, is all too obviously a piece of exposition. Indeed, the
whole shows that Jane Austen started with a bare factual ground

plan and then set to work to give it life and individuality by a careful process of refining and revising. But there are passages in **The Watsons** that could not be improved, which give us a glimpse of the great Jane Austen, especially of her moral perceptiveness. Tom Musgrave is subtly exposed by a number of small touches; his patronising manner with the Watsons till he notices that Emma is admired by Lord Osborne, his unwillingness to appear at the ball till he can steal in at the tail of the Osborne party as a part of it. Yet Jane Austen does him justice. She notes how dull the evening is at the Watsons' till he arrives: vulgar though he may be, he has the ease and spirit to make a stiff party relax. Jane Austen's detached sense of justice also shows in her picture of Emma. She is not a snob. She finds Lord Osborne's manners too aloof to be agreeable and is not afraid to admit it to herself. But she is not inhumanly unsnobbish: she finds it pleasant to be noticed by someone in Lord Osborne's position and to feel a little embarrassed when he calls unannounced and sees in what humble surroundings she lives. Here is an example of Jane Austen's unique fairness; the fairness which led her to recognise that the Miss Bingleys though ill-natured could be very agreeable, and that the odious Mrs. Norris would have been a more useful wife to an impecunious sailor than her silly kindly sister Mrs. Price.

Jane Austen's moral insight displays itself more extended in the scene at the ball:

At the conclusion of the two Dances, Emma found herself, she knew not how, seated amongst the Osborne set; and she was immediately struck with the fine Countenance and animated gestures of the little boy, as he was standing before his Mother, wondering when they should begin,—"You will not be surprised at Charles's impatience," said Mrs. Blake, a lively pleasant-looking little Woman of 5 or 6 and 30, to a Lady who was standing near her, "when you know what a partner he is to have. Miss Osborne has been so very kind as to promise to dance the two first dances with him."—"Oh! yes—we have been engaged this week," cried the boy, "and we are to dance down every couple."—On the other side of Emma, Miss Osborne, Miss Carr, and a party of young Men were standing engaged in very lively consultation—and soon afterwards she saw the smartest officer of the set, walking off to the Orchestra to order the dance, while Miss Osborne passing before her, to her little expecting Partner hastily said— "Charles, I beg your pardon for not keeping my engagement, but I am going to dance these two dances with Col. Beresford, I know you will excuse me, and I will certainly dance with you after Tea." And without staying for an answer, she turned again to Miss Carr, and in another minute was led by Col. Beresford to begin the set. If the poor little boy's face had in it's happiness been interesting to Emma, it was infinitely more so under this sudden reverse;—he stood the picture of disappointment, with crimson'd cheeks, quivering lips, and eyes bent on the floor. His mother, stifling her own mortification, tried to sooth his, with the prospect of Miss Osborne's second promise;—but tho' he contrived to utter with an effort of Boyish Bravery "Oh! I do not mind it"—it was very evident by the unceasing agitation of his features that he minded it as much as ever.—Emma did not think, or reflect;—she felt and acted,—"I shall be very happy to dance with you Sir, if you like it," said she, holding out her hand with the most unaffected good humour.—The Boy in one moment restored to all his first delight—looked joyfully at his Mother and stepping forwards with an honest and simple Thank you Ma'am was instantly ready to attend his new acquaintance.—The Thankfulness of Mrs. Blake was more diffuse;—with a look, most expressive of unexpected pleasure, and lively Gratitude, she turned to her neighbour with repeated and fervent acknowledgements of so great and condescending a kindness to her boy.—Emma with perfect truth could assure her that she could not be giving greater pleasure than she felt herself—and Charles being provided with his gloves and charged to keep them on, they joined the Set which was now rapidly forming, with nearly equal complacency,—It was a Partnership which could not be noticed without surprise. It gained her a broad stare from Miss Osborne and Miss Carr as they passed her in the dance. "Upon my word Charles you are in luck, (said the former as she turned him) you have got a better partner than me"—to which the happy Charles answered "Yes."

This is an admirable scene. How perfectly it reveals Emma's warm heart and also her lack of conventionality! Her very words, "I shall be happy to dance with you Sir," indicates her quick sensibility to the boy's feelings, his wounded pride. This is Jane Austen the moral realist at her best.

There is nothing so good in her second unfinished work **Sandition;** but its general level is higher. Left unfinished at her death, **Sandition** is a sketch for the first chapters of a satirical novel about a watering place: and consists mainly of a gallery of comic portraits seen through the eyes of a young girl, Charlotte Heywood. It is a light-hearted work, Jane Austen the comedian is more in evidence in it than is Jane Austen the moralist. Here it differs from **The Watsons.**

Equally, however, **Sandition** is a proof that Jane Austen did not show her quality fully in her first drafts, that her particular kind of perfection is the result of second thoughts. But because **Sandition** is more satiric in tone, its imperfection shows itself differently. **The Watsons** tends to be a little drab compared with a finished Jane Austen novel. **Sandition** is too full of robust fun to be drab. But compared with a finished Jane Austen novel it tends to be crude. Its comic figures sometimes seem exaggerated. We must imagine that their creator, had she had time, would have softened and subtilized them the better to reconcile comedy with reality. As it is, the effect of **Sandition** is curiously old-fashioned. It is a warning against judging dates by internal evidence: for on internal evidence we should be inclined to say that Jane Austen had written it in those early days when she had depicted Mr. Collins and Mary Bennett. The objects of her satire, too, recall her youth. For, as in **Northanger Abbey,** she is making fun of romanticism. Here she mocks it in the person of Sir Edward Denham, a would-be Byronic baronet, full of picturesque despair and dishonourable designs on young ladies. Moreover, Charlotte the heroine, like Catherine Morland, has a weakness for romantic fancies, though she knows better how to curb them. Yet **Sandition** has the virtues of its defects: with a youthful crudeness it has a youthful exuberant sense of fun. What could be more entertaining than the conversation of the young and hypochrondriac Mr. Arthur Parker introduced to Charlotte Heywood:

Such was the influence of Youth and Bloom that he began even to make a sort of apology for having a Fire. "We should not have one at home, said he, but the Sea air is always damp. I am not afraid of anything so much as Damp—" "I am so fortunate, said C. as never to know whether the air is damp or dry. It has always some property that is wholesome and invigorating to me—" "**I** like the Air, too, as well as anybody can, replied Arthur, I am very fond of standing at an open Window when there is no Wind—but unluckily a Damp air does not like **me.**—It gives me the Rheumatism.—You are not rheumatic I suppose ?"—"Not at all." "That's a great blessing.—But perhaps you are nervous." "No—I believe not. I have no idea that I am."—"**I** am very nervous—To say the truth Nerves are the worst part of my Complaints in **my** opinion. My Sisters think me Bilious, but I doubt it.—" "You are quite in the right, to doubt it as long as you possibly can, I am sure.—" "If I were Bilious, he continued, you know Wine would disagree with me, but it always does me good.—The more Wine I drink (in Moderation) the better I am.—I am always best of an Evening.—If you had seen me today before Dinner, you would have thought me a very poor Creature.—" Charlotte could believe it—

What then do Jane Austen's lesser works tell us about her ? First, that she was a deliberate craftsman who did not trust to first inspiration but got her effects by working over her material often and carefully. Secondly, we discover that her basic inspiration was comic. From her earliest days she wrote primarily to express her comic vision of the world. Thirdly, the style in which she expressed this comic vision was with her from the start. Many great writers have begun by copying others, they find their own manner later. Jane Austen's characteristic manner is present and formed in her juvenilia: the smiling irony of **Love and Freindship** is the smiling irony of **Sandition.** Nor did her point of view alter. Anti-romantic when young, she is anti-romantic in middle age. Her moral view, it is true, did not emerge fully in her earliest works, for it was only in her maturity that she allowed herself to be sufficiently serious for this to happen. Yet our general impression is that all her life Jane Austen the author was unmistakably herself. Already in her childish flights we hear the amused irresistible accents of her voice.

David Cecil

THE JANE AUSTEN SOCIETY

Report for the Year 1965

Fireplace in the Parlour at Jane Austen's House at Chawton

THE JANE AUSTEN SOCIETY

(Founded in 1940 by Dorothy G. Darnell)

THE JANE AUSTEN SOCIETY

Report for the Year 1965

———o———

Membership

Ninety-seven new members joined during the year, of whom 22 became Life Members. In addition 13 old members became Life Members. One hundred and nine members live in the U.S.A. Total membership in now 1061.

Members are reminded that subscriptions are due on 1st January, and that this Report is the only reminder that they will receive. The Hon. Secretary would much appreciate prompt payment of the 5/- Annual Subscription, and will gladly provide a Bankers' Order Form.

Annual General Meeting, 1965

The Annual General Meeting was held at Chawton House, by kind permission of Major and Mrs. Edward Knight, on Saturday, 17th July. The Duke of Wellington presided and about 450 members and their friends were present.

In opening the meeting, the President said that it would be the last occasion on which he would preside. In August he would reach the age of eighty, and felt that it was no longer right that he should cumber the ground. This news was greeted with dismay.

The President asked that the minutes of the last Annual Meeting, having been published in the Annual Report, should be taken as read. This was agreed. There were no matters arising.

The Hon. Secretary presented the Report for 1964, and stated that there were now over 1000 members. This was seconded by Mrs. Sitwell, and carried.

In asking Mr. B. F. C. Hall, the Hon. Treasurer, to present the accounts, the President said that Mr. Hall was resigning his appointment, as he had left Alton, and offered the thanks of the Society for all he had done during the last six years.

It was proposed by Mr. Hugh Powell, seconded by Mrs. Towell, and carried, that the accounts be adopted.

The Duke of Wellington announced that Lord David Cecil, C.H., had agreed to accept the office of President of the Society, and proposed his election. This was carried with acclamation.

Sir William Makins then addressed the meeting, expressing the sorrow of members at the Duke of Wellington's resignation, their gratitude for his services to the Society, and their gratification

The Duke of Wellington, K.G.

at the appointment of his successor. On behalf of the Society, Miss Beatrix Darnell, a founder member of the Committee, presented the Duke with a small ivory bust of the 1st Duke of Wellington.

Sir William Makins proposed that Mr. T. Edward Carpenter and Mr. John Gore be re-elected Vice-Presidents and that the Duke of Wellington be elected a Vice-President. This was seconded by Lord David Cecil, and carried.

The Duke of Wellington proposed that Sir William Makins be re-elected Chairman of the Society, and that the Committee be re-elected en bloc. This was carried.

Sir William Makins then spoke to the Society concerning the Annual General Meeting in 1967. He said that the 150th anniversary of Jane Austen's death fell on the 18th July that year, and that the Committee had considered holding the Annual General Meeting in Winchester, on one of the Saturdays nearest to that date. This was put to the meeting, and was agreed to in principal.

The meeting was then addressed by Mr. L. P. Hartley, whose theme was "Jane Austen and the Abyss."

A vote of thanks was proposed by Mr. Noel Blakiston, seconded by Mrs. Hickman, and carried.

The Duke of Wellington then closed the meeting, and thanked Major and Mrs. Knight for once again lending Chawton House for the meeting. Teas were provided in aid of Chawton Church funds, when about £75 was raised.

A change of President

At the Annual Meeting on July 17th, 1965, the Duke of Wellington, K.G., who reached the age of 80 in August, announced his resignation as President to the great regret of the Society. Lord David Cecil, C.H., agreed to take his place.

The Duke became President in 1949 and for more than 15 years played a vital part in the growth and success of the Society. At all times his advice was readily available to the Secretary and Committee and his wide experience helped to solve its problems and guide its policies. He seldom failed to preside at the Annual Meeting when his witty and efficient handling of the formal business invariably made it a pleasant prelude to the address.

He usually brought over from Stratfieldsaye a party of enthusiastic Janeites, which some times included the lecturer, and on occasion himself gave an address.

His consent to become a Vice-President affords the hope that for some years to come the Society may have the benefit of his experience and see him every year at the Annual Meeting.

It was recognised that his place would be hard to fill and the

Society was lucky indeed to find an ideal successor ready to hand.

Lord David Cecil, C.H.

Lord David Cecil, Goldsmith Professor of English Literature, Oxford, from 1948, established his position in contemporary English letters at a very early age and has long been an acknowledged authority on Jane Austen's art. The only lecturer who has twice addressed the Society, his discourses have been among the most popular in a remarkably able succession. The Society therefore can look forward with confidence to the continuance of a Presidency of an ideal kind, **suaviter in modo, fortiter in re.**

J.G.

Annual General Meeting, 1966

The Annual General Meeting will take place at Chawton House, at 3 p.m., on Saturday, 16th July, when Dr. C. V. Wedgwood, C.B.E., will be the speaker.

Birth of a Legend

In 1958 I saw, outside a first-floor room in the Rutland Arms, Bakewell, a notice saying that Jane Austen had stayed there in 1811 when she was revising **Pride and Prejudice,** and had made that particular room the scene of two episodes in the novel. Taken aback by these statements, I telegraphed to the late Dr. R. W. Chapman to ask if there were any truth in them, and he replied: "No evidence that she was ever north of the Trent."

I then asked the management of this excellent hotel from where this notice had come and was referred to the hotel's owners, Stretton's Derby Brewery Ltd., from one of whose directors I had a courteous letter, saying that the text of the notice had been written by Mrs. Elizabeth Davie of Stanton Park, Matlock, Derbyshire.

One of the company then wrote to Mrs. Davie, asking her to be so kind as to give her grounds for what she had so fully related, and forwarded her reply, to which I will refer presently. Then, I regret to say, owing to various preoccupations, I abandoned the matter, though knowing that I ought to have gone on with it. During the last few years, however, so many people have spoken or written to me of this wonderfully interesting, and to all of us, quite new information about Jane Austen's life, that I have at last laid the matter before the Committee of the Jane Austen Society, who felt unanimously that the whole thing should be dealt with in the forthcoming Report.

The notice composed by Mrs. Davie, with minor omissions, is as follows:

"In this room in the year 1811, Jane Austen revised the MSS of her famous book **Pride and Prejudice.** It had been written in 1797, but Jane Austen *who travelled in Derbyshire in 1811* (our italics) chose to introduce the beauty spots of the Peak into her novel. The Rutland Arms Hotel was built in 1804, and while staying in this new and comfortable inn we have reason to believe that Jane Austen visited Chatsworth only 3 miles away and was so impressed by its beauty and grandeur that she made it the background for Pemberley, the home of the proud and handsome Mr. Darcy.... The small market town of Lambton is easily identifiable as Bakewell, and any visitor driving thence to Chatsworth must be struck by Miss Austen's faithful portrayal of the scene.... Elizabeth Bennet had returned to the inn to dress for dinner, when the sound of the carriage drew her to the window. She saw a curricle driving up the street, undoubtably Matlock St., which these windows overlook, and presently she heard a quick foot upon the stairs, the very stairs outside this door. So, when visiting this hotel and staying in this room, remember that it is the scene of two of the most romantic passages in **Pride and Prejudice.**"

It will be seen that three statements are made here:

1 That Jane Austen stayed at the Rutland Arms in 1811.

2 That the description of Pemberley is a "faithful portrayal" of Chatsworth, and Lambton "easily identifiable as Bakewell."

3 That the Rutland Arms was the inn at Lambton in which Darcy visited Elizabeth.

To consider first points 2 and 3 :

The similarity between Pemberley and Chatsworth lies in their nearness to Bakewell and in the features of their parks. The XVIII century print of Chatsworth shows so plainly the details of Jane Austen's description: the winding river in front of the house, the lawns sprinkled with timber, the bridge, the wood-crowned hill rising behind the house, that we publish it to demonstrate how easily Jane Austen could have gained a vision of the park from any of the numerouse illustrated guides, Northern Tours or views of Gentlemen's Seats then available. When, however, she describes the house itself, we submit that the resemblance to Chatsworth stops short. She says: "It was a large handsome stone building standing on rising ground." It had a picture gallery and a saloon; "the rooms were lofty and fine, and their furniture suitable to the fortune of their proprietor." It was, clearly a large country house, the dwelling of a man whose income was said to be £10,000 a year. (The "very likely more" we may set down to Mrs. Bennet's joyous optimism, £10,000 is near enough). But £10,000 a year even in the 1800's would not have gone far in maintaining Chatsworth. Chatsworth is a palace. The Rev. Mr. R. Ward who published one of the early 19th century guides to the Peak of Derbyshire, gives some idea of the house's size: "The building is in the form of a square containing a court, within it having a fountain with the statue of Orion seated on a dolphin in its centre, and a colonnade to the north and south sides of it. The south front of the house is 190 feet in length and is enriched with pilasters . . . . . The west front is 172 feet in length and enriched in a similiar manner . . . . . Over the colonnade to the north side of the quadrangle is a gallery nearly 100 feet in length, the walls of which are covered with a very numerous and interesting assemblage of drawings by the most eminent masters." The size of the building and the treasures it contains, make it, one would have supposed, perfectly clear that no argument could be based on the resemblance of Pemberley to Chatsworth being so strong that Jane Austen must be assumed to have seen the latter.

As for the details of the park mentioned by her, not only are they those that could be gathered from a contempory print or description, but they are, in fact, common to at least one other house and park in Derbyshire.

Sir William Makins has been told by Mary, Duchess of Devonshire, that in the Chatsworth neighbourhood it used to be said

Chatsworth in the 18th Century.

that Willersley, near Cromford, was the original of Pemberley. Reading Mr. Ward's description of it one can see why. He mentions the winding river—"beyond it is seen a lawn, on the further side and on a very elevated part of which stands Willersley Castle, backed by high ground and wood." Ward describes a stone bridge with three arches, and says: "behind this and further to the east, rises a very elevated, woody country."

Mrs. Davie's assertion that Lambton is "easily identifiable as Bakewell" needs no dispute since it arises from a misreading of Jane Austen's text. Bakewell and Lambton were envisaged by Jane Austen as two separate places. When the party consisting of the Gardiners and Elizabeth had seen the famous beauties of the district, they "bent their steps" towards Lambton, the scene of Mrs. Gardiner's youth: "and within five miles of Lambton, Elizabeth found from her aunt, that Pemberley was situated. It was not in their direct road, nor more than a mile or two out of it. In talking over their route the evening before, Mr. Gardiner expressed an inclination to see the place again." That night Elizabeth heard from the chamber maid that the family were not in residence at Pemberley. They went, therefore, to Pemberley on their way towards Lambton, and the place from which they set out was Bakewell, though it is not named until Elizabeth says to Darcy: "Before we left Bakewell we understood you were not immediately expected in the country." When they leave Pemberley they go straight to Lambton, for Jane Austen says of Mrs. Gardiner: "They were now approaching the scene of her former pleasures," and that after dinner, tired as she was, she set off to call on her former acquaintances.

The fact that Jane Austen did not describe Bakewell as Lambton, makes nonsense of Mrs. Davie's contention that Mr. Darcy's curricle, said to be arriving at the Lambton inn, was "undoubtedly" driving to the Rutland Arms up Matlock St., the direct route from Chatsworth.

That anyone who has read **Pride and Prejudice** and seen Chatsworth, should feel that the resemblance between the latter and Pemberley is so strong that it can only be accounted for by Jane Austen's personal presence in the neighbourhood, must strike the rest of us as odd, but does no one any harm. Nor do misreadings of **Pride and Prejudice** greatly matter, since the book is there for everyone to read. The really serious aspect of the affair is the, as we believe, completely baseless statement, on which the rest of this is built, that Jane Austen "travelled in Derbyshire" and stayed at The Rutland Arms in 1811. Mrs. Davie justifies this as follows :

"In writing the notice about Jane Austen for the Rutland Arms, I based it chiefly upon the information in the "Official Guide to Bakewell" published in April, 1936. This encouraged me to make very careful comparison between the description of "Pemberley" and the landscape at Chatsworth. We have, in chapter XLII of **Pride and Prejudice,** mention of Matlock, Chatsworth, Dovedale and the Peak, also of "the little town of Lambton" ...... and within five miles of Lambton Elizabeth found from her aunt that Pemberley was situated. This fits perfectly the description of the park at Pemberley, the drive, the setting of the house, except for one wood, which might perhaps have been felled or be an addition of Jane Austen's, all fits so well that it seems incredible that she should not have seen it herself. (Chapter XLIII of **Pride and Prejudice).** In this same chapter we find "before we left Bakewell."

As I believe that The Rutland Arms was built in 1804/1806, and the manuscript of **Pride and Prejudice** revised in 1811, *surely it is more than logical conjecture* (our italics) to conclude that she saw Chatsworth and described it in her revision ? Unfortunately the author of the Bakewell Guide is now dead, so nothing more can be learnt from that quarter."

The Reading Room of the British Museum does not contain a copy of the 1936 guide quoted by Mrs. Davie, and I am obliged to rely on my memory of reading this at Bakewell in 1958 and on the note I made at the time. According to this, the writer merely stated, with no supporting evidence whatever, that Jane Austen travelled in Derbyshire. He did not even dignify his statement, new to all of us, by the name of local tradition. Such a statement as it stands is of course valueless, and what we may perhaps call the negative evidence against it is very strong. Jane Austen's life largely owing to her own letters, is unusually well documented. There is, indeed, the painful gap from May, 1801 to September, 1804, and there are gaps of six months, a year, or eighteen months, when no occasion for letter writing arose, as the sisters were in the same house. There are, in fact, no letters from April, 1811 to November, 1812. But few people who have read the letters with their minute details of events will believe that such an experience as a visit to the Peak could have been enjoyed by Jane Austen without one word of it surviving in any letter or in her copious family traditions. In the circumstances, if it cannot be positively asserted that she never went to Derbyshire, far less can it be asserted that she did. Until evidence of such a visit can be found, we feel that to make the statement and erect such an elaborate structure on it, is altogether irresponsible. The mischief is already spreading like dry-rot. In 1964, Mr. Denzil Batchelor, in all good faith, wrote an article for the Weekly Telegraph Coloured Supplement in which he described The Rutland Arms. The management had shown him not only the room "where in 1811, Jane Austen worked at **Pride and Prejudice,**" but "her bookcase, still on the wall, her desk by the window," where she wrote the love scene, sitting "looking down across the Wye." This supplement is published in America as well as here, and the article reached me from Washington.

This, though not unique, is a particularly flagrant example of the growth of legend. In 50 years time this stuff will be appearing as fact in the official biographies of Jane Austen, in 100 years it will need a real effort of scholarship to eradicate it. We have no expectation of checking it effectively, but since one of the arguments frequently used in favour of such tales is: It's never been contradicted, we want to place it on record by the only means open to us, that the Committee of the Jane Austen Society regard the notice, long, confident and circumstantial as it is, as entirely without foundation.

Elizabeth Jenkins

The Marriage Registers at Steventon

The Form of an Entry of Publication of Banns.

The Banns of Marriage between *A. B.* of *L...* and *C. D.* of *.......* were duly publifhed in this Church for the $\begin{cases} \text{firft} \\ \text{fecond} \\ \text{third} \end{cases}$ Time, on Sunday the Day of in the Year One Thoufand Seven Hundred and

$$\begin{array}{l} \textit{J. J.} \text{ Rector} \\ \qquad \text{Vicar} \\ \qquad \text{Curate} \end{array} \Big\}$$

The Form of an Entry of a Marriage.

A. B. of *.......* and *C. D.* of *.......* were married in this Church by $\begin{cases} \text{Banns} \\ \text{Licenfe*} \end{cases}$ this Day of in the Year One Thoufand Seven Hundred and by me

$$\begin{array}{l} \textit{J. J.} \text{ Rector} \\ \qquad \text{Vicar} \\ \qquad \text{Curate} \end{array} \Big\}$$

This Marriage was folemnized between us *A. B. C. B.* late *C. D.* **in the** Prefence of *E. F. G. H.*

* Infert thefe Words, viz. *with Confent of* $\begin{cases} \textit{Parents} \\ \textit{Guardians} \end{cases}$ where both, or either **of the Parties** to be married *by Licenfe*, are under Age.

The entries here reproduced are from the Marriage Register of Steventon, where Jane Austen's father was Rector from 1761-1805. The Committee of the Jane Austen Society thought that members would be interested to see photographs of them.

The rather faint entries are as follows:

The Banns of Marriage between *Henry Frederick Howard Fitzwilliam* of *London* and *Jane Austen* of *Steventon.*

And:

The Form of an Entry of a Marriage. *Arthur William Mortimer* of *Liverpool* and *Jane Austen* of *Steventon.*

The Marriage was solemnized between us, *Jack Smith, Jane Smith, late Austen,* in the presence of *Jack Smith, Jane Smith.*

In the second part of this entry, the name of the original bridegroom has been altered to Jack Smith, and the bride and bridegroom have been made to act as the witnesses of their own marriage.

Who wrote these entries and when?

The writing looks like Jane Austen's. Her brother James wrote a hand very much like her own, but the gravity, not to say melancholy, of James Austen's dispositions seems to exonerate him from playing a childish prank with the register, especially as he became acting Rector of Steventon when his father retired in 1801.

If the writing be Jane Austen's, as we believe, the dating is a matter of some difficulty. Of the facsimiles of her handwriting that are readily available, there is the page of "Love and Freindship," written when she was 16, reproduced by B. C. Southam in Volume the Second. (Clarendon Press 1963). This writing, though formed, seems still to show a trace of childish roundness, which has vanished altogether from the elegant script of the Entries. Are we, then, justified in assuming that these latter were written some time after the age of 16? If this seems rather too old for a daughter of the Rectory to be larking about in her father's register, it must be noted that the leaf on which the Entries are made is not a part of the register proper: it is a specimen sheet, filled in AB, CD, etc., to show how entries should be made, and incidentally does not supply any evidence of date, as a page of the actual register might have done.

It is perhaps worth noticing that Mr. Henry Frederick Howard Fitzwilliam, the hypothetical gentleman whose banns were to be published, bore the names afterwards given to Henry Crawford, Frederick Wentworth, the Mr. Howard who was to marry Emma Watson, and Fitzwilliam Darcy.

Elizabeth Jenkins

The Misses Selby and Steele

The sisters Lucy and Nancy Steele no reader of **Sense and Sensibility** will forget. Only a devoted reader of **Sir Charles Grandison** will remember the sisters Lucy and Nancy Selby, though they are the heroine's cousins and Lucy her principal correspondent. Jane Austen, however, "remembered every circumstance related" in Richardson's last novel and particularly dwelt on what was said and done in the cedar-parlour at Selby House. (J. E. Austen-Leigh, **Memoir of Jane Austen** second edition p.84). Her interest in the minor figures of the book included even Lucy's and Nancy's unimportant brother. (**Letters of Jane Austen,** editor R. W. Chapman, p.140). She must have known that she was calling the Steele girls after the Selbys; investigation of the likenesses between the two pairs suggests that the Steeles, though they have most triumphantly outgrown their origins, began as caricatures of the Selbys. Both Steeles and Selbys come into the story as cousins of a leading character (Mrs. Jennings, Miss Byron). Neither is shown with parents, both have uncles (Mr. Pratt, Mr. Selby) with whom they stay. The Lucies are prettier, sharper-witted and altogether more important than the Nancies; they make good matches, the Nancies are less marriageable. It is a matter for surprise when Nancy Selby is at last not without a "humble servant." (**Grandison** VII.1v.) Nancy Steele had her hopes of the doctor, though it is known that she never caught him. The Steeles are accomplished toadies; the Selbys pay studied compliments to their social superiors. (e.g. **Grandison** VII I.) Lucy Selby is a great letter-writter; Lucy Steele's style of letter-writing is shown to us, though admired only by Mrs. Jennings.

Although Richardson approved of his Lucy and Nancy, and thought them "well acquainted with propriety," a good deal of what they say and write would hardly satisfy Jane Austen's more exacting notions of what was amiable and refined in Richardson's creation it is likely that they often saw them in another light than that Richardson intended: and so it was with Lucy and Nancy Selby.

A hint of the Steeles' origin as a private joke for readers of **Sir Charles Grandison** remains perhaps in **Sense and Sensibility,** Vol III, Ch. 11, where Jane Austen endows them with "friends" of the name of "Richardson." It may be significant that we hear of these at the moment when Nancy Steele is outraging Elinor's nice sense of honour by repeating a conversation between Lucy and Edward heard by "listening at the door." Nancy reports that Lucy has "never made any bones of hiding in a closet or behind a chimney-board" in order to learn secrets. In Jane Austen's novels only such characters as the Steeles spy and peer. A heroine of Richardson's, even in High Life, can spy through a keyhole on a misbehaving maid and not incur her author's disapproval.

Reproduced, by courtesy of the Publishers, from The Times,
10th September, 1964

Address given by Mr. L. P. Hartley at the Annual General Meeting
1965

———o———

When the Secretary of the Jane Austen Society did me the honour of asking me to give the address at their Annual Meeting, I accepted without too much misgiving, for I remembered a saying which my father was fond of quoting, and which he attributed, I believe mistakenly, to Lord Melbourne, to the effect that "every man has the ability to do a job he has the ability to get."

This consoling dictum sustained me for some time, but as the zero hour drew nearer it began to lose its hold. Someone said "Culture is the sediment of things forgotten." If that is so, no one could be more cultured than I am about Jane Austen. But merely to have forgotten something is not enough; and what could I possibly say about Jane Austen that has not been said, and said better, before? The discouraging epigram, "What is true is not new, and what is new is not true," began to ring in my ears. At last I consulted a friend who told me, "Jane Austen knew nothing about the Abyss."

I pondered over this, and the question at once arose, what exactly **is** the Abyss? How does one define it? The term was vaguely familiar, but it was a modern conception and susceptible of more than one interpretation. If it was a collective Abyss, the Abyss that the Atom Bomb has dug in our conciousness, even whether we are aware of it or not, the threat of universal extinction, then it was historically impossible for Jane Austen to know about it. Such a threat was not implicit in the French Revolution or the Napoleonic War. Careless readers have made the sweeping assertion that Jane Austen never mentioned the latter, which is quite untrue. There is a reference in **Persuasion** to Trafalgar, and to the action of San Domingo in 1806, and there are many other indirect allusions: the prize-money won by sailors—by Captain Wentworth, for instance. And even if she did tend to disregard it, the Napoleonic War was not the international catastrophe that the two world wars of our century have been, still less the catastrophe that a third world war would be. One cannot imagine a Duchess of Richmond giving a ball on the eve of the descent of the hydrogen bomb, supposing we had been given warning of its descent.

No, that kind of Abyss could not have been known to Jane Austen. It has been suggested that she had an intuition of coming calamity and for that very reason kept her pen and her thoughts away from it, I do not find this argument convincing, for the pen no less than the tongue, goes to the sore place. But most of the Janeites I consulted said, "Nonsense, of course she knew nothing about the Abyss, if there is one, and thank goodness she didn't.

Thank goodness we can bask in the sunshine of her mind and the inspiration which commonsense and confidence in the social order helped to give her, without indulging in such dark preoccupations."

But supposing the Abyss represented not a cosmic but a personal catastrophe ? As far as I know Jane Austen only uses the word abyss once, when she puts it into the mouth of Henry Tilney, perhaps the most amiable and attractive of her heroes. Catherine Morland says that in Bath she sees a variety of people in every street but at home in the country she can only go and call on Mrs. Allen. Mr. Tilney, we are told, was much amused. "Only go and call on Mrs. Allen !" he repeated. "What a picture of intellectual poverty ! However, when you sink into this abyss again, you will have more to say. You will be able to talk of Bath and of all that you did here." So the Abyss was, for Henry Tilney, the intellectual void represented by a social call on Mrs. Allen.

But I think there are much stronger evidences of its existence in Jane Austen's novels, even if the word itself is not used. I first read them in 1913, when I was at school, and she at once became my favourite novelist. I preferred her immeasurably to Dickens. She wielded a much finer pen than he did; as regards style and construction, she was infinitely his superior; her characters were portraits, not caricatures, and the subtlety of her humour made his seem obvious and exaggerated. Her world was real to me, and his the world of make-believe. Not that I didn't enjoy Dickens, but I felt that he used his genius as a conjuror might, to create illusions, whereas she used hers to irradiate the unchanging surface and texture of life; by her selectiveness she enhanced its meaning and by her humour she banished its humdrumness. It was her humour that especially appealed to me, for I felt it was a kind of universal solvent, that could be applied to any experience and, by making it comic, could make it comprehensible and even enjoyable. One only had to look at things the Jane Austen way and all would be well. Life at a public school was not always easy or pleasant, I felt unconsciously that had Jane Austen chosen to describe it she could have made it a subject for comedy without romanticising or distorting it, but simply by seeing its comic side, as she had seen the comic side of **The Mysteries of Udolpho**, whose terrors I could never take seriously after I had read **Northanger Abbey**. Public schools do not come much into Jane Austen's books—Eton and Westminster are mentioned—but I felt she would have understood them by her unrivalled knowledge of the strains and stresses of a stable and conventional society—and what more stable and conventional (as it seemed then) was there than public school life ? It did not occur to me that Jane Austen who was self-educated, except for one year's schooling at the gatehouse of Reading Abbey, which ended when she was nine, would not have written a school-story. I didn't then know about the two inches of ivory to which she (perhaps mistakenly) confined herself. I thought that her attitude of mind—her prevailing sense of life as a subject for comedy—could be applied to any set of circumstances. I did not realize that it implied respect for certain social rules and regulations—for civilized living, in fact—and if she had doubted these values, moral and social, her exquisite art might have fluttered with a broken wing. As Blake said,

> If the sun and moon should doubt,
> They'd immediately go out,

and it is the same with the artist, if he loses his fundamental conviction.

The War came, and as Gunner Hartley I went into the Army, which had its rules and regulations, indeed, but not such as I understood, nor do I think Jane Austen would have understood them, for civilised living had gone by the board. Although I never went overseas, Army life did seem at the beginning a kind of Abyss; a chaos without sign-posts or landmarks, in which dread and bewilderment reigned. I think that during that time my confidence in Jane Austen as an interpreter of life must have been severely shaken, and though I read some escapist literature, I did not return to her. Instead, I read **The Brothers Karamazov** with intense excitment, for it seemed to show what life was like in the raw—the kind of life into which I had been pitchforked, though I never experienced its ultimate horrors.

After the war my taste in fiction inclined, or declined to the romantic. I returned to the Brontës, who had been an early love of mine, and it was then that I read Charlotte Brontë's letter to her publisher, W. S. Williams, dated 1850, about Jane Austen. Had I read it before the First World War I should have dismissed it with indignation or irritation or perhaps with a smile, but in the light of my more recent experience it impressed me deeply. I am sure you all know it, but I will read it again, for it puts Charlotte Brontë's case against Jane Austen with incomparable force.

"I have also read one of Miss Austen's works—**Emma,** read it with interest and with just the degree of admiration which Miss Austen herself would have thought sensible and suitable. Anything like warmth or enthusiasm, anything energetic, poignant, heartfelt, is utterly out of place in commending these works; all such demonstration the authoress would have met with a wellbred sneer, would have calmly scorned as outré and extravagant. She does her business of delineating the surface of the lives of genteel English people curiously well. There is a Chinese fidelity, a miniature delicacy in the painting. She ruffles her reader by nothing vehement, disturbs him by nothing profound. The passions are perfectly unknown to her, she rejects even a speaking acquaintance with that stormy sisterhood. Even to the feelings she vouchsafes no more than an occasional graceful but distant recognition—too frequent converse with them would ruffle the smooth elegance of her progress. Her business is not half so much with the human heart as with the human eyes, mouth, hands and feet. What sees keenly, speaks aptly, moves flexibly, it suits her to study; but what throbs fast and full, though hidden, what the blood rushes through, what is the unseen seat of life and the sentient target of death—this Miss Austen ignores. She no more, with her mind's eye, beholds the heart of her race than each man, with bodily vision, sees the heart in his heaving breast. Jane Austen was a complete and most sensible lady, but a very incomplete and rather insensible (**not** senseless) woman. If this is heresy, I cannot help it."

Well, this diatribe had a disturbing effect on me, as it may have had on other devotees of Jane Austen, and it certainly strengthens the case of those who think that she knew nothing about the Abyss. But great novelists are apt to underrate each other (did not Henry James speak of 'poor little Hardy'?) and to imagine that an intention that differs from their own must be misguided.

Writing to G. H. Lewes, in January 1848, Charlotte Brontë says: What a strange lecture comes next in your letter! You say I must familiarise my mind with the fact that Miss Austen is not a poetess, has no 'sentiment,' you scornfully enclose the word in inverted commas, no eloquence, none of the ravishing enthusiasm of poetry! And then you add I **must** learn to acknowledge her as one of **the greatest of artists, of the greatest painters of human characters,** and one of the writers with the nicest sense of means to an end that ever lived—the last point only will I ever acknowledge.

'Can there be a great artist without poetry?'

Charlotte Brontë was in her way a fair-minded woman; but she was critical and censorious, as witness the passage in her introduction to **Wuthering Heights,** in which she wonders if it is wise to create human beings like Heathcliff. Except for the Duke of Wellington, in whom she could find no fault, her armour of partisanship was by no means flawless.

In a letter to W. S. Williams she writes: "I had a letter the other day announcing that a lady of some note, who had always determined that whenever she married, her husband should be the counterpart of Mr. Knightley in Miss Austen's **Emma** had now changed her mind, and vowed that she would either find the duplicate of Professor Emanuel" (in **Villette)** "or remain for ever single!"

At another time she asked him, "Whenever you send me a new supply of books, may I request that you will have the goodness to include one or two of Miss Austen's? I am often asked if I have read them, and I excite amazement by replying in the negative. I have read none except **Pride and Prejudice**. Miss Martineau mentioned **Persuasion** as the best."

In January 1848 she wrote to G. H. Lewes, "If ever I do write another book I think I will have nothing of what you call melodrama, I **think** so, but I am not sure. I **think** also, I will endeavour to follow the counsel which shines out of Miss Austen's 'mild eyes' 'to finish more and be more subdued.'

"Why do you like Miss Austen so very much? I am puzzled on that point. What induced you to say that you would have rather written **Pride and Prejudice** and **Tom Jones** than any of the Waverley novels?"

"I had not seen **Pride and Prejudice** since I read that sentence of yours and then I got the book. And what did I find? An accurate, daguerreotype portrait of a commonplace face; a carefully fenced, highly cultivated garden, with neat borders and delicate flowers, but no glance of a bright vivid physiognomy, no fresh air, no blue hill, no bonny beck."

Granted that any novelist, of lesser stature than Charlotte Brontë, would have been annoyed to be told to study the works of another novelist, especially another woman novelist, her verdict on Jane Austen's is still surprising.

Of some forgotten novelist of the day she writes that she is 'as shrewd as Miss Austen but not so shrewish.'

I think that the explanation must be that Charlotte had only read **Emma** and **Pride and Prejudice**, the two novels of Jane Austen in which the sunlight much exceeds the shadow. Had she read **Sense and Sensibility**, or **Mansfield Park**, or **Persuasion**, her opinion would surely have been different.

Pride and Prejudice and **Emma** are favourites with Jane Austen's readers, perhaps because in them she realizes most fully her gift for comedy and approaches most nearly to the perfection at which, as Flaubert did, she always aimed. She kept within her range of experience, or of the experience which she could best translate into art.

But re-reading her novels after so many years, I rather wonder if this perfection has not been achieved by the exclusion of other qualities that would have jarred on or even imperilled it. Perfection is, one would think, an absolute quality: there cannot be degrees of perfection. Yet no one would say that an object by Fabergé, however perfect, could be compared, in artistic value, to a painting by Rembrandt, however faulty. **Madame Bovary** is a great novel, one of the greatest and perhaps the most perfect; but its perfection depends on rigid exclusion of some of the most precious (and incidentally the commonest) human qualities. There is only one nice character (I apologise to the shade of Henry Tilney, who was justly critical of it, for using the word 'nice'), there is nothing in **Madame Bovary,** as Matthew Arnold said, to rejoice or console us. Perfect it may be, as a work of art, but it takes a one-sided view of life. And it might be argued that the perfection of **Emma** is partly due to the absence, or at any rate the rare appearance, of anything that might not rejoice or console us.

> Faultily faultless, icily regular, splendidly null,
> Dead perfection, no more—

this is not true of **Emma,** whose life-enhancing qualities will never cease to delight, but it is a warning against the dangers of perfection—or the quest for it. I have been told, but do not vouch for its truth, that Persian rug-makers (those of the Mahometan faith) always leave some part of the pattern flawed or incomplete, so as not to challenge comparison with Allah, in whom alone perfection lies. I don't say this to belittle **Emma,** the most perfect of Jane Austen's works (and, incidentally, the one most vulnerable to Charlotte Brontë's criticism), but as a plea for those that are sometimes considered less good, **Sense and Sensibility, Mansfield Park,** and **Persuasion.**

Re-visiting the world of Jane Austen in 1965, I got a very different impression of it from the one I had in 1913. Then I rejoiced in the comedy; Mrs. Norris could not be too grasping and disagreeable, or Miss Bates too garrulous and fatuous, for me. I longed for their re-appearances, Mrs. Charles Musgrove, in **Persuasion,** was another of my favourites, and her complaint that her sore throats were worse than other people's, has delighted me down the years, because I thought (perhaps with more reason than she had) that mine were worse, too. The tribulation of the lovers (of the heroines, I should say, for they suffered much more than the heroes), I didn't take very seriously, for I knew that all would come right for them in the end, and the social background I took for granted, as I took for granted the map of Europe; it had been, was, and always would be, just the same as Jane Austen painted it.

I re-read the books with different feelings. They did not seem so funny as they had seemed. The change was not in Jane Austen, it was in me; my sense of humour had dwindled, and I could no longer see human life in the aspect of comedy. Nor, I think, am I alone in this. It is said that human nature doesn't change, but I think it does, and has, and not least in its sense of humour. I remember a friend of mine, a novelist, saying to me "There is no sort of joke now except a bad-taste joke," and she was no mean exponent of jokes of that kind. 'Sick' humour is the order of the day. Jane Austen was quite capable of sick humour; she had been condemned as unfeeling because of a joke in a letter to Cassandra about a miscarriage which anyone might have made if they had the wit to make it; and who would escape the charge of ill-nature if it was founded on some malicious remark in a letter to a close relation?

But if I didn't find Mrs. Norris and Miss Bates and Mr. Collins as funny as I once had, I marvelled anew at the cleverness, the subtlety, and the economy of the means by which Jane Austen makes her effects—the beauty of single sentences and the wonderful chapter-endings, which miraculously combine a faint note of finality with a stirring of expectation for what is to come. And I found many more instances than I expected to find of visual images and feeling for Nature—the 'March that was more like April,' and so on. And if I could not look at Pemberley with the rapt excitement of Elizabeth Bennet, I could still see, with my mind's eye, what she saw. Those shrubberies! What a nostalgia they evoke! I should like to plant one myself, if my age and the size of my garden did not make the project what Jane Austen might have called 'imprudent.'

But what struck me most (and this brings me back to the edge of the Abyss), is the sadness to be found in all the novels, except perhaps in **Emma.** There is more sunshine than shadow, of course, but there is more shadow than I remembered from my confident pre-war days. Many, many years ago an artist told me that every picture should have a passage in it 'as black as paint can make it'—otherwise (I suppose he meant), the colours would lose their relative value. I don't know if this rule still holds but it seemed to hold then; I studied a great many pictures, and always seemed to find a black patch somewhere. Indeed, I have seen a modern painting which was **entirely** black. Is the presence of a black spot essential to serious fiction?—for Jane Austen is a serious novelist. She cannot be likened, say, to Shakespeare or Thomas Hardy, without their tragedies. The two inches of ivory included much more than that.

As Lord David Cecil has said, there are no deaths, or deaths that matter, in her novels. (There are eight in WUTHERING HEIGHTS). What deaths there are have mostly taken place beforehand, and left only a legacy (sometimes a disappointing one) of **money,** to influence the story.

Money is discussed much more openly in Jane Austen's novels than it would be now. Mr. Rushworth had 12,000 pounds a year, Mr. Darcy 10,000, Mr. Bingley 4,000, and the Bennets, I think, a mere 2,000, which were anyhow entailed on Mr. Collins. Multiplied by ten, as I suppose they should be to bring them in line with the value of money today, and being more or less tax-free, (though Jane Austen does once refer, I think, to some tax-problem), these figures represent a great deal of money and money plays a great part in the marriages of Jane Austen's heroines.

How was it that she herself never married? Someone, I think it was Miss Mitford, described her as a 'husband-hunting butterfly,' and she cannot have been a dull woman. We hear of attachments to various men, Mr. Blackall (ominous name) was one, but none which is properly authenticated, and both she and her sister Cassandra died unmarried. The most obvious explanation is that neither had a large enough dot to tempt a suitor, for Jane Austen's father, who had seven (or was it eight?) children, had, I think, only £750 a year to bring them up on and provide for their futures.

Did Jane Austen really **want** to marry? All her novels are about **getting** married, and marriage might be thought the be-all and end-all of her heroines' existence; but as someone has pointed out, despite this strong emphasis on the bliss of **getting** married, there are few completely happy marriages in Jane Austen's novels: Mr. Bennet certainly did not enjoy being married to Mrs. Bennet.

"Oh dear, let him stand his chance and be taken in. It will do just as well. Everybody is taken in at some period or other."

"Not always in marriage, dear Mary."

"In marriage especially. With all due respect to such of the present company as chance to be married, my dear Mrs. Grant, there is not one in a hundred of either sex who is not taken in when they marry. Look where I will, I see that it **is** so."

Perhaps Jane Austen, whose mind was so fully occupied with other things, did distrust the married state; perhaps, like Fanny Price, she would not marry someone she did not love; but I can't help thinking that lack of money and the 'consequence' that money brings, may have been at the bottom of it.

Why, otherwise, are there so many Cinderellas in the novels? Fanny Price, Catherine Morland, even Elizabeth Bennet, are handicapped, matrimonially and emotionally, by mixing with people much better off than themselves. To be a man was a great advantage; to be a rich man was a still greater advantage, compared with the lot of the unmarried woman. Not all novelists project themselves into their novels, but the majority do, either from the wishful or fearful-thinking which, more than any other single factor, enables a novelist to unite his material with his sensibility.

These heroines, then, or some of them, suffered from an inferiority-complex which made Elizabeth Bennet pert, Catherine Morland gauche, Fanny Price submissive, Anne Elliot resigned. It did not embitter them, however, still less did it make them delinquents. I saw a case the other day in which some teenage malefactor pleaded (I think successfully) in his defence that as a child he had suffered tortures from a sense of social inferiority. Jane Austen would have thought this nonsense. A friend of mine said she lacked compassion—which is not true, she had plenty of compassion, and although she generally withheld it from evildoers, she sometimes extended it to them. Wickham gets off more lightly than he deserves, and as for that odious General Tilney! I cannot forgive Catherine Morland, or Henry Tilney, for forgiving **him,** on the grounds that his daughter's marriage to a peer had put him into a better temper.

On Jane Austen's monument in Winchester Cathedral, (a favourite building with her, we are told) is quoted from the **Book of Proverbs,** "In her mouth was the law of kindness." Someone said that you cannot expect truth from a lapidary inscription, and I think this one went rather far, as regards Jane Austen the author, if not as regards Jane Austen the woman. As an author she was not particularly kind, but she was just: justice is a quality that shines out of her works. She was a stern moralist—perhaps of all novelists the most moral. She makes it quite clear if she dislikes this or that character, but in company with Shakespeare, who put so many *bons mots* into the mouth of (say) Iago, she allows the most unpleasant or the most stupid of them to say a good thing now and then.

But I am wandering from my point, which was the element of sadness in several of Jane Austen's books. She did not write about Belsen and Buchenwald; she did not, like Dostoievski, depict a human soul in the last stages of despair and dissolution, but she was acutely aware of suffering and sorrow; and sometimes, I think, in portraying them, she overruns the two inches of ivory which was the limit she set herself. Suffering, of course, is relative; but how acutely one feels for Catherine Morland, so cruelly turned out of Northanger Abbey without the money to pay her fare. Catherine expected something horrid to happen at Northanger Abbey, and she finds it, though not in the guise she expected. With consummate skill Jane Austen plays on the reader's apprehensions, just as she plays on Catherine's; now allaying them with the discovery of a laundry-list, now renewing them with partial but disquieting revelations of her host's sinister nature; and when the catastrophe comes, it comes, as always in Jane Austen, with dramatic suddenness. The evil in Northanger Abbey was not a supernatural matter of cabinets and tapestries and long-forgotten documents. It was quite natural, a rather frightening middle-aged man, who caused her more suffering than any phantom would have. Of which of Jane Austen's characters is it said, "He is black, black, black,"? I can't remember, but how flat **Northanger Abbey** would be without this sudden irruption of blackness at the end.

"Happiness," Jane Austen is credited with saying, "is a dull thing to write about." For myself, in my later years, I find the darker passages often more satisfying than the social chit-chat, the Court Guide to Bath, the references to money, the importance of 'consequence' and precedence—all of which were so well within her range that she could do them on her head, without always avoiding the danger of self-imitation. The irony which shimmers over her books is one of the most delightful qualities, but it can pall—it can suggest that we need take nothing seriously as long as we see it in the aspect of comedy; and no one, however vigilant his sense of humour, can see life like that, as if all experience was something that could be laughed or shrugged off. Charlotte Brontë's gibe, that Jane Austen ignored the 'unseen seat of life' is untenable; nearly all her characters (Lady Russell in **Persuasion** is one of the exceptions) are very much alive, even if it isn't the kind of life with which Charlotte Brontë had most sympathy. The charge of 'nothing heartfelt' would be easier to sustain. I fancy that Jane Austen would have thought that to unbosom oneself to the public, even in a work of fiction, would be a breach of good manners. But there are times when she discards the mantle of irony—in the passage in **Northanger Abbey,** for instance, where she defends the novel against the charge of triviality. In this (though irony is present) she commits herself to what she is saying; we hear the true voice of feeling, the voice of personal conviction, as we hear it, still more clearly, in the famous conversation between Anne Elliot and Captain Harville, as to the relative fidelity, in emotional relationships, of men and women.

"God forbid," says Anne (and it is one of the few times when the word God is mentioned in Jane Austen's novels), "God forbid that I should undervalue the warm and faithful feelings of any of my fellow-creatures ! I should deserve utter contempt if I dared to suppose that true attachment and constancy were known only by women . . . .All the privilege I claim for my own sex (it is not a very enviable one, you need not covet it) is that of loving longest when existence, or when hope, is gone."

With Jane Austen, almost less than with any other writer except Shakespeare, can one assume that her characters voice her own opinions; but one feels that Anne is speaking for Jane Austen here.

At the end of **Mansfield Park** occurs another, equally famous passage, and this time Jane Austen is speaking with her own voice. "Let other pens dwell on guilt and misery. I quit such odious subjects as soon as I can, impatient to restore everybody not greatly in fault themselves, to tolerable comfort and to have done with all the rest."

This is all very well, but Jane Austen's pen has been dwelling on guilt and misery for a great many pages, and prior to the Crawford episode there has been what Mr. R. W. Chapman has called the 'long-drawn agony of Fanny Price.' "That great, black word **miserable** ! . . . .Her mind was all disorder. The past, present, future, everything was terrible. But her uncle's anger gave her the severest pain of all. Selfish and ungrateful ! To have appeared so to him. She was miserable for ever. She had no one to take her part, to counsel, to speak for her. Her only friend was absent. He might have softened his father; but all, perhaps all, would think her selfiish and ungrateful. She might have to endure the reproach again and again; she might hear it, or see it, or know it to exist, for ever, in every connection about her. She could not but feel some resentment against Mr. Crawford; yet, if he really loved her, and were unhappy too !—it was all wretchedness together."

Surely this passage gives us a glimpse of the Abyss, if it does not take us into the Abyss itself.

In its physical aspect Jane Austen's world was much safer than ours. There was very little danger to life and limb from accidental causes. Motor-cars did not run over people; aeroplanes did not crash; and as far as I can remember, even horses did not run away. Yet there are moments when the outside world shows its teeth, and how vividly Jane Austen describes them ! The Cobb at Lyme Regis: I have often negotiated those few unperilous steps, and wondered how Louisa Musgrove could have fallen down them, though I had no one to 'jump' me. Yet what a tremendous experience Jane Austen makes of it—just as she does of the incident of the gypsies in **Emma,** another irruption of the irrational and dangerous into Jane Austen's well-ordered world. Here was a group of juvenile delinquents, "half a dozen children headed by a stout woman and a great boy, all clamorous and impertinent, in look though not absolutely in word." Poor Harriet could not follow Miss Bickerton, 'who had given a great scream,' because she suffered from cramp after dancing. Frank Churchill arrives in the nick of time to save her and escort her back to Hartfield, where she immediately fainted away.

The phenomenon of violence, so familiar to us, hardly came into Jane Austen's purview at all; but it is clear that she knew how to describe it when she wanted to. Her world was ruled by reason, by moral considerations: when anything goes wrong, it is somebody's **fault;** they have acted, to use a familiar phrase, without due care and attention—not to the dangers of the roads but to the dictates of prudence, reason, conscience and religion—and for that they are punished.

Most people would agree with G. H. Lewes that her novels are deficient in poetry, though there is much more of it than she is given credit for. A more serious lack, I think, is that she makes almost no allowance for the **irrationalism** of much of human behaviour, an element of which **we** are only too painfully aware, and should be, even if Freud had not emphasized it, and perhaps encouraged it. Nor does she recognise the existence of evil as something to be reckoned with; there are a few villains in her novels, but very few villainesses, except that very black one, Lady Susan, who might have come out of the pages of **Les Liaisons Dangereuses,** via **Clarissa Harlowe,** which we know Jane Austen read; or at any rate, we know that she bought it, for the bill exists. All the great novelists, except Jane Austen, have recognised the importance of the irrational as a factor in human behaviour, and the greatest of all, Cervantes, made it his subject; for what is **Don Quixote** but a study in unreason.

Sense and Sensibility is sometimes regarded as the least successful of Jane Austen's novels, but to me it is one of the most satisfying, simply because it does recognise, however distantly and disapprovingly, the force of unreason in human life. Marianne Dashwood is one of my favourite characters in fiction. I like her for herself (she was nice to her mother and had many other amiable qualities besides), and I like her because she does **not** act from prudential considerations. She does not feel (in the beginning, at any rate) that money should be the sine qua non of marriage, or that love must be founded on esteem (an idea Jane Austen seems to have held, though it is, and always has been, unsupported by experience). "I have never yet known," Mrs. Dashwood says, "what it was to separate esteem from love." It is generally thought that Jane Austen was on Elinor's side, the side of sense, against Marianne's side, the side of sensibility. But I wonder. Her mind may have condemned Marianne, but her feelings did not: Marianne, with all her faults, her disregard of public opinion, her anti-social tendencies (playing the piano whether other people wanted her to, or not), her determination to go her own way and be herself—all these things endear her to me. I cannot think that when Charlotte Brontë wrote the letter about **Emma** she had read **Sense and Sensibility**. For surely here the 'unseen seat of life' is defined as clearly as it ever can be, and the 'sentient target of death' (though it never gets a shot in the bull's eye) is **not** ignored; it is present throughout Marianne's illness, the wonderful account of which, with its harrowing alternation of hopes and fears, its complete lack of sentimentality, its insistence on the medical and mental aspects of the case, would give it a high place in any anthology of sick-bed scenes.

In her last illness, Jane Austen was asked if she wanted anything, and she replied "Only death." That was in 1817, a year before the birth of Emily Brontë, who also died young and who also, apparently, at the end wanted only death. As women, and as novelists, the two might be thought the antitheses of each other the one loving society, the other solitude. Someone said to me, "If Jane Austen knew nothing about the Abyss, Emily Brontë knew nothing about anything else." The social background which meant so much to Jane Austen meant nothing to Emily Brontë. Only Mr. Lockwood ever called at Wuthering Heights, no one ever called at Thrushcross Grange, unless Heathcliff can be regarded as a visitor, when he spent the night in the garden knocking his head against a tree and howling like an animal. The only concession, the only recognition, that **Wuthering Heights** vouchsafes to society is when Catherine Earnshaw tells Nelly Dean that one reason for marrying Edgar Linton is that she would then be the 'greatest woman of the neighbourhood.' One has to laugh, for what neighbourhood, in the social sense, was there round Wuthering Heights? Some ghosts, no doubt. But all the same, there are many points of resemblance between Marianne Dashwood and Catherine Earnshaw, apart from the fact that the one nearly dies of love and the other dies of it. Each was determined to be herself, cost it what might to herself and those who loved her; many of their remarks would, mutatis mutandis, be interchangeable. Marianne recants, and apologises to Elinor, to society, and to God, for her errors, whereas Catherine dies impenitent, only asking Heathcliff for forgiveness. Yet they both hold our sympathy, or at least they hold mine, by each possessing a quality of incorruptibility which can be summed up in one of Emily Brontë's few recorded remarks, "I want to be what God made me."

Catherine was not happy with her dull husband, Edgar Linton. Was Marianne likely to be happy with her dull husband, Colonel Brandon? He was fairly well-off no doubt, but as Marianne (in her unregenerate stage) said to Elinor, "What have wealth and grandeur to do with happiness?"

Northhanger Abbey is a satire on one aspect of the Romantic Movement; Sense and Sensibility is a much more subtle and serious criticism of it. Even if we sometimes suspect that Jane Austen is trying to convince herself, she means to convince the reader.

To Emily Brontë as to Marianne, Autumn was a season rich with romantic yearning. Emily shows it in a poem, Marianne in a conversation between herself and Elinor. Emily writes, as always, from the heart, and Jane Austen seems to make fun of Marianne's feelings—but they are none the less moving. The subject is falling leaves, and Emily's poem reads:

> Fall leaves, fall; die, flowers, away;
> Lengthen night and shorten day;
> Every leaf speaks bliss to me
> Fluttering from the autumn tree.
> I shall smile when wreaths of snow
> Blossom where the rose should grow;
> I shall sing when night's decay
> Ushers in a drearier day.

"And how does dear, dear Norland look?" cried Marianne.

"Dear, dear Norland," said Elinor, "probably looks much as it always does at this time of year. The woods and walks thickly covered with dead leaves."

"Oh!" cried Marianne, "with what transporting sensations have I formerly seen them fall! How have I delighted, as I walked, to see them driven in showers about me by the wind!

What feelings have they, the seasons, the air, altogether inspired !
Now there is no one to regard them. They are seen only as a
nuisance, swept hastily off, and driven as much as possible from
the sight."

"It is not everyone," said Elinor, "who has your passion for
dead leaves."

"No, my feelings are not often shared, not often understood.
but sometimes they are."

There is no doubt that Elinor gets the better of this encounter,
but it is Marianne's words, which, at any rate for me, linger longest,
however exaggerated their sentiment may be.

I feel that Marianne was a tragic character and (with all
respect) that **Sense and Sensibility** should have been a tragic novel.
That Jane Austen could have made it one, had she wished, I have
no doubt; the ingredients are all there, and she had nothing to do
but change the emphasis at the end. The danger for a novelist of
straying outside his range is really no greater, if in a different
way, than when he sticks inside it. Who would have prophesied
that Dickens would have made such a success of **A Tale of Two
Cities,** a novel that was quite outside his ordinary beat ? To
experiment, in fiction may be disastrous, but it may open up veins
of imagination that the author did not know of.

But before I fail to prove my point that Jane Austen might
have been a tragic novelist, may I quote a letter that I recently
received on this very subject ?

"I found **Adam Bede** a tragic book, and poor Hetty Sorrell
had all my sympathy, but **Sense and Sensibility** unearthed too
vividly that awful period of desolation, rejection, and humiliation . .
It is extraordinary. I have wept reading this book, and I thought
my tears had dried up years ago."

L. P. Hartley

ANNUAL REPORT, 1965

The article "The Misses Selby and Steele," printed on
page 296 of this Report, was written by E. E. Duncan-
Jones, and was first published as a letter to The Times
Literary Supplement on 10th September, 1964.

INDEX TO ADDRESSES AND ARTICLES
in alphabetical order of Authors

311

INDEX OF REFERENCES TO JANE AUSTEN'S WORKS

(In the case of the longer Addresses and Articles published in the " Reports ", in which individual Works are frequently mentioned, references are, in general, to first pages only.)

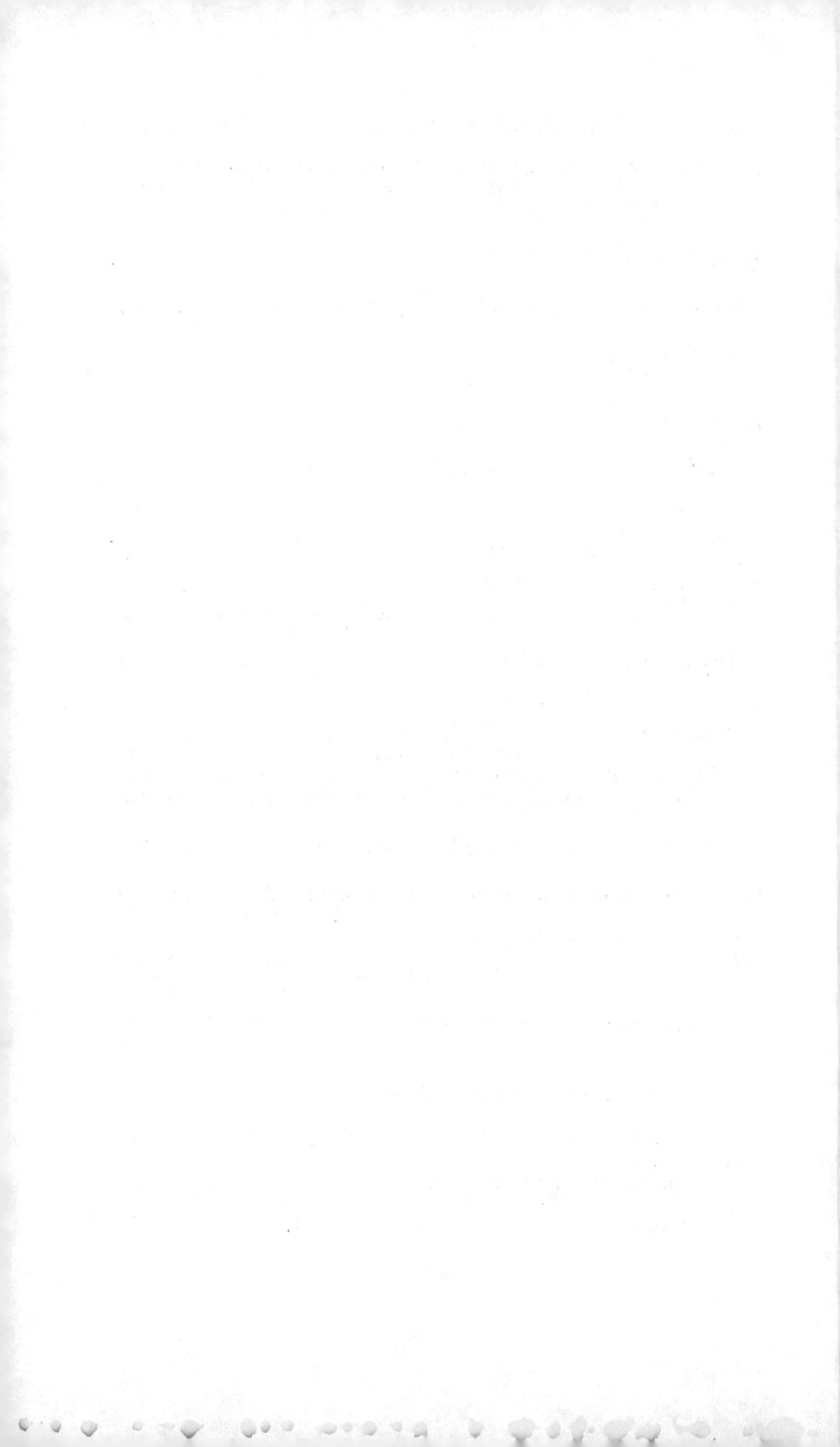

GENERAL INDEX

316

(Indexes compiled by Wing Cdr. P. F. Weller, R.A.F. (Retd.) who apologises for any
inadequacies.)

317